THE FIGHTING SOUTH

John Temple Graves (*Courtesy The Birmingham News*)

The Fighting South

JOHN TEMPLE GRAVES

With an Introduction by
Fred Hobson

THE UNIVERSITY OF ALABAMA PRESS

Library of Congress Cataloging in Publication Data

Graves, John Temple, 1892–
    The fighting South.

    Reprint. Originally published: New York : Putnam, 1943.
    Includes index.
    1. Southern States—Civilization. I. Title.
F215.G76 1985   975   84-16320
ISBN 0-8173-0245-X
ISBN 0-8173-0246-8 (pbk.)

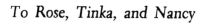
To Rose, Tinka, and Nancy

CONTENTS

	Introduction by Fred Hobson	ix
ONE	The Fighting South	3
TWO	Forever and Ever, Amen	19
THREE	Highlight and Low	39
FOUR	Centripetal Force	49
FIVE	"I Got Shoes"	65
SIX	Fever	70
SEVEN	December Seventh	84
EIGHT	Under the Oxygen Tent	104
NINE	Of One Blood	119
TEN	You Can Hear Their Voices	138
ELEVEN	"For the Advancement of Colored People"	151
TWELVE	Forty Feeding Like One	162
THIRTEEN	The Land Is Bright	177
FOURTEEN	Far Light	193
FIFTEEN	The Aristocratic Tradition	203
SIXTEEN	Woman Is Pleasing	212
SEVENTEEN	Here We Rest!	226
EIGHTEEN	"—And the Democratic Party"	238
NINETEEN	Lord God Almighty	251
TWENTY	Free For All	263
INDEX		278

Introduction

FRED HOBSON

IN THE 1930S AND EARLY 1940S, IT SEEMS, NEARLY EVERY prominent Southern journalist was planning or writing a book about Dixie. North Carolinian Jonathan Daniels traveled around the Southern states, then wrote *A Southerner Discovers the South* (1938), a charming mixture of description and social commentary. That same year transplanted Tar Heel Gerald W. Johnson produced *The Wasted Land*, a less hopeful picture of the late Confederacy. Three years later Wilbur Cash of Charlotte came forth with his Southern classic, *The Mind of the South*, and the next year Virginius Dabney of Richmond wrote *Below the Potomac*, a portrait of the newest of New Souths by a certified Southern liberal. Lesser known journalists such as Clarence Cason of Alabama (in *90° in the Shade*) and Stetson Kennedy of Florida (in *Southern Exposure*) also contributed to the development of this new Southern literary genre. And in 1943 another Alabamian and notable journalist, John Temple Graves of Birmingham, finished his book about Dixie and called it *The Fighting South*.*

Graves, like Daniels, Dabney, and Johnson, was a prominent member of the Southern liberal establishment, a man

*For biographical information about Graves, I draw on Margaret E. Armbrester, "John Temple Graves and the New Deal, 1933–1940," M.A. thesis, Vanderbilt University, 1967; and Armbrester, "John Temple Graves II: A Southern Liberal Views the New Deal," *Alabama Review*, XXXII (July 1979), 203–13. I have also benefited from discussions with Professor Tennant S. McWilliams, who is currently working on Graves.

widely known as a newspaper columnist and a lecturer. A native of Rome, Georgia, he had grown up near Atlanta where his father, the elder John Temple Graves, was a newspaper-man and orator of note. In 1889 the elder Graves had given the funeral oration for that prophet of the New South, Henry Grady.

The younger Graves attended Princeton, where he became a strong supporter of the university's president, Woodrow Wilson. After Princeton he took a law degree at George Washington University and, after serving in World War I, went to work for the Federal Trade Commission in Washington. Although in 1923 he wrote a little-acclaimed novel, and demonstrated other interest in writing, he might have remained a Washington bureaucrat if his father, who had become an editorial writer with the *Palm Beach Times*, had not become ill and needed his son's assistance. So in 1925 the younger Graves moved to Florida, began to write editorials for the Palm Beach and then the Jacksonville newspapers, and thus launched his career in journalism.

It was a career that took off rapidly. In 1929 he joined the editorial staff of the Birmingham *Age-Herald* and in the 1930s became—as *Newsweek* described him in 1937—the "first successfully syndicated Southern columnist." A self-described "good Woodrow Wilson Democrat," he preached the Wilsonian gospel of education, internationalism, and economic progress while holding, as Wilson had, to traditional Southern social values. When Franklin Roosevelt became president in 1933, Graves became an enthusiastic New Dealer, largely because he saw FDR as a reformer within the Wilsonian tradition. But by the mid-1930s he had come to question many aspects of the New Deal, and after 1937—and Roosevelt's attempt to pack the Supreme Court—Graves turned against most of the New Deal. He became critical of FDR's widespread relief program, his "planned economy," and, in particular, the TVA which he had earlier supported. Feeling that the New Deal had been a series of necessary emergency measures that had remained in effect after the emergency, Graves wrote in 1938, "The New Deal has been dealt." He supported Wendell Willkie, not FDR, in 1940. When national Democratic politics conflicted with his professed loyalty to the South, Graves came down on the side of traditional loyalties.

It was against this background of New Deal skepticism and Southern allegiances that Graves came to write *The Fighting South*. What stirred him more immediately, however, was the war raging in Europe and the Pacific in the early 1940s. At the time he wrote his book, he was working for the Southern Council on International Relations, an organization that strongly supported the war and Great Britain. His position was similar to that of other Southern liberals during the war: like Virginius Dabney, Mark Ethridge, and other liberal spokesmen, he strongly supported the war effort at the same time he was openly critical of Negro efforts to take advantage of the war to achieve full equality. He believed the American South could not fight a war abroad and also handle racial conflict at home—conflict he was certain would result if blacks pushed too hard for rights during wartime. Dabney expressed the same fear in a favorable review of *The Fighting South* published in the *New York Times*. So did Gerald Johnson, who wrote in the *Saturday Review* that Graves was a "realist" on race—although Johnson, who had described Dixie as the "Wasted Land," felt that Graves's estimate of Southern health was "rather . . . on the optimistic side." The anonymous reviewer in the *Nation* was most laudatory of all. "This seems the most genuinely revealing of the several books of the past few years by Southerners about the South," he wrote. "It describes rather than theorizes, and is particular rather than general. . . . [Graves] lays bare the shortcomings of the South while preserving a warm natural belief . . . in what every Southerner regards as the qualities of the South."

One might differ with the *Nation's* estimate that *The Fighting South* was the most revealing Southern book "of the past few years"; Cash's *The Mind of the South* had appeared just two years before, and Graves's book posed no serious threat to Cash. Graves wrote a book not nearly so ambitious as Cash's— whose grandiose title suggested the extent of his enterprise and the nobility of his attempt. But *The Fighting South* was a book, like Cash's, written with one eye on Europe and with a realization that the war might radically change the South. Cash had concluded *The Mind of the South:* "It would be a madman who would venture [prophecies about the South] in the face of the forces sweeping over the world in the fateful year of 1940." Graves was even more conscious of Europe, because the war that Cash anticipated as he wrapped up *The Mind of the South* in late 1940 Graves saw as a reality in 1941 and 1942. Thus he attempted to bring together the subjects of war and the American South, and he found a point of departure in the polls that showed that Southerners, between 1939 and 1941, had been far more eager to go to war than had other Americans. Graves sought to discover why, and investigated the influence of the South's militant tradition, its poverty (and thus, supposedly, its having little to lose), its Anglomania, its lack of a German populace, its propensity to violence, and thus its habit of living dangerously. But most of all, Graves determined, the South was "pure of heart." It still held honor and chivalry more highly than other Americans did; it was ready to jump in and fight to protect the right.

But by "the Fighting South" Graves means not only a South ready to jump into World War II. The South was ready to "fight" for its rights on the home front too. Dixie had long been "fighting mad" at certain offenses it had suffered at the hands of the rest of the United States. John C. Calhoun, Henry Grady, and other Southern leaders had begun as nationalists but had become more pro-Southern when they saw that the nation did not heed the Southern position. In the

1940s the South was fighting mad over matters ranging from federal discrimination in freight rates and the selling of steel to the nation's attitudes toward Southern racial problems. The Southerner had "developed a chronic chip on his shoulder as a result of his long belief that he is not fairly treated or well understood."

As he proceeds in his story, Graves professes to describe what "the Southerner" thinks and feels, how he responds to outside stimuli—but after a while it is clear that the Southerner the author describes is often himself. He emerges in his narrative as a Southerner of the variety Daniel J. Singal describes in his recent book *The War Within* (1982), a study of Southern intellectuals in the early twentieth century caught between Victorianism and Modernism. Graves is indisputably a Southern Victorian, almost a classical Victorian—and in this book World War II is particularly ominous to him because it threatens the certitudes of a Victorian childhood. It is to this childhood that Graves devotes his second chapter, in many ways the most heartfelt and appealing chapter in the book. Growing up Southern in College Park, Georgia, around the turn of the century was the best of all possible worlds as Graves describes it. It was a simpler time, a time in which people knew their places and absolutes still reigned. Graves came of age under the influence of the Southern Lost Cause (although he insists he really did not hate Yankees) and "the eternities of Queen Victoria, Robert E. Lee, and the Lord God Almighty." A product of a "good family"—related to John C. Calhoun and a number of other notable Southerners—he early developed a regard for class distinction. He also came to view Negroes according to the requirements of *noblesse oblige*, that code to which his family, along with other "better" white Southerners, subscribed. The blacks of College Park considered his father "the best friend the colored people had in the country"; they "put themselves in his hands for advice and protection." Later in the book Graves insists, "The friendship of the white liberal Southerner is the Negro's basic hope." Racial paternalism might have a bad name in the late twentieth century, but in the year 1900—or even 1940—it was better than any alternative the white South had to offer.

Graves's Victorianism—his regard for form and manner, for people and things in their place, his basic sentimentality, but his equal regard for high thinking and right action—pervades *The Fighting South*. Earlier, in an essay entitled "The Eternal South"—which had served as an introduction to *A Book of the South* (1940), which he had helped to edit—he had sounded more like Thomas Nelson Page than a hard-minded Southern journalist. "In the secrets of its own soul," he had written, "there is one South, an eternal South, surviving through yesterday, today and tomorrow . . . never ceasing, never ending." In *The Fighting South* he again displays his love of high sentence and noble sentiment—and of hierarchy. The South consisted of "the classes" and "the masses," and it was clear that Graves himself was of "the classes." His world was largely made up of Southern ladies and gentlemen, in their places. The Southern male was "nearly always" the "master or slave" of Southern woman, "rarely her comrade." But Southerners could be gentlemen regardless of class, or even location, since by "gentleman" Graves meant one possessed of nobility, breadth of vision, and regard for women. Even in 1943, he insisted, "there is such a thing as a Southern gentleman. He may live in Chicago. He may wear overalls. But he exists and his tribe must increase if we are to get anywhere in the years to come." The war, Graves believed, was accompanied by a breakdown of the gentlemanly ideal. But "there will be a call for gentlemen when the atom is split."

Graves's notions of religion, competition, and the condition of society were equally high-minded. Possessing the Victorian love of order and of individual responsibility, he inveighs against both "the anarchy of our 1920's and the socialism of our 1930's." His code of competition—clean, civilized, and governed by rules—could have come from the public schools of mid-Victorian England: "Civilize the plays, put a just umpire over them, educate the players, respect the rules, set limits in decency, and the fighting world becomes the free world." Finally, the religious temper of the Victorian is never far away in *The Fighting South*, particularly in the latter part of the book. Graves concludes his book written in those perilous times of the early 1940s with a prayer for "one more chance to be beautiful—and American—and alive—O God, our strength and our redeemer!"

Graves, indeed, was one of those many Southerners of the mid-twentieth century who would have felt more comfortable in an earlier age. But at the same time he protested change, he possessed a flexibility—an intellectual recognition of the necessity of change—that distinguished him from certain other Southern Victorians and gentlemen. His remarks about the Mississippi aristocrat William Alexander Percy are telling. Percy, two years before, had produced *Lanterns on the Levee*, a poetic defense of the life of the educated, cultivated Southern planter and a lament for the passing of Southern aristocracy as Percy knew it. Graves was one of a large number of Southern liberals—Dabney, Daniels, Ralph McGill, and Cash were others—who admired the conservative Percy, partly because of the nobility of the man but also, one suspects, because Percy's paternalism in race relations was not really so far from their own views. But despite his regard for Percy, Graves wrote of him: "The tragedy of Will Percy, it seems to me, is that he surrendered when it wasn't necessary. He never was able to believe the 'tradesfolk' could become the aristocrats for whom he was saying goodbye."

Graves, that is, possessed a certain adaptability that Southern aristocrats like Will Percy lacked, an ability to accept with his head a change that he might find difficult to accept with his heart. He too might be called an aristocrat, but the aristocracy he preferred was one of merit, not necessarily of birth. He showed the same common sense in approaching those other intellectual forces in Southern life of the 1930s, the Nashville Agrarians and the Chapel Hill Regionalists. The Agrarians—John Crowe Ransom, Allen Tate, Donald Davidson, Robert Penn Warren, and eight other Southerners—had in 1930 written *I'll Take My Stand,* an unapologetic defense of the Southern agrarian tradition. They looked backward, not ahead; they protested, variously, industrialization, random progress, public education, and a modern God without thunder. They championed a traditional Southern sectionalism, by which they meant (or at least their most vigorous spokesman, Davidson, meant) putting the South first and the nation after it. In many ways Graves—essentially the social conservative—must have been attracted to agrarianism. In his book he praised the purity of spirit of the Agrarians and their "immortal volume"; but he also acknowledged their "bad economics," and in other parts of his book clearly pledged allegiance to the Southern Regionalists, that group centered in Chapel Hill and associated with sociologist Howard W. Odum which advocated sweeping social change and put the nation ahead of Dixie. "Sectionalism" and "Regionalism" were words tossed back and forth in the 1930s, and Graves made clear where he stood in the debate: "Sectionalism in the South, happily on the way out now, is a silly thing, sentimental always and looking backward. It is very different from regionalism. Regionalism is a recognition of facts of geography, economics, history, etc. . . . with resulting contribution to national variety." Howard Odum could not have said it better. Graves himself may often have been sentimental, but all the same he distrusted sentimentality in others. Soft-hearted, he was also hard-headed.

The Fighting South is, in the final analysis, a book not so much about the South as about the good life as Graves perceives it; and he believes the American South has had certain elements of that good life, and can contribute still others. Despite Graves's regard for the past, his book, finally, is one that looks ahead—for, unlike Cash and Percy when they completed their books in 1940 and 1941, Graves is pretty certain the Allies will win the war and America will determine its own destiny.

Also, despite Gerald Johnson's largely correct assessment that *The Fighting South* was not particularly prophetic—that the author left "prophesying to the prophets"—at times Graves *does* play the prophet. He anticipates Howard Zinn's thesis in *The Southern Mystique* (1964) that the South is a sort of distorted mirror image of the rest of the United States, a place where American vices and virtues are magnified. "The best and the worst of this nation are cartooned in the not-so-solid land between the Potomac and the Rio Grande," Graves writes. "The best land . . . the worst land. . . . More hating and more loving." He also anticipated, correctly, that the Agrarians' *I'll Take My Stand* would someday be more highly regarded than it was in the 1930s when many thinking Southerners ridiculed it as a testament of racial, religious, and economic conservatism. The Agrarian manifesto, Graves believed, was "a thing for the future out of the past." He suggested, as well, that there were certain qualities in Southern life, primarily a regard for manners and politeness, that in the future might make for more harmonious race relations in Dixie than elsewhere—although at the same time he was one of those myopic Southern liberals who could never have imagined that, thirty years after he wrote, the South would be racially integrated, and peacefully so.

Finally, Graves saw in the South a regard for leisure, an appreciation of simplicity, a distaste for bigness and certain elements of progress, a respect for individuality—in short, a regard for living as much as *making* a living—that the rest of the nation would come to appreciate in the later third of the twentieth century. His hope, as he expressed it in *The Fighting South*, was that "something defeated at Appomattox [would] come back to victory in our atom's splitting, that a dignity and balance in living which were the Old South's tradition [would] become the order of a New World's day . . . "

THE FIGHTING SOUTH

Chapter One

THE FIGHTING SOUTH

THIS IS A BOOK ABOUT THE UNITED STATES AND THE years to come. The writing has been done in that ever so dark and bright corner room which looks out upon the Atlantic and the Gulf, but the concern is with the whole house. No matter what a title seems to say I am not here to sing of the South's willingness to fight. I am here to examine the fact of that willingness as it relates to some raw material and finished stuff on hand below the Potomac for the America we hope to make. If Southern problems and depravities are mentioned, if notice is taken of lynchings and loud talk, cussedness, killings, malaria, and meanness, they are incident to a point about the nation that may be. If there is a little moonlight, a memory, and an ounce of glory, they belong to the same point.

Things that were wrong and things that were right need examining in cool science as we go about the making of a civilization near the heart's desire. Most of them are on exhibit in the South, and that is a good place to have them now that geopolitics is locating that region no longer at the shank of a continent but in the heart of a Western Hemisphere. Most of them are in the South —these evil things that must go, these fine ones that must flower. Most are identifiable, too, in circumstances which

3

had the South war-minded long before the attack on
Pearl Harbor made a fighting people of us all.

Week after week in the period from September, 1939,
to December, 1941, the South was the first on the Gallup
poll's regional list in friendliness for the British cause and
in disregard of consequences. There was Senator Reynolds, of course, but the North Carolinian was a specialty, not a rule. The expression of the South which the
polls reflected was found in the attitudes of Carter Glass,
of Virginia, and Claude Pepper, of Florida, two gentlemen whose disagreement on the New Deal advertised
the more their harmony against Hitler and their willingness to accept not only a shooting war but a declared
one. When anything hit the South hard enough in those
days to make New Dealers and anti-New Dealers forget
each other, that was hard hitting. And the war in
Europe did that to a lot of Southerners. Not to all of
them. There were New Dealers in the South, as elsewhere, who believed that the defense effort created both
an opportunity and a need for pushing the New Deal
further on all fronts. There were anti-New Dealers in
high estate whose hate of Hitler was only a secondary
affair with them; they were sure that Mr. Roosevelt had
already killed American democracy and was about to kill
the capitalist system in America, and they wondered
what all the shooting was about.

But the South, as the South, was for putting Hitler
down. And the South was for war if that should be the
only way to save England. The Gallup poll of early October, 1941, asked this question: "Which of these two

things do you think is the more important, that this country keep out of war or that Germany be defeated?" Seventy per cent of the American people as a whole, according to the cross-section questioned in the poll, thought beating Germany was more important. Eighty-eight per cent of Southerners thought so. This was typical of all the Gallup polls that had gone before and of polls taken by other organizations. It bore out the observation of Southern editors and politicians. It was reflected in the higher "morale" of Southern selectees in training camps. It recalled the strikingly larger proportion of voluntary enlistments by Southerners before the draft was organized, and the comment of Alabama's Congressman Luther Patrick, that "they had to start selective service to keep our Southern boys from filling up the army."

What was the explanation of this greater belligerency of the South in the days before Pearl Harbor? Dorothy Thompson said it was poverty, that Southerners had less to lose and were readier therefore to take a chance. Erskine Caldwell, professional discoverer of the worst, told an America's Town Meeting of the Air audience in February, 1941, that Southern ignorance was the explanation. Mr. Henry L. Mencken, when I asked him, came alive with old invective against the "Sahara of the Bozart." He even rephrased my question: "The unusual susceptibility of the South to English propaganda," he put it, "is in part, I suppose, an inheritance from Civil War days, and in part simply one more proof of the high voltage of Southern credulity. The English, to be sure, deserted the Confederacy when the going became dangerous, as they desert all their clients in like case, but they gave it some useful help so long as the business was safe and profitable. This set up an Anglomania in the South that still survives more or less. . . . But the main reason is probably the marked and almost pathological Southern capacity for believing in bogus messiahs. It was in the South, not in the North, that the Ku Klux buffoonery flourished most prosperously after the last war to save democracy, and in the South that the Anti-Saloon League collared the largest battalions of true believers. It is in the South today that the evangelical clergy maintain their only remaining hold on American public opinion, and it is the South that has always been easiest for such frauds as Bryan. The relative poverty of the region is largely a function of that insatiate will to believe. There is nothing more expensive on this earth than believing in the palpably not true. Contrariwise, poverty has an undoubted effect on credulity. The poor man is always easier to fool than the fellow who is well heeled. Skepticism is the brat of security. It is a surplus value."

The wonderful time Mr. Mencken had making this answer hurrahed between its lines. Nevertheless, believing in things, especially in a better world, while it may have sinful results, is hardly a sin. In fact, it may be the virtue which will give the democracies the élan they will need to survive this war and its aftermath.

Jonathan Daniels liked the poverty theory too, but was nicer about it and more sociological. " 'Have-not' people are all more inclined to belligerency than 'have' people," he wrote. "This war shows that. The comfortable in possession don't want to fight. This present belligerency in the South in terms of the European war may indicate a belligerency which is not limited to that. People in other regions of America may find that the young South as a 'have-not' region will have a belligerent push in it beyond this war. It may mean that we've got to put more meaning in democracy throughout America if that belligerency is to help us and not hurt us."

Other Southerners and observers of the South offered other theories. These had to do with the Anglo-Saxon blood and tradition of the South, the surviving psychologies of the Confederate War, the memory of England's sympathy in that war, the Southern climate and what it does to tempers and imaginations, the Woodrow Wilson influence, Southern loyalty to the Democratic party and the New Deal, the business of being agricultural, the long business of selling cotton to British mills, British money invested in some parts of the South after 1865, and, what most impressed me, a general psychology of danger and defense created in the South by all of its experiences, military, economic, and social. In offset to the uncomplimentary theories of Mr. Mencken was one that the South's feeling resulted from sheer virtue. "My notion," wrote Senator Carter Glass, "is that the attitude of the South is due both to superior character and to exceptional understanding of the problem involved."

Virginius Dabney, editor of *The Richmond Times-Dispatch*, named "the South's predominant Anglo-Saxon origins, its martial tradition, its dependence upon foreign markets for its cotton and tobacco, and its realization of what it means to be conquered." Editor Douglas Freeman, of *The Richmond News-Leader*, offered "first, our English stock; second, our martial tradition; and third, our knowledge that some things are worse than war." Mark Ethridge, of *The Louisville Courier-Journal*, thought a reason was "that we know better than anybody else that war settles questions. . . . Another is that our heroes in the South have always been military. . . . I feel, too, that climate has something to do with temper. We have never been a stolid people. . . . Perhaps deeper than anything else is the homogeneity of the Southern people. They come from pretty much a common source, their traditions are the same, including the tradition of fighting against political and religious oppression, and they understand that it is necessary to fight to preserve anything that is precious." Clark Howell, of *The Atlanta Constitution*, named "gratitude" and suggested, also, that "we of the South have once been a defeated and invaded country and we have learned just what this means. . . . Our friends in the West have never had the invader set his foot upon their soil, and possibly this is why there is not the unanimity among them to defeat Hitler on the other side of the Atlantic rather than wait for him to come over here." D. Hiden Ramsey, of *The Asheville Citizen*, wrote that "blood is thicker than ersatz." Also, that "Woodrow Wilson is still the major political prophet of the South," and "the South has never been fond of Germany or the German people. . . . Southerners are spirited folks . . . most of the great generals were of Southern birth . . . isn't it also true that the less urban a people are, the more willing they are to fight for their country? . . . The Anglo-Saxon tradition comes nearer than anything else to explaining." Governor Frank Dixon, of Alabama, James E. Chappell, of *The Birmingham News-Age-Herald*, and James G. Stahlman, of *The Nashville Banner*, stressed the same tradition.

The belief that Southerners are, for one reason or another, closer to American fundamentals, had emphasis in other replies to my inquiry. "The people of the South," wrote George Fort Milton, of Tennessee, historian of the Confederate War and its aftermath, "probably have the closest contact with the true fundamentals of democracy of any portion of our national citizenship. We have had fewer lush days to lead us into forgetfulness of the early faiths." Senator Burnet R. Maybank, of South Carolina, agreed. "An instinctive patriotism," he called it, "an immutable determination vigorously to defend the security of their country and their sovereign rights against unjust and unwarranted inroads from any quarter. . . . These characteristics are not engendered by any adverse material or educational conditions." Senator Lister Hill, of Alabama, made a similar point after mentioning the English stock and tradition and the "imprint of the War Between the States." He thought "Southerners are more belligerent not just about this war but about everything that pertains to their rights and their country . . . not merely because they are a people quick to action once their emotions are aroused but because they are willing to make a great sacrifice in this struggle for democracy just as their forebears risked their lives." A prominent physician of South Carolina said it was "realism," that "underneath the Southern superstructure of manners and romance is a habit of facing facts—and the fact was that Hitler had to be put down." Chancellor Oliver Cromwell Carmichael, of Vanderbilt University, believed that "the greater belligerence of the South towards this war is due to its greater abhorrence of dictatorship and greater love of liberty and freedom. . . . The spirit of Andrew Jackson and of Robert E. Lee is still reflected in the background and thinking of the mass of Southern peoples and expresses itself in the vitality of its opposition to tyrannical systems."

Margaret Mitchell, who is so modestly afraid of being expected to write another epochal novel that she dodges all debate about the South or things Southern, wrote that she "honestly" hadn't "the slightest idea why this [greater Southern belligerency] is true." But Stark Young, author of the South's other best-seller, "So Red the Rose," suggested "the traditional connection between the Southern conceptions and the English, the relation of our typical past to that of the landed class in the British Isles. With this is directly connected the tradition, not entirely dead yet, of a leading class from which other classes took the lead, as illustrated during the War Between the States by the way farmers and modest people without slaves or anything to lose or to gain by secession or war yet followed, partly by habit, the lead of the landed class. There is the remembrance that in that war the ruling class in England sided with the Southern cause, though in the end their advocacy was neutralized by other elements. . . ." Mr. Young mentioned, also, a theory that modern German methods of invasion and destruction derived from ones used against the South in the Confederate War. "Many a Southerner, reading the news of the German war over England, has by inheritance a certain added perception of its impact." He quoted James Truslow Adams' "America's Tragedy":

"In 1870, when Germany was fighting France, Sheridan had gone over as a private observer but was received by Bismarck and other high officials, both civil and military. Doctor Busch, the biographer of Bismarck, notes that at a dinner given by the Chancellor the discussion turned to the recent conduct of some of the German forces, and Councillor Abeken thought that war should be conducted in a more humane fashion. Sheridan denied this, says Busch, and expressed himself roughly as follows: The proper strategy consists in the first place in inflicting as telling blows as possible upon the enemy's army, and then in causing the inhabitants so much suffering that they must long for peace, and force their government to demand it. The people must be left nothing but their eyes to weep with over the war. The German noted in his journal: 'Somewhat heartless it seems to me, but perhaps worthy of consideration.' During the

World War the Bishop of London, in an address quoted the words of the American general but attributed them to the Kaiser."

The late Clarence Cason of the University of Alabama, whose book "Ninety Degrees in the Shade" was given to proving that nearly everything good, bad, or indifferent about the South is due to the number of months Southerners spend annually in hot weather, would have said of this question, no doubt, that when there is a war going on Southerners have ninety degree tempers and ninety degree imaginations and also that they think of themselves as a fighting people. Captain Joseph Haskell, aide to Major-General Richardson in the Louisiana war games in the spring of 1941, told of a conversation with an old man to whose farm he went for some local information during the maneuvers: "You think we'll git into this war?" the old man asked. When Captain Haskell wasn't sure, he added: "Well, if we do, I'm wondering if them Yankees is goin' ter he'p us."

The comparative poverty of the South, giving it less of vested interest and landed estate to lose than other parts of the country, may indeed have been a factor in its attitude towards the war. Yet in the Gallup polls the area which ranked next to the South in this pre-war belligerency was the monied East. And the poll of October, 1941, showed, for the country as a whole, the "upper income" people voting 76 per cent, the "middle income" 74 per cent, and the "lower income" only 65 per cent on the affirmative side of the proposition that it is more important to defeat Germany than to stay out of the war. There was the fact too, that, poor or not, Southerners are traditionally opposed to changing their ways or having their established order upset. Tenant farmers and sharecroppers may be little concerned for a status quo which has no real estate for them, but the farmers who own land and the villagers and townsmen who do their own little business feel as vested and landed about it as anyone in the world. Attend a Rotary luncheon in any small Southern town or a Farm Bureau meeting in any village school house and you will find little of the detachment from sense of material establishment that was supposed to make Southerners more willing to take a chance on war.

The "Anglo-Saxon blood and tradition" theory, to my mind, explained the attitude of some of the Southern classes but not that of the masses. It explained the intellectuals, perhaps, and the romanticists and the people in whose lives history and ancestry play a big part. These add to quite a total but they are outnumbered by Southern masses in whom there is no sense of England for better or worse. The average Southerner doesn't feel kin to the British through blood, experience, common tradition and institution, or service rendered. He knows more about English people than he does about Germans, but part of what he knows is what George Washington did to them at Yorktown and Andrew Jackson at New Orleans. And that King's Mountain affair. And the Mecklenburg business. As for the sympathies and help in the Confederate War, appreciation of these is obscured if not lost in the quantity and quality of memories nearer home. The diplomatic relations of the Confederacy rank with the Confederate navy as very small parts of the story upon which the South loves to dwell. To my mind, it was not the existence of an Anglo-Saxon tradition which explained the Southern position so much as it was the non-existence of a Germanic tradition. In the East and the Middle West immigrants from Germany, and second, third, and fourth generation descendants of those immigrants, had stamped Germany on the face of many affairs political, social, cultural, sentimental, nomenclative, and gastronomic. It was true that the Germany they represented was not the one of Hitler or the Prussian Junkers. It was rather the home-loving, music-loving, sentimental, intellectual Germany. But the stamp was there and it made for bonds with the Fatherland and natural sympathies which did not exist in the South. That was why it was possible to say that the South's greater belligerency came not of ties with any country across the sea but of a lack of ties.

Woodrow Wilson, the Democratic party, the New Deal—Southerners have been passionately loyal to all of these for one cause or another, and all were involved or recalled in the Roosevelt Administration whose war policy the South was supporting. They were factors in explanation, undoubtedly. But it wasn't for the War of 1917 or the League of Nations that the South loved Wilson and loves him still. It was for being a Democrat and a Southerner in the White House and a great man in the world. As for the Democratic party, Southerners had learned through the politically solid years to vote for it without liking everything it did or all of the people allowed in it—Tammany, the anti-Prohibitionists, the Catholics, and such. Party loyalty might have explained a Southern acceptance of the war policy but it did not explain Southern enthusiasm for the policy. Much the same could be said of the loyalties to Roosevelt and the New Deal. They were loyalties which had been compelled to ignore the New Deal championship of the Negro, which had already gone much farther than the white South liked. And they were loyalties which did not exist among some of the Southerners who were most clearly all-out for the war policy—Carter Glass, for example.

The War Between the States, with its scars and memories and the introspections that came of them, contributed much to the Southern attitude, it seemed to me. The contribution was psychological. The psychology was one of defense and living dangerously. So many things have been taken violently away from the South in the course of time (or lost to the South) that Southerners, as a people, have a violent aversion to losing things by violence. They may want and need better things but, more than that, they want to keep what they have. They withhold nothing in defense, and they are ready to defend by attacking when that is indicated. And danger, whether it be physical or economic, is a thing to which they are so accustomed in their history and present way that, while they do not court it, they stand in no such dread of it as do more prosperous and peaceful parts of the country. The fact that the murder capital of

America moves annually from one Southern city to another speaks not only of the carelessness with which Southern Negroes cut and shoot each other but of the comparative indifference of the South to violence. Living dangerously is not a philosophy with the average Southerner, but it is a habit.

The psychology of defense, the habit of dangerous living—and one thing more. That is the capacity for being pure of heart. There is guile in the South, and selfishness, and plain meanness, and disregard of law, and a full measure of hypocrisy and subterfuge. But when the subject is something learned in youth, something which possesses the imagination through such words as "patriotism," "religion," "honor," "manliness," "love," there is a knack of going all-out, of standing on no consideration of self, of being one hundred per cent in purehearted affirmation. (That is the thing Mr. Mencken can't stand.) All people are like that, more or less, but Southerners are especially given to such affirmation, perhaps by way of making up for being mean under other stimuli. Howard Odum, author of "Southern Regions," has analyzed better than I can this compound of defense, danger, and wholeheartedness. Agreeing that there was no one explanation for the greater belligerency of the South, he wrote me:

"One explanation is the South's ideology of patriotism and loyalty. Southerners give the appearance of wanting to believe in something and when believing in it, to fight for it. . . . Much of our belligerency is against those who do not believe as we do. It is defense.

It is also a left-over from the cultural conditioning of the Civil War and its Reconstruction. . . . There are so many things which we Southerners do not do that we are inclined to set up ideals and to fight for them as a substitute for doing more difficult and concrete things. The South, for instance, is sincere when it is willing to fight for Christianity and when it boasts of being the most Christian of the regions. . . . However, we fight to defend this larger faith more than we fight to see that our minority groups are given the benefit of our Christian doctrine. Hitler is anti-Christ, anti-individualistic, anti-American, and the fact that we ourselves in the South are Fascistic and dogmatic has nothing to do with the logic of our believing in the principle of Americanism and fighting for it. . . . Another elemental factor may be the continuing frontier culture of the South, not a retarded frontier as the sociologists call it but a continuing frontier of folk culture and folkways, and always, the spirit of war and fighting and defense. . . . There is another partial explanation in the fact that the South still retains the ideology of honor and a certain type of chivalry. . . . The South, with these ideologies of loyalty and defense and honor would not be consistent if it did not rise to a patriotic level."

Dr. Odum added that "the South has been invaded so often since the Civil War by thousands of reformers and accusers that it is automatically prepared to defend itself."

Southerners don't necessarily want to fight, but they don't mind very much, and they do think there are things worth fighting for. They got themselves into this frame of mind and heart by having a lot of trouble and being sorry for themselves and not too sophisticated. And all under a warm sun. And living out of doors, doing manual things, mostly on the land. That summed up the Southern situation, it seemed to me. I think it was a very good thing for the country and for the South that this attitude towards the war existed. It was good for the country because the country had a job on its hands which called for degrees of faith and fervor at home. It was good for the South because that region had been growing pathological in contemplation of its problems and in practice of hates to which the problems gave rise. Forgetting them for a time in favor of the primary problem of the world was good exercise.

Chapter Two

FOREVER AND EVER, AMEN

WHEN ANYTHING HITS WENDELL WILLKIE IN HIS FUN-
damental democracy he comes clean. We Democrats
concede him that. Mr. Willkie is pure-hearted about
things basic to his country. As a lawyer, he has been
glib with tricks of the courtroom. As a public utility
executive he has been up to all the defense mechanisms
and maneuvers which that much-mooted industry has
considered necessary. As a politician running for President he was as rough-and-tumble as anybody. But when
something comes up which concerns things he learned
as a boy, something plainly to do with such shining abstractions as liberty, democracy, and the like, he responds
with a nothingwithholding totality. When I wrote as
much of him editorially in the months when he was a
dark horse for the Republican nomination, he sent me a
little note indicating that this was his own theory of
himself: "I never read a better interpretation."

The Chinese were correct when, on the occasion of
the Willkie visit to Chungking in 1942, they gave him a
name which, translated, meant "Powerful Foundation."
The Chinese are too polite to have meant anything
physiological. A man of full quotas in sophistication, he
has the pure-heartedness about total things that comes

from childhood. It is a quality possessed by many Southerners, too, and, as I have suggested, explained in part their willingness to make this their war. Southerners carry through their lives more remainders from childhood than most people do, I believe. It makes them silly about some things, magnificent about others. The belligerence which has been advertised as "the Fighting South" derives in part, I think, from these native returnings, from circumstances that take Southerners back to first days when great events occur, and from an atmosphere about the childhood of many Southern men now in prime that was at once faithful and fighting.

The childhood of Southerners of the middle and upper classes whose attitudes still dominate the South had for its climate the rules, fixities, devotions, dramatics, acceptances, and eternities of Queen Victoria, Robert E. Lee, and the Lord God Almighty. Form ruled their world, and faith. These can be killing things when the form is worn out and the faith has no warrant. But unless there is some sort of form there is no container for living. And unless faith in something exists the driving powers of democracy grow as feeble as ours did in sick years before this war. When Descartes said the mind of a new-born child has nothing written on it but that its blank sheet does and must have ruled lines for writings to come, he said a thing too many of us forgot in the anarchies that were considered maturities before the war.

When I was a boy in College Park, Georgia, at the century's turn it was a time for the South of what W. J. Cash has called "easing tensions and quiet years." The

Populist revolt was dead. The aristocrats who had killed it were giving way to the "little foxes," hard-boiled descendants of Scarlett O'Hara who were going to win at any price. Industrialism was on the way, born of a cheap labor which didn't seem cheap by the standards of the agrarian South. Half in hope of what this industrial development would mean, half in disillusion because of agrarian hopes that had died, the Southern masses were patient again in their colonial lots. Tom Watson, the Georgia Populist, was giving up statemanship as a thing that didn't work, turning to bigotry. The problems which industry was bringing and which were destined to rank Number One in the nation were not yet distinct. A company house to live in and fifty cents a day for wages were tokens of something that had vaguely to do with progress, with Henry Grady's vision of a New South. But the changes that were coming were for the time being a tide "too full for sound or foam." Indeed, good feeling, or, rather, absence of bad feeling, covered the whole country. Imperial fervors of the Spanish-American War added to the good will. By 1907 my father, who had some rank in Democratic Party councils, attended a big one at Chattanooga and proposed to William Jennings Bryan that he inaugurate an era of national political amity by withdrawing from the Presidential race in favor of the Republican war hero, Teddy Roosevelt, who had made as many noises against "the corporate interests" as Bryan had. Bryan was very nice about it, insisted on letting my father make his speech after lieutenants had tried to censor it. But he

wasn't interested. He said "not as at present advised."
One of the Atlanta papers picked up the expression for
a cartoon in which a number of unlikely things were
given the same phrase. "Will New Orleans win the pen-
nant? Not as at present advised!" (It was last in the
Southern League.) "Will cotton hit twenty cents? Not
as at present advised!" (It was eleven cents.)

In those days my younger brothers and I would sometimes climb the big chinaberry tree outside the pantry
window and make illegal entry to steal shredded wheat
biscuit. Often in our thieving I would be troubled dimly
by the legend on the box—"Tell Me What You Eat and
I'll Tell You What You Are!" I couldn't tell him what
I ate because I ate everything. The question suggested a
set of problems, a series of differentials, discriminations,
inequalities, and introspections that troubled me. It
was my first contact with the stomach-aches of civilization.

We were dependent on our own inventions and fan-
cies then. From the same chinaberry tree, I remember,
we built a home-made railway with wooden two-by-fours
for rails and with flat-cars whose flanged wheels were
cotton mill spools cut in half. There were switches, sid-
ings, and graded curves. Railroading was the most fascinating of all phenomena for us, and we intended to be
locomotive engineers when we grew up, preferably on
the Atlanta and West Point Railroad.

Is it a sin to be remembering your childhood in days
of war and economics and fearful maturity? I think not.
And so much can be remembered. The games we played

there in College Park, my brothers and sisters, the Mc-
Crory and Willingham children and I. "Stealing Sticks,"
"Anthony Over," "Run, Sheep, Run," "Leapfrog,"
"Pop the Whip," "Hop Scotch," "Postoffice," "Drop
the Handkerchief," "Clap In, Clap Out," "Going to
Jerusalem," and many a home-made one without a name.
We played a game with marbles called "Knucks Down,"
and wrapped the agates in grease to get the nicks out.
There was "Shinny" with clubs made of the root and
lower part of a hickory sapling. We had a game of throwing tops to split other tops with the sharpened point or
to "null" chewing tobacco tags. Sling-shots, kites, bows
and arrows, acting poles—we had them all and all were
made at home. And string "telephones" rigged with pa-
per-bottomed tin cans and a waxed cord. And the things
we did on our bicycles. I can remember the wondrous
"zoon" of a rubber band stretched between the handle-
bars as I rode at top speed in the wind. We saved soap
coupons for a prize, and the shiny tin tags from chewing
tobacco, and photographs from cigarette packages, and
the bird pictures that came in soda boxes, and stamps,
and butterflies. Putting straws in doodle-bug holes, lightning bugs in bottles, June-bugs on a string. Going to
school with a tin lunch box and your books strapped
together. Whistles and blowguns made of hickory bark
or reeds from the canebrake. The deviltry of smoking
rabbit tobacco, dried corn silks, or plain string. And that
fateful, fascinating book "Slovenly Peter" in which appalling things happened to those who would not eat their
soup or cut their fingernails. The pain and thrill of be-

ginning to go barefooted each April, and of putting on shoes again in October. Sometimes we would want to go before it turned warm enough for us to change from long underwear. My father would say we could do it if we would wash our feet and legs in cold water on the morning of the proposed release—a bargain we were likely to consider too hard because bathing in cold water was an atrocity in those days.

Once I had a hand printing press and published a little weekly paper called "The College Park News" with my sister Laura for society editress. My brother De-Graffenreid was "circulating manager." He ran the errands. There was the era of magic lanterns and scroll saws. And dabbling in electricity, feeling Edisonian when we learned to wrap wire around a core to make a magnet. There were adventures in photography, with "Brownie kodaks," developing pictures in a dark room by a mystic red lantern, the "hypo fixing solution," printing the negatives on "solio" paper by day or "velox" by night. There was a game called "Greenie" which my sisters played. You had to have something green in your possession always and display it when commanded by your opponent. It went on for weeks. They were always cutting out paper dolls, too, Laura and later on "little Anne." And having candy pullings, play-houses, mud pies. They cooked small flour wafers on a charcoal burner. They would make music with tissue paper folded over a comb. They had parties and were grown-up ladies. They made clover chains, hats and aprons of leaves pinned with twigs, crowns of plaited clover. They read

"The Five Little Peppers and How They Grew," "Diddie, Dumps and Tot," "Little Women," and so did I, but the book I liked best was about a faithful, hard-fighting sheep dog. It was called "Bob, Son of Battle."

We children called our father "Papa" and our mother "Mama" until we moved to New York and changed to "Dad" and "Mother." Now my younger daughter calls me "John" and her mother "Mammy." My youngest brother had to be named for so many relatives and friends that he ended up as Cothran Calhoun Carter Smith Graves. My father was famous at the time of his marriage because of his speech at the death of Henry W. Grady. President Grover Cleveland wrote him a letter which was framed and is still a fixture on my family wall. "As I look back upon the years that have passed since God in His infinite goodness bestowed upon me the best of all His gifts—a loving and affectionate wife," wrote Mr. Cleveland, "all else, honor, the opportunity of usefulness and the esteem of my fellow countrymen, are subordinated in every aspiration of gratitude and thankfulness."

> You are not wrong, therefore, when you claim, in the atmosphere of fast-coming bliss which now surrounds you, kinship with one who can testify with unreserved tenderness to the sanctification which comes to a man when heaven-directed love leads the way to marriage. . . . Since this tender theme has made us kinsmen, let me wish for you and the dear one who is to make your life doubly dear to you, all the joy and happiness vouchsafed to

man. . . . You will, I know, feel that our kind
wishes can reach no greater sincerity and force than
when my wife joins me in the fervent desire that
you and your bride may enter upon and enjoy the
same felicity which has made our married life "one
grand, sweet song."

> Very truly your friend,
> Grover Cleveland.

My father's father, General James Porterfield Graves,
and my mother's mother, lived with us. She was twenty
years younger but he considered her an old lady. Every
day before midday dinner they played backgammon and
resumed the game after the meal. They would play, too,
at other hours. That more or less eternal backgammon
game, with the sound of the cups clicking the dice down,
my grandfather reciting his throw aloud and calling
threes "trays" and twos "deuces," my grandmother saying "Your move, General" rather sharply when he would
be slow—was one of the undercurrents of time, as much
a fixture as the flowered porcelain clock on the mantle-
piece. The competition was eager but formal. Each felt
enough younger than the other to make allowances.
Grandmother considered herself old enough and seemed
to want to be. It was just that she thought the General
so much older. She wore her hair parted straight down
the middle. She was always making things, clothes,
cakes, needlework, knitting. Her lemon pies were a tradition. They were supposed to be wonderful and I suppose they were. I never questioned it, but I have not
liked lemon pies since I grew up and it must be that sub-

consciously I didn't care for grandma's. She had some of the literary gifts of her brother, Major Charles E. Smith (who had written for *The Atlanta Constitution* under the name "Bill Arp"). Her vivid stories of days as a young mother in Rome, Georgia, when the Yankees occupied the town during the Confederate War were the first dramas I knew. Grandfather was less communicative. He loved to work about the place with a hoe or rake in the mornings. All afternoon he would doze in his room or sit in a big chair by the window and look at the girls on the campus of Cox College across the road. My father bought him a telescope to see them better for he was very fond of them and they made a pet of him. He believed my father to be the greatest man alive. Once when he went into Atlanta to attend a banquet in my father's honor he drank too much. He told me sorrowfully the next morning that he was "the degenerate sire of an illustrious son." But he had his toddy every night before supper all his life, and lived to be ninety-six.

The McCrory's next door were like members of our family. Malcolm McCrory and I were the same age and did everything together, including fighting. The fighting was generally with rocks. One day as we were slowly retiring from a rock battle, throwing as we went, his struck the ground in front of me, bounced up and broke two of my front teeth. There was a frightful two-family commotion. Mother was overcome. My beauty was spoiled for life. As she weepingly ministered to my cut lips in the bathroom Mr. McCrory brought Malcolm into our back yard and whipped him conspicuously with a cane, hoping that would make mother feel better. But we always felt that the McCrory's whipped too hard. In our family only mother did any whipping, and she used a little peachtree switch which was more humiliating than painful. Malcolm was destined to become one of the most successful business men in the South. He had it in him from the beginning. I remember that when I was given a fine bone-handled pocket knife for my birthday he swapped with me for his shiny, figure-handled one. When I came home with my new knife they told me it wasn't worth a fourth as much as the bone-handled IXL. But it was beautifully shiny, and I still feel satisfied with the bargain. From Malcolm I had my first lesson in finance. He taught me to match pennies and each time I won he would offer to match again "double or quits." I won and won. He owed me $1.28 and I marveled at his daring when he offered to match once more. He won that time so it was quits, but I believed I had come near a fortune.

Another member of the family was Uncle Steve. He was black with the matured blackness that seems aged in wood. Everything that had to be done out of doors about the place—the barn, the garden, the grass, repairs, chickens, wood-cutting, driving, errand-going—he did. He worked for us always. His only vice was getting drunk once a week and that was understood and provided for. I remember him best for his coming in on dark winter mornings before dawn to make the fires. Especially when something eaten or read had upset my imagination and I would have been lying awake a long time imagining lions at the window, burglars under the bed, nameless "things" behind the big chair, or a sinister man on horseback riding around the backyard. Then would come the soothingly definite sound of Uncle Steve at the door with his coal scuttle and kerosene-soaked kindlings, the first little flare of light outlining him squatting there to put the heavier wood and coal on, then his calm departure, and the flames of the fire coming more and more alive, making comfortable flickers and shadows on the wall, making the world kind and safe, with the man on horseback miles away.

I remember Uncle Steve, too, for the way he would turn up around the corner of the house with an axe on his shoulder on occasions when my father was away on lecture trips and passing tramps to whom mother had given food became "impudent." Uncle Steve wouldn't be threatening white men with an axe. But there he was, just happening by on his way to the woodpile.

There were bad Negroes but we children didn't know anything about them. All the wickedness we knew was white—tramps, burglars, horse-beaters, and the villains in books we read. The Negroes in College Park lived in a section called Darktown, but Uncle Steve lived with us. In September, 1906, there were race riots in Atlanta after several criminal attacks on white women by Negroes. Much blood was shed. There were stories of Negroes thrown headlong from the high viaduct on Whitehall Street who would jump up and run away as soon as they touched the ground. Wild rumors went around, and out in College Park we didn't know what might happen.

Sunday afternoon while my father was in Atlanta writing his Monday editorials and mother and I were sitting on the long front porch we saw a group of Negroes approaching the far edge of the big lawn around our place. Mother was much disturbed and sent me in to get the repeater shot-gun Uncle Charlie had given us in case of trouble. But when I came out with it she was smiling. The group had come near enough for the beaver hat the leader was wearing to be seen. Negroes didn't wear beaver hats for trouble. That hat meant a formal occasion, and it was. Formally the Negroes of Darktown, led by their Baptist preacher in the hat, had come to tell my father that they considered him the best friend the colored people had in the country and to put themselves in his hands for advice and protection. Because he was editor of *The Atlanta News*, which had printed the criminal attack stories on its front pages, New York papers were holding him partly responsible for the riots. John D. Wade repeated the charge in his sketch in the Dictionary of American Biography and it was mentioned in some distinguished books about the South later. But the colored people of Darktown didn't think so.

No one was very rich in College Park but no one was seriously poor either. Our nearest contact with Poverty was Miss Kitty Dukes. Miss Kitty was a little, dried-up, humpbacked old maid with a sharp tongue. She would come hopping along into our backyard every now and then for an interview with mother which had to do with "gittin' some vittles." Where she lived I never knew but we were told that she was "very poor" and had to be provided with food and old clothes. We children were afraid of her. Because of the independent way she talked we thought of her as a superior rather than an inferior person. Her poverty was something on which we had no judgment. It appealed only as a vague and interesting condition, like having a baby or being a hundred years old. I believe she felt that way about it herself.

Family singing was a part of our life in College Park. Mother played the piano beautifully, and in time my sister Laura did too. After supper at night we would all sing, but my father would fall out early because he couldn't carry a tune. The music in him was for words. He would always call for a song called "Absent." Mother taught Laura and me to sing a duet, "Nearest and Dearest," but the songs I liked best were "A Warrior Bold" and "Only an Armour Bearer." Not until I grew up did I learn that it was "armour bearer;" I sang it "Only an army barrel, proudly I stand" and "Surely my captain will depend on me—Though but an army barrel I may be." The sense of something faithful to the point of inanimation was enhanced by the mistake. But it was to the "Warrior Bold With Spurs of Gold" that I thrilled most. The brave knight in armour bright who went so gaily to the fray, fought the fight but before night his "soul had passed away." And the "plighted ring he wore" and the way he remembered as he died his love who was so "bright and fair" and had such golden hair—

> So what care I, though death be nigh,
> I've lived for love—and for love—I—die!

A girl with golden hair and blue eyes and an ethereal appearance—her name was Frieda Ashe—lived next door to us. I was desperately and nobly in love with her several times a day, but she never knew. I exercised the emotion from a distance and always in warrior-bold armour.

Because my father was a famous Southern orator and I was his oldest son he wanted me to be one some day, too. He made me read "Beacon Lights of History" in summer vacations, and memorize poetry. It was always heroic poetry. I loved to "speak" it when I could be far enough away from people to feel unobserved. My favorite place was the top of a ladder that led to my acting pole. I would stand there and shout "Marmion and Douglas"—

> And darst thou then to beard the lion in his den,
> The Douglas in his hall!
> And hopest thou hence unscathed to go—
> No! By St. Bride of Bothwell, no! . . .

There was a tragic one called "Allen Bayne," too, which began: "They're taking me to the gallows, mother, they mean to hang me high, they're going to gather round me there and watch me till I die . . ." But the poems that counted most were ones in favor of Robert E. Lee and the Lost Cause. "In vain the Tennessean set—his breast against the bayonet"—I could put a passion into that "et." And "The Sword of Lee"—

> Forth from its scabbard, high in air,
> Beneath Virginia's sky—
> And they who saw it gleaming there

And knew who bore it knelt to swear
That where that sword led they would dare
To follow and to die . . .

I was always at my most sing-song when my father
would listen. I could see that he feared I would never
amount to anything, but he loved me anyhow. And the
heroic belligerencies of the verses were in me, even if
their meters bound me too close. The enemy varied but
it was usually the Yankees. I didn't really hate the
Yankees; they were just a target, I think. But the Lost
Cause was something in all my imaginings. The fact of
being lost was not an end to it but an extra quality, a
something pitiful and proud without which it would not
have been so alive. Even when the Spanish-American
War provided more contemporary enemies I never could
feel that they amounted to much in comparison with the
Yankees. There was a diversion, though, when I read
Conan Doyle's "The White Company." We organized
one of our own to do noble and dangerous deeds, with a
tree house for headquarters. The only approach was by
a hanging rope that had to be climbed hand-over-hand.
There was a countersign, too.

Next to Robert E. Lee was the Lord God Almighty.
God was not a white-haired old man or anything like
that but He was real, and always to be reckoned with.
On Sundays we went to Sunday School at nine, church
at eleven and Prayer Meeting at night. There was Wednesday night Prayer Meeting, too, and the Earnest
Workers Society. And "Now I Lay Me Down to Sleep"
prayers at bedtime, and blessings before each meal. We

were allowed to look at the pictures in Dante's "Inferno" and "Paradiso" on Sunday but never the funny papers. The Katzenjammer Kids, Happy Hooligan and Little Nemo had to wait for Monday morning. My sense of relationship with God was confused at times because of the way Brother Martin prayed in church. Telfair Martin was an insurance man on weekdays but on Sunday mornings when Dr. Mack, our minister, would call on him to lead in prayer he was God's best friend. An enormous man with much blood in his face and vivid black hair, he would stand with head thrown backward in a sweating exaltation while torrents of variegated sound poured from him. Every now and then he would extend both arms heavenward in graceful appeal while his great voice rolled on. He undertook the whole gamut of relations with the Deity, and had an inflection for each. Now he would thunder as the ally of an Almighty God. Now he would whine a way to the ear of a Tyrant God. Now wheedle a favor from a strangely Gullible God. He would befriend against his fellowman's neglect a Lonely God, sing adoration to a Sentimental God, patronize a God-Who-Was-Doing-His-Best, and finally trumpet a victory over evil for a Napoleonic God whose heaviest artillery, surely, must boom with sounds like Brother Martin's. My grandmother, who considered us Presbyterians different, didn't care for Brother Martin's praying. She said he sounded more like a Baptist.

In addition to my other religious activities, I pumped the organ which mother played in church. It was a small organ with a foot pump where the pedals are on a piano.

I would stand there beside her and sing as I pumped, sometimes enjoying my singing so much I would leave the pipes without enough air at a critical moment. Brother Woods White had to speak to me about it.

But my deeper contacts with God were when the sun would set in summer evening glory behind Cox College across the road from our home. My grandfather would be looking at the college girls with the telescope my father had given him but, lacking his maturities, I would be looking at God in red, blue, and gold, in seashores of pink ranked shells the clouds would make, in lines of radiance from below the horizon. That was where God was, and he wasn't a white-haired old man and he wasn't Brother Martin's Best Friend, and he wasn't a member of the Earnest Workers Society or even a Presbyterian. He was a Glory. He was a terrible, eternal, righteous Beauty. He was the Form into which all life was fitted. He was all the things in the world that didn't die. He was something you got lost in and didn't know you were lost. He was yourself all swelled to infinity and dealt around the universe. He was the Impossible that was possible. And most of all He was the winner in a brave battle with the Yankees, the Spaniards, and the Devil.

There are measures in which my boyhood was not typical of Southern ones at the century's turn. There are other measures in which it was typical not only of the South but of all America. What is very typical of the South, it seems to me, is my joy in remembering this boyhood and the extent to which it conditions my mental and spiritual reflexes today. Youth is indeed a pure-hearted time. Those who carry its stamp and are subject to its call through all their other years—as so many Southerners are—will be giving their hearts in toto on occasion, no matter how halting and half-measured their ordinary ways may be. And if there were Lost Causes, Robert E. Lees, God Almightys, Yankees, Men on Horseback, rock battles, and White Companies—and a home so loved and full of love that any threat-to-home gives defense mechanism an automatic start—the response is sure.

Why do Southerners remember their childhoods so lovingly? They have no monopoly on big families or youthful joy. Perhaps it is for the contrast those childhoods make with adult days, with the greater hardship and less return of economic life in the South. Perhaps it is the Southern poverty of which so much is said. But it is something else, too, I think. It is the long conservatism of the South reacting to a world of appalling change in which the sin of breaking the rules to win is the sin of all mankind, with Hitler only the ranking sinner. That Victorian Southern world of my childhood was a stable one for me, with affirmations and acceptances, plus signs, faith, law, things eternal. It was wrong in a million ways, of course, and I remember that Woodrow Wilson was the one who let me know. The burden of his presidential address to my freshman class at Princeton in 1910 was that this is "a dynamic, not a static" universe and that things move on.

But I remember, too, that in my senior year the British poet, Alfred Noyes, who was visiting professor, talked much of what he called "putting the temporal into relation with the eternal." As often as he would recite for us his favorite "Go Down to Kew in Lilac Time—It Isn't Far from London," he would tell us about putting the temporal into relation with the eternal. It was the secret of literature and of life, he said, and I believed him. I felt that Woodrow Wilson would believe him too.

We who have called ourselves liberals through the anarchies of America's 1920's and the denials of her 1930's, who wish to move men forward and make them free, may have to go in for more of the eternities with our temporals when this war is over and a world is being put together. We may have to save our spiritual and mental health and our driving power with a psychology that has acceptances as well as refusals, plus signs with the minuses. We may have to make men free not only by changing lives and chances but by restoring arenas and rules of the game, senses of adventure in the play, things eternal as the play goes on. We may have to find it in our hearts to say again, as long ago: "Forever and Ever, Amen."

There is a limit to high explosion. In the summer of 1940, when Belgian forts were blown apart and dive bombers and panzer divisions were taking France, the dissipations of trinitrotoluol seemed to have no end. We know better now. The slayers who think they slay are faced everywhere with resurrection. The will to live and be free multiples against attack. The spirit of man carries on. Guns can't shatter it, submarines can't sink it or dictators order it down. In the end it will conquer merely by existing. This certainty of things that do not die is a comfort and a spur to those who are fortunate enough to possess it. It will be a possession more precious when the war is won. It comes more by what we feel than by what we know, by what we remember than by what we perceive, more from childhood's pure impression than maturity's complex.

Chapter Three

HIGHLIGHT AND LOW

BECAUSE I WAS BORN AND SPENT MY CHILDHOOD IN THE
South and then went away for enough years to have distance give both enchantment and perspective, and because my return happened to come in the midst of a jazz
age which was followed by a time of trouble and psychopathic cases everywhere, I am an extremist. Having spent
one-half of my life thinking the South wonderful and the
other half being taught it was terrible, I am forever finding it both. And, as luck would have it, I am right. The
best and worst of this nation are cartooned in the not-
so-solid land between the Potomac and the Rio Grande.

There is the best land this side of the Valley of the
Nile. In the areas on both banks of the Mississippi below
Memphis which they call the Delta cotton grows as tall
as corn. The soil wealth of a continent has been filtered
down on those bottoms in annual orgies of the river,
supporting in grace the late William Alexander Percy
and all the fine people before him and their lanterns
on the levees. There is the worst land, too, spread about
the South, growing more so with every rain that gullies
away its small remainders of topsoil. Dreary, damned,
lost land as hollowed-eyed, thin, and sick as the people

who try to make a living on it for themselves and a down-at-the-heel landlord.

There are the most listless people and the most animated. Only about 135 miles from "Tobacco Road" is the City of Atlanta. Whether they came from coca-cola or gave to it, the animations of Atlanta are like none other in these United States. People of all walks and both races live in a state of blood pressure that makes a profession of the impossible, conceive all things within their province and achieving, approach every issue in a spirit of razzle-dazzle and, without half the substance of less frenzied communities like nearby Birmingham, win on nerve, verve, and self-assertion. Long before there was a jazz age anywhere else there was one in Atlanta, and long after that age has passed from hideous sight and sound its hangovers will be driving pulses on Peachtree Street. An area of equal life and more grace is New Orleans. Of Atlanta it is said that it would be gay until the heavens fell. But of New Orleans it may be said that it would be gay long after heaven had fallen and all hope gone. The liveliness of Atlanta is pendant on assurance and bright hoping, but the Crescent City's is in the blood, a relic of history, an in-bred way, a resistance turned chronic to low altitudes, wet temperatures, and hard times, a Latin touch that will have no commerce with Anglo-Saxon heaviness.

There is the animation, too, of those sun-dried Floridians with bright eyes and scrawny necks and high-pitched voices who insult the legend of their semi-tropics and the habit of their neighbors with sleepless energies that seem to come of some concentration from the sun. And there is the animation of a certain other type of Southerner who has come to live almost bodilessly on something in his mind, the nourishment of crowding ideas or a driving task. Men like Gilchrist B. Stockton, of Jacksonville, former American Minister to Vienna.

Southern accent and speaking have this range from best to worst, too. The sounds that come from some of the larynxes differ in content but not monstrosity from what Hollywood and the stage once made them out to be. Voices of syrup, voices that drone like a nauseated bee, whine, squeak, and saw the nerves, voices thick as a cornfield darky's, voices thin as paper. And others from the same land that sound like mankind at its best. Smooth, with music in them, educated, exact, soft without being weak, civilized against every harshness, dropping final "g's" without losing them just as the French remember but do not mention their final "n's." Turn on a radio in the South. You may hear a heavy-breathing evangelist, grunting, shouting, going crazy in God's name, having a fit on the Heavyside Layer—and wonder if it is Africa you have got, not Alabama. You may hear a whine-voiced female reading her piece with wrongly-accented sentences as occurrent as wrongly-accented words, and first syllables made to sound like the whole thing. *Inn*-surance, *Dee*-troit, *Ice* Cream. But sometimes you get something else. You get a glory in speech. You hear the poised flow from which a musical and ease-taking land has taken every discord, smoothed every obstacle. You hear the most civilized speech this side of France.

Affection and disaffection have their extremes, too, below the Potomac. There is more hating and more loving. For best examples, the two subjects which most inspire bad feeling among present-day Southerners—union labor and the Negro. Southerners excel all others, I believe, in the sums total of hate they put into the two troubles. But they excel, also, in affection between employers and employees, between white men and black. The terms of the affection may be wrong, there may be no equity in it nor any solution of the immense problems, but it is a genuine condition. And even though it does not give the answer that must be given to racial and industrial quarrels, it is surely one of the predicates to the eventual right answering. It relates to the answer even if it does not make it. The Negro in the South suffers many injustices at the hands of white majorities and as a race is hated by many Southern whites. But as an individual he is liked, and that may not be said of him elsewhere in this country. The Southern employee, too, is more often known and liked by his employer even though that employer's hate of labor leaders and organized labor may lead him to unlimited hostilities and even though under the competitive drive in a comparatively poor region intolerable working conditions have sometimes been permitted. The personal touch is a hold-over from slave days, and paternalism is the bad name for it. But affection is its good name and it belongs somewhere on the list of American assets for a better world.

There is the matter of statecraft. Southerners work hard at their politics. They put more native talent into it, care more, get more pleasure out of it, than most people. It is their passionate pastime. They are very good at politics and very bad in the uses they make of politics. In Mississippi, I believe, there is a greater incidence of talented politicians than anywhere else in the world. And among these politicians there is a more nearly even division between demagogs and statesmen. In that state and the other Southern ones appears the peculiarly Southern type of misleader of the people—the demagog who believes in his stuff, hypnotizes himself with his public, is as earnest in his evangelism as he is scoundrelly in his method. Tom Heflin wasn't fooling when he told Alabama's farmers that the Roman Catholics in Washington had bought up all the high pieces of ground and put high walls around them to hide gun emplacements for the day when the Pope would signal the taking over of this country. He honestly believed it and those strangely shy blue eyes of his showed it as he talked. Eugene Talmadge believed in the Negro menace, even though he believed equally in the political effectiveness of inciting the white man against the black. It is possible to guess that the ablest demagog of all—the Louisiana Kingfish—had bewitched himself at the time of his taking away into a belief that he would really make every man a king, even though he must have had against that eventuality ample plans for letting his imperial lieutenants fleece the kings good and proper. But the Southern states have produced, too, and in this century, men of

conscience and dream in statecraft whose political passions were born in the light and who would not com-
promise in the representative ideal of a people's will in a
statesman's way. Woodrow Wilson may have owed his
education and philosophy to other influences but the
flame in him was kindled through Calvinistic generations
in the South. His burning idealism was Southern, come
with the lights of his first day at Staunton, Virginia, and
even though the principle of umpired competition for
which he stood in both foreign and domestic policy was
never examined enough in the South to have meaning
there his stands at Armageddon and his "battle for The
Lord" thrilled Southerners with a sense of a great kins-
man in action. As unyielding in his way as Woodrow
Wilson was another Southern statesman of this century
—Mississsippi's John Sharp Williams, who left Washington of his own volition in 1923 swearing he would
"rather be a hound dog and bay at the moon from any
Mississippi plantation than remain in the United States
Senate." And Oscar Underwood, of Alabama, who
might have had the Presidency if he had been willing to
be silent against the Ku Klux Klan at the Democratic
Convention of 1924 ("Alabama casts 24 votes for UN-
derwood!") And Carter Glass, of Virginia, whose intelligence, patriotism, and courage in long office-holding
have not been questioned even by those who have
doubted his social-mind. And Tom Watson, of Georgia,
who may have succumbed at last to the creeping sicknesses of the South but who was a brave and great leader
in his time. Josephus Daniels belongs in the statesman's

roll, too, I believe, for intelligent humanitarianism in many high places. These and other Southern names have been respected at Washington in this century for capability in office. And the ten recent years in the saddle have given Southerners an experience in power—especially congressional committee power—which has brought forth as many statesmen as blatherskites and blow-hards. Two of the most nimble-witted and effective men ever to serve in the Senate are James F. Byrnes, of South Carolina, and Hugo L. Black, of Alabama, both of whom were appointed from that body to the Supreme Court. Mr. Byrnes resigned from the Court in the fall of 1942 to become Wartime Director of Economic Stabilization. With no college education, making his way all the way, he has learned as he has lived. Black, almost as self-made, carried through days of opportunistic politics a habit of study and a passion for the underprivileged which are making him at once a just judge and an humanitarian one, still in love with social ends but no longer persuaded they justify any and every means.

The South's best foot foremost in statecraft is Cordell Hull of Tennessee. He has the homespun and humility of a Lincoln and he can be in his way as rough-and-tumble as Andrew Jackson. With these qualities he has served the Wilson philosophy of free competition throughout the world with Wilson's passion and persistence and without Wilson's intellectual arrogance. Intelligent enough in statecraft, right enough in political thinking, the extra something which makes him great is his character, the massive salt of him.

Democracy, subject-matter of two wars in this century, is a thing both honored and despised in the South, both lived and denied. There is the pure democracy of a man like President Frank Graham, of the University of North Carolina, so pure that it gets him into as much (and much the same) trouble as would the practice of pure Christianity. And there is the un-democracy of the Ku Klux Klan, of the flag-waving lunatics, the Fascist-minded wearers of shirts and feathers, and certain industrialists who are sure that the masses must be kept ignorant, non-voting, and unorganized because real democracy won't work, not in the South at any rate. Of liberty, equality, and fraternity it may be said that the South denies equality, practices fraternity and, at least, sings liberty. The same Southerners who insist on a permanence of inequality between white man and black, worker and employer, landlord and tenant, rich and poor, may practice more than any others the fraternities between races and classes that astonish people from other parts of the country. The white man may treat the Negro like "kinfolks" even if he won't treat him like a fellow citizen. The employer and the employee may be "Bill" and "John" to each other even though their group relationship is paternalism on one side and professional unionism on the other.

There are extremes in music. Out of New Orleans en route from Africa and the Igorottes came the awful one-one-one concatenations, the dreadful tin pans, the adenoidal horns, the demoniac drums. But out of the cotton fields and kitchens came the Negro spirituals. Outlanders love them objectively as expressions of a strange world of longing, trouble, resignation, passion, and faith. But Southern white people love them introspectively as well. They love them with a half possession of the same histories, emotions and imaginations that gave them being. Indeed, according to Prof. George Pullen Jackson, of Vanderbilt University, who has made a specialty of the study, Negro spirituals are nothing out of Africa or originating in race experience but adaptations of old camp meeting songs of the early white settlers.

When I think of the total of contradiction in the South I find it summed up for me somehow in the whole circumstance of Huey Long's address to the Cajans in the Teche country under the Evangeline Oak. It was when he was running for governor of Louisiana in 1928. The words most on Huey's lips, probably, were "son-of-a-bitch." And the King's English was for him something to be killed in the presence of those sweating masses whom he promised to make kings. But when the spirit moved him or the occasion came he could be a purist and a poet. He was both on that morning beside the famous tree. "And it was here," he told them, "that Evangeline waited for her lover Gabriel, who never came. This oak is an immortal spot, made so by Longfellow's poem, but Evangeline is not the only one who has waited here in disappointment. . . .

"Where are the schools that you have waited for your children to have, that have never come? Where are the roads and the highways that you spent your money to build, that are no nearer now than ever before? Where

are the institutions to care for the sick and disabled?
Evangeline wept bitter tears in her disappointment. But
they lasted through only one lifetime. Your tears in this
country, around this oak, have lasted for generations.
Give me the chance to dry the tears of those who still
weep here."

The best and the worst. Demagogs and poets, lovers
and betrayers, sickness and health. They are not exclusive properties of the South, and in many instances their
superlatives are not there. Best and worst are everywhere
in America. But they are more visible in the South because the lines are clearer and there is less of intermedi-
ate. America in highlight and lowlight—the America
which pulled itself together after Pearl Harbor and
which will have been more advertised and warned by
this war than in all its centuries before—may be looked
at in the South. Especially because this South is a fighting South, one which, without telling itself so, accepts
the play of contradiction and opposing force as history's
way, nature's way, and the way of human pulses.

Chapter Four

CENTRIPETAL FORCE

THE FIRST NATION-SIZED AMERICAN TO CALL THE SOUTH
poor was not Franklin Delano Roosevelt in 1938. It was
John Caldwell Calhoun in 1850. "The South, the poor
South!" were the Nullificationist's last words. In the beginning there had been no more total an American than
this gaunt-eyed man of the South. When he entered
Congress from South Carolina in 1810 and became
chairman of the committee on foreign affairs he was a
super-nationalist. He it was who introduced the resolu-
tion of war upon England in 1812, and in the conduct
of that war he made himself so invaluable that they
called him "the young Hercules who carries the war on
his shoulders." Then and for many years after he was a
big navy man, a big army man, a friend of the national
bank, an advocate of internal improvements by the
Federal government. He was even a protectionist. Over
and over he spoke for national unity, deprecated sectional feeling and what he—of all people!—called "re-
fined arguments on the Constitution." John Quincy
Adams said of him in those days: "He is above all sectional prejudice more than any other statesman of this
Union with whom I have ever acted."

If Calhoun became later the first professional Southerner, the profession was not of his choosing. It came to him out of developing circumstance. What he thought of as the excesses of Northern states in rivalry with the South, of industry serving itself at agriculture's expense, turned him at last from America as a whole to the South in particular, and from a scorn of fine-spun theories about the Constitution to theories of his own spun masterfully fine to defeat the economic inequities he believed to have been established against South Carolina and the other Southern states. These produced his Doctrine of Nullification, his theory of secession, his call for Southern blocs to defend Southern rights. The tariff excesses of 1828 and the greater ones of 1832 seemed to him to be "making geographical divisions of a nation," "making two of one nation." When, like Lee in 1861, he saw that the divisions had been made and the two created, he gave himself to his own half.

In January, 1849, the year before his death, Calhoun called a conference of Southern Senators and Congressmen and begged them to hold this Southern situation above party allegiance. He predicted a tragic era for the South if the North was permitted to have its majority way on these economic matters. But his fellow Southerners were not convinced. Only a minority of them would sign his manifesto, and a political stand which might have saved the subsequent one at arms was denied.

On the moral issue of slavery the South deserved to be defeated in that stand at arms. And the defeat served a purpose of such point to the whole developing principle of human liberty that it may have been worth the evil consequences of the conquest of one part of a nation by another. But the consequences have been evil, and more and more Americans were facing the fact when the Second World War began. And more and more Southerners, in the years since Calhoun, had been forced along Calhoun's path from nationalism to sectionalism because of what the Southern section was suffering at the hands of others. There was Georgia's Henry W. Grady in the years after Reconstruction. At the time of his death in 1889 this brilliant Georgian was known to the nation for shining championship of "the New South," a South inviting and joining hands with industry from the North, forgetting its quarrel, forgiving its wounds. Grady, whose father died in the Confederate service, was intensely a Southerner even though for most of his life he saw the South's future in terms of concessions to Northern points of view. For this Thomas W. Watson, the agrarian, classed him with "those who would betray the South with a Judas kiss."

My father said of Grady that he had "died literally loving a nation into peace." The words are on the Grady statue in downtown Atlanta, visible every time they clean away the soot. But there is reason to believe that my father was wrong about the condition of Grady's heart at the time of his death. Only 39, Grady was going the way of Calhoun. Like Calhoun, his last words were not of the nation but of the South. "Tell her (his mother) if I die, that I died while trying to serve the South, that land that I love so well." Would they have

been his last if he had died three years before at the time
of the speech to the New England Society of New York
which made him famous? I doubt it. Gallant, dramatic,
looking upon the Civil War as a thing decisive of Southern destiny, he had stood before the New Englanders
and vowed that the South would come back in whole
heart to the Union of States. It was a speech free of all
sectional antagonism. He spoke of Abraham Lincoln—
"came he who stands as the first typical American, the
first who comprehended within himself all the strength
and gentleness, all the majesty and grace of this Republic. . . ." He renounced Negro slavery and Southern theorizing about the Constitution. He welcomed
the North to the South, abolished the Mason and Dixon
line, took his stand upon the proposition that the South
was about to make a victory out of her defeat: "We have
found out that in general summary the free Negro
counts more than he did as a slave. . . . We have
sowed towns and cities in the place of theories, and put
business above politics. . . . We have learned that one
Northern immigrant is worth fifty foreigners. . . . We
have wiped out the place where Mason and Dixon's
line used to be. . . . The South found her jewel in the
toad's head of defeat."

He could be amiable even with General William Tecumseh Sherman, the gentleman who was not the hero
of Margaret Mitchell's "Gone With the Wind." The
general was at the banquet table. Turning to him, the
eloquent Atlantan declared: "I want to say to General
Sherman, who is considered an able man in our parts

though some of our people think he is kind of careless about fire, that from the ashes he left us in 1864 we have raised a brave and beautiful city."

He was the South's first industrial pleader, its foremost conciliator, its champion of progress, its "No North— No South" proclaimer. (He was, also, the first of a long and multiplying line of Atlanta boosters.) In its last lines alone was there any hint of reservations in his speech, but those are significant: "Now, what answer has New England to this message? Will she permit the prejudice of war to remain in the hearts of the conquerors when it has died in the hearts of the conquered? Will she transmit this prejudice to the next generation, that in their hearts, which never felt the generous ardor of conflict, it may prepetuate itself? Will she withhold, save in strained courtesy, the hand which, straight from his soldier's heart, Grant offered to Lee at Appomattox? Will she make the vision of a restored and happy people, which gathered above the couch of our dying captain, filling his heart with grace, touching his lips with praise and glorifying his path to the grave, will she make this vision on which the last sigh of his expiring soul breathed a benediction, a cheat and a delusion? If she does, the South, never abject in asking for comradeship, must accept with dignity its refusal."

But for these final words the Grady speech at Boston in 1886 was so perfect in nationalism that some of his critics in the South, including Thomas E. Watson, interrupted the country-wide acclaim with sour talk of a sell-out. Did something come over Henry Grady in the three remaining years of his life? Something which told him that the South was as much in need of his championing as the nation was of his loving into peace? I believe it did. I believe that it came with no bitterness, for his was a buoyant soul. I believe there came to him in his last years a conviction that if Southern poverty was to be overcome and a real peace of economic equity and social balance attained for the nation, the South must be permitted to express itself and its special circumstances. "If then it be provincialism that holds the South together," he was saying at Dallas in 1888, less than two years after the New England dinner, "let us outgrow it; if it be sectionalism, let us root it out of our hearts; but if it be something deeper than these and essential to our system, let us declare it with frankness, consider it with respect, defend it with firmness, and in dignity abide its consequence."

In December of 1889, a few days before his death, he came once more to New England, but this time with a different note. Henry Cabot Lodge's Force Bill was up. Grady stood before the Boston Merchants Association with a speech which he had said was going to be his greatest and which he may have known was going to be one of his last, for he was ill already. There was a challenge this time, a warning that the South would take its stand: "We wrested our state government from Negro supremacy when the Federal drumbeat rolled closer to the ballot box and Federal bayonets hedged it deeper about than will ever again be permitted in this free government. But, sir, though the cannon of this Republic thundered in every voting district of the South, we still should find in the mercy of God the means and the courage to prevent its reestablishment." "Meantime," he went on, "we treat the Negro fairly" (the pity is that he was so wrong on this point) "we treat the Negro fairly, measuring to him justice in the fullness the strong should give the weak, and leading him in the steadfast ways of citizenship that he may no longer be the prey of the unscrupulous and the sport of the thoughtless." Then, reporting more truly, "The love we feel for that race you cannot measure nor comprehend."

Within the week he would be dead. But on the morning after the speech to the Merchants of Boston he made another—to the Bay State Club. It was to be his last. Poverty—Southern poverty in nature's plenty—and death were on his mind. He told of a funeral he had attended once in Pickens County, Georgia. There can be cheerful funerals, he said, "but this funeral was particularly sad. It was a poor 'one-gallus' fellow, whose breeches struck him under the armpits and hit him at the other end about the knee—he didn't believe in décolleté clothes. They buried him in the midst of a marble quarry; they cut through solid marble to make his grave and yet a little tombstone they put above him was from Vermont. They buried him in the heart of a pine forest, and yet the pine coffin was imported from Cincinnati. They buried him within touch of an iron mine, and yet the nails in his coffin and the iron in the shovel that dug his grave were imported from Pittsburgh. They buried him by the side of the best sheep-grazing country on the earth, and yet the wool in the coffin bands and the coffin bands themselves were brought from the North. . . .

". . . The South didn't furnish a thing on earth for that funeral but the corpse and the hole in the ground. There they put him away and the clods rattled down on his coffin, and they buried him in a New York coat and a Boston pair of shoes and a pair of breeches from Chicago and a shirt from Cincinnati, leaving him nothing to carry into the next world with him to remind him of the country in which he lived and for which he fought for four years but the chill blood in his veins and the marrow in his bones. . . ."

In these last speeches, delivered so shortly before his death that the North had no time to catch their significance before it was called to praise a great Southern nationalist dead, Henry Grady was not a nationalist. He was a challenging, aggressive, stand-taking man of the South. He was a Southern regionalist, still loving a nation into peace perhaps, but instructing that love in the problems, tasks, and poverties of his part of a nation.

The ashes of the Confederacy are blown with the winds of two World Wars. A new world is making, and its dimensions are so small with science that there is no place for big talk about a little pocket called the South. If Calhoun, who led the South into the Civil War, was a nationalist turned sectionalist, if Grady, who led the South out of the Civil War, was going through the same turn, what does that have to do with the hope of salvation in 1943? The answer is that a centripetal force which through all history has been driving Southerners back upon the South, making professionals of them often against their will or plan, is entitled after this war to more study and understanding than it has had before, if the South is to be taken, as I propose, for awful example, shining proof and glittering chance. It is a centripetal force which was in play even as the greatest war involved our land. Resurgence of race trouble in the months after Pearl Harbor, and contentions that the South was being denied both the indulgence to which its long-suffering agriculture was entitled and the share of war production plants which its industrial hope contained—were putting the same force into play. The force comes of two persisting facts, the fact of comparative poverty and the fact of a race problem more difficult than perhaps any other people ever had. The poverty has been identified as coming in large part as a result of national policy. The race trouble has been deemed so incapable of settlement from outside that interference has been a call to arms. The way of Calhoun and of Henry Grady has been the way of many in the South who have come after them. When the New Deal became the Democratic Party and claimed as such the loyalty of the South and when its genuine solicitudes for Southern masses was made known in such earnest that an additional claim was established, there were many Southern New Dealers with a separate place in their thinking for the special problems of the South as distinguished from the general ones of the nation. They were willing to join anti-New Dealers when purely regional matters were involved and when one of the ancient discriminations or failures to discriminate came into issue. An example was Mark Ethridge, of Kentucky, great and good friend of the President and his national policy, who found himself as caught by the centripetal force as Calhoun and Grady when the economic and racial issues were raised during the war. When he appeared on an America's Town Meeting of the Air program in February, 1941, and addressed himself to the theme "Are We A United People?" his argument was that we were not and that a major factor of disunity was discrimination against the South. And when he sat with his fellow members of the President's Fair Employment Practices Committee in Birmingham in June, 1942, he associated efforts to get the Negro a fair share of war jobs with a statement that "there is no power in the world—not even in all the mechanized armies of the earth—which could now force the Southern white people to the abandonment of the principle of social segregation." It was Grady before the Boston merchants again.

The South came to war in 1941 more aware of itself as a region than it had been since 1861. A major item of awareness, happily, was of its sins. It was confessing to bigotry, neglect, injustice, and sloth. But another item was a conviction of discrimination, old and new, which made the South special where it did not deserve to be, along with a lack of discrimination in matters that were indeed special. The old discrimination—as the South had seen it from Calhoun on and as most of the country's economists had come to see it—of tariffs. Nothing has ranked with the tariff in the region's long complaint against national economic policy. An agricultural land, exporting great percentages of the cotton and tobacco which have been its staples, it has always thought itself cursed with the policy which forced it to buy in a protected market and sell in an open one. Especially when, after the first World War, the policy was responsible in part for American balances of trade which limited the dollar exchange necessary for foreign purchases of the Southern staples. More recently, and ranking next, have been freight rates. It is true that some Southern industries do not subscribe to the theory that the South and West are discriminated against in a national freight rate structure which makes the per-ton-mile rate lower in so-called official territory (the East and North) than elsewhere. They point to the facts that this situation exists only as regards the so-called "class rates," that a greater tonnage of Southern production moves under so-called "commodity rates" and that these are actually lower in the South than in the East and North. But the Southern governors and economists who have been protesting say that it is in the development of new industries, which are small and take the class rates, that the South is limited by freight rate discrimination. They agree that in such established industries as coal, cotton, and steel upon which commodity rates have been set the South does not suffer and even has an advantage. But in rates on the thousand and one new industrial products which the region will need to be manufacturing after the war to integrate its industry and give it volume and value, the class rate discrimination is a very great handicap, they say. And they insist that the handicap is not justified in relative operating costs.

There has been the discrimination in the system of selling steel, too. Even though the so-called "Pittsburgh Plus" arrangement has been abolished twice in the last twenty years, its return once may mean its return again. This is the device by which Pittsburgh's national market for certain standard steel products has been protected from encroachments of growing production centers like Birmingham by a monopolistic enforcement upon these centers of an extra selling price. Originally all steel coming out of Birmingham had to be sold at the Pittsburgh price plus an imaginary freight from Pittsburgh to the delivery point. The steel might go from the mills at Birmingham to a point no farther from that city than Mobile, but the delivered price would include freight all the way from Pittsburgh. This meant that Pittsburgh could compete on even terms with Birmingham at Mobile and all over the South. The imaginary freight charge was finally eliminated in favor of a flat five dollars a ton added to the Birmingham price. When the Federal Trade Commission ordered this whole "Pittsburgh Plus" system eliminated as unfair, the steel people managed to keep it nevertheless by substituting for the imaginary freight an arbitrary three dollars a ton on Birmingham steel above Pittsburgh's. In 1936, after an intensive campaign against the practice by Southern newspapers and trade organizations, the United States Steel Corporation removed the three dollar differential of its own accord. Since that time the growth, integration, and capacity operation of Birmingham and other Southern mills have developed strikingly, and the Birmingham district was able to take a very large place in the war production that began in 1939. It is interesting to note that shortly before this discrimination was eliminated (for the time being at any rate) the United States Steel Corporation had as president of its Birmingham subsidiary, the Tennessee Coal, Iron and Railroad Company, an·exceptionally catholic-spirited and sales-hearted gentleman. He was John·Lester Perry, now president of the corporation's Carnegie-Illinois Corporation in Pittsburgh. During his brief stay in the South, Mr. Perry made a point of appearing personally as often as possible wherever Southerners assembled for business conference and trade councils. Everywhere he went his philosophy grew. It was that "the Tennessee Company will grow as the South grows." In that estimate he gave his effort to developing the South, using the purchasing power of his commissaries, the science and persuasion his company's wealth commanded, for encouraging Southern farmers to grow products for which a market could be made, and for finding these markets where they existed and developing them where they did not. In his economics, which surely must prevail after this war if the peace is to be a true one for American free enterprise, the production of great companies like his could no longer be confined to commodities but must run to customers as well. The manufacture of customers was the final integration as he saw it. That manufacture is the law of our economy of mass and machine. And it is the South's practical appeal to post-war America.

Another discrimination which has made the fighting South fighting mad is against oleomargarine, a product of cottonseed oil. Not only is there a discriminatory federal tax against this product but some of the dairying states of the North Middle West levy prohibitory taxes of their own. In the same voice with which they propose thus to limit the domestic market for Southern cotton they ask protection against the growing competition of a Southern dairying and livestock industry which is the most significant present economic development in that region.

As oppressive as these discriminations, in Southern opinion, are certain refusals to discriminate. The circumstance of having a Negro population almost as large as the white but below the white in advancement (no matter whose the fault), the circumstance of being an agricultural land with two staples predominating, the circumstance of having attained what industrial development has come to it on a basis originally of cheap labor (which was nevertheless not so cheap as the agricultural living from which it was drawn)—make a special set of problems and opportunities, Southerners believe, and suggest realms in which general rules may not fairly or productively be applied. The Negro problem is not dealt with justly or successfully yet in the South, but it is a problem which is separate from the one involving the smaller and more advanced Negro minorities in other parts of the country. The development of wage scales and labor organization in the South may warrant much Southern skirmishing, but it can never be settled fairly by either a national government or a national labor union which insists on arbitrary, over-night elimination of Southern wage differentials. Southern industry has been built on a presumption of these differentials. Without them much of Southern industry and the labor it employs would be destroyed. The poll tax in the South is an abomination and ought to be abolished, but if the national rather than the state government is permitted to do the abolishing there is opened a field of federal interfering which is sure to ignore harmfully to all parties concerned the delicate and special set-up involved. Lynching is a crime without necessity or excuse, but it was almost extinct in the South until the war-time racial agitators provoked it again, and the realism of the matter is that a federal law would create so much Southern resentment that racial hostility and violence might actually increase.

Miss Dorothy Thompson may have been right in part when she named poverty as an explanation for Southern willingness to get into the war. But I do not think she was right when she said it was because the Southerner felt he had so little to lose. I think it was because the Southerner has been subjected through history to the centripetal force of his special regional facts. He has developed a chronic chip on his shoulder as a result of his long belief that he is not fairly treated or well understood. He fights not because he thinks he has nothing to lose but because he thinks he ought to have more.

When Jonathan Daniels lectured in Birmingham in

1938, Colonel William S. Pritchard of that city asked him from the audience if he didn't think "the South could come into its own now if the North would take its foot off our neck." Mr. Daniels' apt and sensible reply was that "there are two feet on our neck—and one is our own." The acrobatics were questionable but not the point. Greed on top, bigotry at the bottom, social incomprehension all around, have accounted for as much trouble in the South as the Yankees have. Many social and economic imbalances need righting by and among Southerners themselves and can be righted in no other way. But the fact remains that not all of the wealth created in the South each year at the time of the war's coming was enough to support a decent economic civilization, no matter how, where, or for what purpose it might be distributed.

Chapter Five

"I GOT SHOES"

NEARLY ALL OF GOD'S CHILDREN IN THE SOUTH HAVE shoes. They wear them whenever they find it comfortable to do so. In the first round of the New Deal Secretary of Labor Perkins made a remark about the need of putting shoes on the people of the South. "When we have put shoes on the South," she said, "the social revolution will have begun." This won from Southern people the scorn it deserved. It was another example of the uncomprehension which aggravates folly with so many who offer to do the South over from outside. Never once have I seen a bare foot at a luncheon meeting of the Birmingham Rotary Club. (It is true that I am not a member and that they may have kept something from me.) Never once have I seen a bare foot among the farm families crowding the streets of the little towns of the South on Saturday afternoons. But what Miss Perkins had in mind was neither uncomprehending nor foolish. She had in mind the comparative poverty of the Southern States in the midst of much natural wealth, and the immense new market to be made for America in lifting the purchasing power of those people to the national level.

Although Miss Perkins' Mr. Roosevelt was not the

first to say the South was poor he was first to say with authority that its poverty should be a national economic problem and that its rank as such was Number One. If he had used the word "opportunity" in lieu of "problem" he could have pleased more Southerners and meant the same thing. I would be bringing a poor coal to Newcastle if I gave this book to discussion of Southern economic conditions. The thing has been done with faithfulness and authority by so many others. The comparative poverty of the South has been attested by such competent present day observers as Howard Odum, Arthur Raper, Rupert Vance, H. C. Nixon, Will Alexander, W. J. Cash, David Cohn, Clarence Cason, R. B. Eleazer, Charles S. Johnson, Frank Graham, Wilson Gee, Francis P. Miller, Clarence Poe, F. D. Patterson, C. Vann Woodward, and Erskine Caldwell. Romping Jonathan Daniels has discovered it. Scholarly Virginius Dabney has examined it. President Roosevelt was only putting a seal on the thing when in a letter to his Conference on Economic Conditions in the South, dated July 5, 1938, he declared: "It is my conviction that the South presents right now the Nation's No. 1 economic problem—the Nation's problem, not merely the South's. For we have an economic unbalance in the Nation as a whole, due to this very condition of the South. It is an unbalance that can and must be righted, for the sake of the South and of the Nation. . . . Without going into the long history of how this situation came to be—the long and ironic history of the despoiling of this truly American section of the country's population—suffice it for the immediate purpose to get a clear perspective of the task that is presented to us. That task embraces the wasted or neglected resources of land and water, the abuses suffered by the soil, the need for cheap fertilizer and cheap power; the problems presented by the population itself—a population still holding the great heritages of King's Mountain and Shiloh—the problems presented by the South's capital resources and the absentee ownership of those resources; and problems growing out of the new industrial era and, again, of absentee ownership of the new industries. There is the problem of labor and employment in the South and the related problem of protecting women and children in this field. There is the problem of farm ownership, of which farm tenantry is a part, and of farm income. There are questions of taxation, of education, of housing and of health."

The point of national interest in this relative poverty of the South was in the final paragraph of a report on the South which was made to the President thereafter by his Conference Committee. This committee, composed of Southerners so divergent in view that they had only the South in common, closed its report with a statement that: "Northern producers and distributors are losing profits and Northern workers are losing work because the South cannot afford to buy their goods."

Purchasing power will be something the South has to offer after the war. It is something which all the poor people, all the poor classes, all the poor lands and nations, must be permitted to offer if the rich are to keep their wealth and have it multiply. That is the rule of technology. Mass production must have its mass consuming. When the nearness is considered with the size, and the absence of tariff walls, language barriers, and international complications, the market to be made through improving the purchasing power of 36,000,000 Americans in the South may be the greatest one of all for American businessmen. It is not a market which would need to be made by subsidy, either. There is natural wealth to pay for the purchases. "The South has an abundance of things the Nation needs," said the Southerners in their report to the President. "Its vast stores of raw materials—forest, mineral and agricultural; its extensive power resources—water, coal, oil, and natural gas; its ample transportation facilities—rail, water and air— and its varied climate, could make the South a tremendous trader with the rest of the Nation. . . ."

The land of problem is the land of promise. To make it worth staying in is a proper objective for all Americans, including those who live there. Both New Deal and anti-New Deal economists suggested in the hard years before the war that Southern conditions might improve if three to six million Southerners were moved away. The economists did not say how these would be chosen for the going. Or where they would go. Or who would be the Moses to lead them into the unidentified Promised Land. In my opinion no Moses worth his bulrushes would lead Southerners out of the South. Rather, I think, he would look around him at the minerals and trees, the rivers, pastures, and rains, the water power and long sun, the brave memories and shining chance, and say, "Here at your feet is your Promised Land—if you till it and have benefit of the tilling. This is your Promised Land, and America's too, if you supplement what God and history have given with what you can give, if you live on it in ways of science, if you balance its agriculture with industry, its cotton and tobacco with food, its physical science with social science. This is your Promised Land if you educate your children in grace to inherit it, if you love it enough to put your own gold in it, if you do justice in it among yourselves, if you honor its laws, hold its laborers worthy of their hire, its farmers of their crops, its merchants of their fee. This is your Canaan if you take your stand in it for entitlements against other lands, if your goods go fairly to the markets of America, if no distant tax or tariff burdens you when you buy or limits you when you sell, if the rent of gold is no greater for you than for other men, and if the fruit of your possessions is permitted to fall into your own laps!"

Chapter Six

FEVER

"THE GERMAN BOMBS HAVE NO MORE EFFECT ON us. . . ."—it is Starzynski, the Mayor of Warsaw, September, 1939. "We are accustomed to them!" A whistle in the awful dark. The supernatural was not summoned. Mind did not conquer matter, nor the spirit of Poland the iron and steel of Hitler. But in that cry from Warsaw was the hope of the world. It was the spirit of man, daring, trying, enduring, believing forever. It could not defeat matter yet in hand-to-hand fight but it never stopped thinking it could. In the thought was humanity's passport. The God-spirit survived the fall of Warsaw. It survived the mutilation of Finland, the kidnaping of Denmark, the betrayal of Norway, the criminal attack on Belgium and Holland, the assassination of France, the ghastly dew on England, the cold killing of Yugoslavia and Greece, the "protection" of Rumania, Bulgaria and Hungary, the treachery at Pearl Harbor, the spearheads in the Caucasus, the infiltrations at Singapore, the encirclements in Egypt, the siege of Stalingrad. It survived them all, stood at Bataan and in the Solomons, multiplied in America, and landed in North Africa.

It multiplied in the rich imagination of the South, making a fever where fever was easy-making. Clarence

Cason, who attributed much Southern phenomena to living at "Ninety Degrees in the Shade," would not have failed to include the phenomena of Southern response to war. Edgar Allen Poe expressed a region as well as a man with his imaginings. So does William Faulkner, of Mississippi, now. Shouting baptismals, the moan of Negro spirituals, camp meeting evangelism, the flaming crosses of the Klan, the passionate fixed idea of vigilantes, the bigot's dream, the Cavalier's tradition, the psychological long results of coffee and coca cola, the 88-year-old climate of a Lost Cause, the 15-year-old tradition of Rose Bowls, love of woman, love of God, the Latin touch, the vitalities of Scotch-Ireland—all made their contribution to fevers of the Southern mind about the war. They were fevers which gave a pulse to dying and living. In the beat of them the events of 1939-43 made a chronology which the cool historian will never tell.

November, 1939:   "River so blue . . . so blue and bright . . . as dawn's pearly hue . . . as dawn's sweet light. . . ." It is the saddest song in the world. It speaks of the world's gracious and gay, the Vienna that was. It speaks of life's exquisites, and the divine carelessness that even at the end said the situation was "hopeless but not serious." Where are all the bright eyes, the moments of tenderness, the whispers, the dancers and lovers the Blue Danube has served? Do they go on through eternity somewhere? Do they cross battle lines for memory's sake? Or are they as dead as the soul of them in a man with a little black moustache who inhabited Vienna once without living there?

December, 1939:   The Finns are supernatural. Short of the stars in their courses, they have used everything in the physical world. Daggers in the Arctic night, spotlights on the snow, holes in the ice, Chicago gangster guns, trees, skis, avalanches blown into the water to make waves that sink the Red ships.

January, 1940:   The Russians retreating. It is 31 degrees below zero. They say the dead will lie frozen until spring. They say the floating mines in the North Atlantic will menace shipping for years. If the corpses in Finland should be preserved indefinitely where they lie, if the mines go floating in the Atlantic for all time, what object lessons!

April, 1940:   Germany invades Denmark and Norway. "Blood has drizzled on Norway's capital." War comes to the enlightened lands. Remember them. Those people love their countries with a love that covets no other, hates no other. Each, strong in himself, and brave, knows how to work with his fellows, build with them, endure, hope, love, plan with them. The world is on its way back to the Dark Ages or forward to Scandinavia.

May, 1940:   The Belgian forts are blown apart. Holland taken. Panzer divisions race through France. The British are nearing Dunkirk. It is a world in which no one is safe any more, no future sure. It surrounds the United States of America. A hundred thousand fighting men of Holland casualties in three days. One-fourth the little land's armed force. Six thousand German planes in the sky. Millions of men seeking each other for the kill across the face of four nations. Lightning war. Hitler over Europe. History so loud you would think to hear its guns, screams, and grinding motors in the farthest corners of the earth. Impossible that such things should be as we tinker with typewriters in America, as people watch the stock market, little boys and girls ride bicycles in the streets, and there is a problem of getting the grass cut.

May, 1940:   Is it an angel or a grinning skull? Millions who face it in France and the Lowlands wonder. Others will already know. To be relieved of ghastly duty, given most honorable discharge from awfulness, is a mercy, a ministry of angels. The skull was invented to frighten living people. It is useful for that in peace, helps the argument against war. But when war has come and there is so much dying, mortals are entitled to the other picture, to be reminded that there is beauty, release, peace from pain. Death is an angel.

In Louisiana that spring an on-rushing "Blue" Army swarmed across the bridge at Vicksburg to stop an "invading" Red one. The road from Talullah through Rayville to Monroe was so congested there was much complaint from motorists. The congestion was not so bad, however, as in Belgium and Holland. The Blue Army had 40,000 men, the Red 30,000. No one was hurt but the mosquitoes were bad.

In Birmingham, at Mountain Brook Country Club where dark pines surround white columns and the old South lives in architecture, captains of industry entertained Sir Louis Beale, K.C.M.G., C.B.E. It was a dinner of the Alabama Committee of the American Branch of the Newcomen Society. Sir Louis was a member of the Anglo-French Purchasing Board. The industrial captains stood right loyally as Sir Louis toasted "the President of the United States." They tried to forget that it was Roosevelt. They stood better as Thomas W. Martin, president of Alabama Power Company, toasted "His Majesty, the King of England!" Sir Louis made a speech. It was beautiful. His voice was low, confidential, yet an impression of much fire was there and you had a sense of oratory. ("As a lad," he told me, "I was taught that the way to make a speech is to imagine yourself talking to one individual, preferably your mother.") England was loved. It was true love, and the delicacy and restraint made it the more certain. The South was England's cousin, more than any other part of America. Broad-faced, stocky, magnetic, Sir Louis made himself at home. He had a soft and masterly eye for the ladies. Over Scotch and soda he was communicative without being indiscreet. About all battles he was pessimistic, about the winning of the war cocksure. Afterward England and France in holy alliance were to force free trade on Europe, keep Germany disarmed. America would be cordially invited. . . . Local editorials made happy reference to the "blessed spot . . . realm, this England" and to people who love their country. There were parties, excursions, inspection trips. After two days the perfect ambassador departed.

The war was just begun. The part America was to play not even the omniscient commencement speakers knew. But it was stirring, something felt. Especially in the South. It was felt on the late afternoon of May 22 when the sun dropped below the stadium's rim at Mississippi State College. As the commencement speaker plodded on and twilight came, the six thousand faces were ennobled in half-darkness. He finished, and one by one the graduating class came by, their names called affectionately and loud by President Humphrey. Each name was a little drama, a collection of memories, ambitions, sacrifices, domestic loves. Beyond the stadium the level plains stretched towards Columbus twenty miles away, calm with grass and soft trees. Candidates for degrees in the School of Education came forward. The evening star was over the stadium, alone in total, cloudless sky. It began to burn there, brighter and brighter, so bright there was no ignoring it when candidates for Second Lieutenancies in the Army Reserve Corps were called. It was the lamp of the universe. The new officers swore to defend their country against enemies foreign and domestic. Officers under the evening star! The young men were going to know some nights without stars. The young men were going to have their lives monstrously interrupted. The young men were going to die. But there was something that could not die. The star over the stadium, the quiet lands around, the recurring pageant of youth, love, hope, and unasking courage, were stuff of time-without-end.

Thirteen days later, over the ruins of Dunkirk, radio carried a salty voice—"We shall defend our island whatever the cost may be; we shall fight on the beaches, landing grounds, in fields, in streets and on the hills, and even if, which I do not for a moment believe, this island or a large part of it were subjugated and starving, then our empire beyond the seas, armed and guarded by the British Fleet, will carry on the struggle, until in God's good time the New World, with all its power and might, sets forth to the liberation and rescue of the old. . . ." The Germans entered Paris unopposed. The Maginot Line was cut off. Premier Reynaud appealed to President Roosevelt for "clouds of planes." When they didn't come he resigned. France refused the offer of merger into a Franco-British Union. On June 17 Marshal Pétain asked the German government for "an end to hostilities . . . as between soldiers, after the fight, and in honor."

July, 1940:   Hitler rides in Berlin along streets carpeted with flowers. He has conquered France. England is going. What sort of world will we have if he wins? This Negro bootblack in New Orleans, whistling at his stand, where will he be? This captain of industry, high in the Brown-Marx building in Birmingham, what will he be doing? This serene debutante, driving her shiny roadster along Atlanta's Peachtree Street, how about her? The baby kicking his heels in his carriage as his nurse rolls him in suburban Richmond, the merchant tidying his shop at Columbia's Five Points, the old lady knitting on the porch of a big brick house in Nashville, the driver of the motor bus hurtling towards Mobile, the milkman making deliveries out Clark Street in Roanoke—where will they be, what doing, how feeling, how many living, how many dead—and if dead, how—if Hitler wins?

The summer of 1940 was two fevers for the South. The falling of France and the Democratic National Convention. To all the little country towns and farm houses of Alabama an impassioned voice came from Alabama's own: "In the name of the people of the State of Alabama, in the name of the people of the whole United States, and in furtherance of the cause of freedom and law and justice in a world that is gripped with chaos—" It was United States Senator Lister Hill, arms lifted at Chicago—"I place in nomination the valiant American, Franklin Delano Roosevelt!" Nazi airmen were raining bombs on England. Premier-Designate Prince Konoye was completing an inner cabinet that would chart Japan's course to the South Seas. But not until the first Wednesday after the first Tuesday after the first Monday in November did Southern attention go undivided again to war. The ordeal of England was paralleled by Mr. Willkie's challenge to "the champ."

August, 1940:   Ghastly dew is over England. How these times draw us to ones we love. How fiercely we look to right and left against what harm may befall them. How tenderly we stand beside them sharing our little corners of a breaking world. What comfort in their very existence. How we treasure each moment that passes with them and may not pass again!

September, 1940:   Two million British soldiers are guarding the English coast. British planes over Germany loose thousands of self-igniting cards soaked with gun cotton and phosphorus which spring into flame. The King doesn't stutter any more. Neither do his people. . . . "Never," vows the salty voice, "has so much been owed by so many to so few." What reward for the Royal Air Force? Make them all lords and dukes—some are already. Give each a bank president's salary for life, require fellow citizens to stand uncovered in their presence, let them hold political office without running. Allow them to break all the laws of England forever. Make it illegal for any woman on whom they smile not to smile back. Let them and their children and their children's children be the new aristocracy of England. Do all this and they will still be unpaid.

October, 1940:   The salty voice again, speaking French: "Good night, then: sleep to gather strength for the morning. For the morning will come. Brightly will it shine on the brave and true, kindly upon all who suffer for the cause, glorious upon the tombs of heroes. Thus will shine the dawn. Vive la France!" France is a woman. When she is wounded every man to whom a woman is dear knows something his heart cannot endure. France is beauty, fragility, femininity, art, love, dawn, sunset, twilight's purple, life's exquisite thing. When she is gone the world is rough, illiterate. France is the civilized world's white shoulder. When she is cut the world bleeds. . . .

In the South devout ones began finding things in their Bibles. From many pulpits the Thirteenth Chapter of Revelation was quoted: "And I stood upon the sand of the sea, and saw a beast rise up out of the sea, having seven heads and ten horns, and upon his horns ten crowns, and upon his heads the name of blasphemy." The "beast, coming out of the sea" was Hitler on the English coast. The ten crowned horns were Baltic, Balkan, Scandinavian, and Low Country states. "And they worshipped the beast, saying, Who is like unto the beast? who is able to make war with him?" That was the despair that swept the democracies when blitzkrieg seemed unstoppable. "And there was given unto him **a** mouth speaking great things and blasphemies. . . ." The radio, of course, and Hitler's noisy speeches, and the pagan German philosophies. "And he doeth great wonders, so that he maketh fire come down from heaven on the earth and in the sight of men. . . ."—the dive bomber. "And he causeth all, both small and great, rich and poor, free and bond, to receive a mark in their right hand, or in their foreheads"—the mark, Germany's coin! —"and that no man might buy or sell, save he that had the mark, or the name of the beast, or the number of his name." Numberings, economic restraints—what could this be but the total state, the planned economy, the regimented life under Hitler's New Order? "Let him that hath understanding count the number of the beast, for it is the number of a man, his number is six hundred three score and six. . . ." Six sixty six! The number was identified in a hundred ways, its digits added, subtracted, reversed. "And power was given unto him to continue forty and two months. . . ." Forty-two months after September, 1939, is March, 1943. The war will end in March, 1943. The Bible says so!

November, 1940:   Greek forces are advancing on Tepelini in Albania. Sneeze-words of Poland, ski-words of Finland, trigger-words of Norway, de-voweled words of Holland, vanishing ones of France, kay ones of Greece, but here at last is a word to love, spell, pronounce, even to rhyme. It is Tepelini—on the road to Valona. A beautiful word, and, oh, so easy. It fits tunes. It is delicious, refreshing. Tepelini! Repeat it over and over if you need rest. It will sing you to sleep. Tepelini!

December, 1940:   Wavell defeats the Italians at Sidi Barrani. The glory that was Greece has the high sign on the grandeur that was Rome.

In Tampa that spring the tears flowed one day in wartime measure. A troop train was leaving for Alaska. They were a company of aviation engineers, going to clear airports under the midnight sun. The small island of Annette off the Alaskan coast was their first destination. Women stood weeping in the sand at MacDill Field, saying good-bye. In a Tampa theater pictures were shown of other mothers' sons from the South uniformed in white, practicing skiing operations for a possible defense of Newfoundland. Florida boys who might never have known more than a few frosts in all their lives—clearing ice from Alaskan fields. Farm boys who might have spent their days at the plow riding heaven with navies of the sky. Office clerks whose years might have been four-walled forever—traveling the earth's face. Indoor men turned out, one-place men finding all places. It may be that the tears at Tampa were well-spent, the fears just. But it may be, too, that in this melee into which American youth was being thrown, America was going to recover its soul for venturing.

April, 1941:   Fort Jackson, S. C., is a community of 50,000 men now. There are the problems of municipality—sanitation, streets, traffic, health, recreation, merchandising, police, fire protection. Yet nothing is far from the sandy earth and surrounding pines. Some of the men have planted grass and shrubs outside their tents. The company yards are neat as laundry. The sentries get an obvious satisfaction in their walkings to and fro. You can see small groups of men off duty—they are comrades. Faces range from soft to tough, mother's boy to nobody's fool, grave to gay, North to South, city to farm. Lawyers peeling potatoes, salesmen cleaning cigaret stubs from the yard. Farmers with growing hands marching up and down with guns. Inferior men giving orders to superior ones, little two-by-fours telling stout fellas where to get off.

May, 1941:   The Germans come down on Crete, Max Schmeling among them. Thousands of them out of the air in parachutes and gliders. Dive-bombers and transport planes roaring, guns all over earth, air and sea. Like inverted poppies the parachutes settle, flowers of death. And the gliders, coming softly, picking a place, crashing gently, and when their occupants have darted forth or died, looking unimportant and peaceful like discarded fruit crates on the ground.

June, 1941:   "Can you doubt what our policy will be. . . ." It is the salty voice, crossing the planet. "Russian danger is our danger." It may be the turning point has come, that Hitler has made the Great Miscalculation the soothsayers have been saying he would make. . . . If the Russians fight half as well and long as the Chinese the German army will be as expended as the Japs. . . . Russian Godlessness does not threaten us as German paganism does. You cannot persuade people to have no God, as the Russians wish. But you can persuade them to worship false gods.

July, 1941:   Hitler over the world. A man with a little black moustache, marching up and down his conquered continent, screaming his unholy orders, has betrayed mankind as it has not been betrayed in 1910 years. . . .

By midsummer when the 1940-41 totals were taken, Southern enlistments in both army and navy were found to have exceeded heavily the national average. In the country as a whole the proportion of army enlistments to inductions as selectees was 49.8. But for Kentucky it was 123.4. For Texas it was 98.6, Georgia 92.6, South Carolina 85.3, Florida 75.9, North Carolina 75.3, Arkansas 71.1, Tennessee 62.5, Virginia 60.9, Alabama 60.6, Mississippi 58.5, Louisiana 43.9. In the same period (1940-41) navy recruiting in the South far exceeded the national average. Comparing with 44 per 100,000 in Northeastern States and 63 in Central States were 121 in the Birmingham district, 111 in the Nashville, 109 in the Richmond, 100 in the New Orleans. The Birmingham record was exceeded only by one of 171 per 100,000 in the Portland, and another of 122 in the Salt Lake City.

September, 1941:   Militaristic insanity is the name for the swaggering little men who lead the armies of Japan. How small a number of people would need to be liquidated to be rid of the tradition that has brought this misery! A handful of Prussians, a few Jap army officers.

October, 1941:   England is gathering power. Our ships are going through. England was too old to die.

In November two vessels of the United States Navy were struck by German torpedoes. They were convoying merchant ships with war material for England. Over Pensacola and Perdido Bay in Florida the naval aircraft played thunderous games. The sands on the beach were white and firm. As blood stained the blue Mediterranean and treasures in ships and goods lay dark on its floor, it was pleasant on the Gulf of Mexico. A blue of its own in the Western Hemisphere. A "mare nostrum" whose destiny might be as storied for the Americas as the Mediterranean had been for Italy, England, and France. The Gulf and the Atlantic from Galveston to Norfolk. Coasts of the South, enclosing a land that had suffered much, sinned much, loved, and fought without ceasing for one thing or another. A land with fevers in its mind, much blood in its heart.

Chapter Seven

DECEMBER SEVENTH

THE DATE CAME INTO HISTORY WITH NOTHING IN ITS dawn or noon to keep Southerners from church. Most of them had the news in an early afternoon radio broadcast. If they had heard it a little earlier while they were still in the presence of their God, they might have thanked Him for the daring and dishonorable attack. It aroused the people of America as nothing else could have done, made them single-minded to gather and loose the whole force of the mightiest nation.

"Praise the Lord," said Chaplain Howell Forgy (or was it Chaplain McGuire?) on his cruiser in Pearl Harbor, "and pass the ammunition." Solemnly but with assurance America went to war. A people grown negative, tentative, minus-signed and soft through ten years of intemperance and another ten of trouble, came back to affirmation. A word they had invented without employing began to be employed. It was "all-out." Because of the grim adventure into which Pearl Harbor sent them the spirit of all adventure began to come back. "They will always remember the character of the onslaught against us," President Roosevelt told Congress. Pearl Harbor was destined to memory for honorable things done for us as well as the dishonorable one to us.

The Battle for the World began. When blitzkrieg had pushed into France, Churchill had said it was "the Battle of the Bulge." For a few pitiful days it was "the Battle of France." After that the summer-long hell-from-heaven was "the Battle of London." America began to count as an arsenal, and against its deliveries the Germans waged "the Battle of the Atlantic." Wavell drove west, was driven east—"the Battle of Africa." The United States established lend-lease aid and priorities—"the Battle of Production." Greece and Yugoslavia were killed, Russia was attacked, it was "the Battle of Europe." But when America and Japan came in, all the latitudes and longitudes were involved, all the continents, every ocean and the North Pole. The Battle of the World was on.

My sister Laura, living on a high place overlooking New York City from Llewellyn Park in the Oranges, her oldest son at nearby Fort Totten, wrote me of the December 9th air raid alarm: "Yesterday was a preposterous, utterly unreal day, beginning with my first shock when I read that 'anti-aircraft guns from Ft. Totten were being distributed and set up all over New York City and manned by the men from the Fort.' That sounded ominous and I was sure Frederick must be one of them. Then, all of a sudden the radio announced that ENEMY PLANES WERE APPROACHING NEW YORK. An air raid situation in New York and New Jersey—the most unbelievable and unreal thing in our whole lives! I even felt a little self-conscious until my cook rushed in to me with her stricken face, and that did make it seem more real (though somewhere in the back of my mind was the memory that last spring she had refused to have her teeth pulled because, she had said, 'What's the use, Hitler's bombs will blow them out soon!'). But this air raid warning—one right after another—grew more real as it went along, and I can't describe to you the terror I finally felt as I stood in my window and looked over at New York knowing the danger to the ones I loved who were there at work. . . . The news broadcasters gave the warnings 'from the mayor,' 'from the Chief of Police,' 'from the Bureau of Public Safety.' Nothing in my life so stark and real since the birth of my two boys. I suppose you read that they evacuated the children from the schools, ordered the people and cars off the streets. . . . Well, at least we now have a rough idea."

Next day a boy from a little house in Madison, Florida, aimed himself in his bomber plane at a Japanese battleship off the Philippine coast. The 30,000-ton *Haruna* went down, and the boy was killed. Captain Colin P. Kelly, Jr., entered history, the first American hero of the Second World War. Beside the mantel in the little house in Madison an old musket lived on as if nothing had happened. The plate on it said: "This gun was used against the British in the Revolutionary War and the War of 1812 and was a menace to deserters and robbers in the Civil War."

Two weeks later the salty voice crackled in the Senate Chamber. "The stakes for which they have decided to play—are mortal." He was the supreme orator of the supreme time, at the top of his career as orator, statesman, soldier, and man. Shakespeare, Cicero, and Richard of the Lion's Heart were together, the literature, the eloquence, the heart fire. " 'He shall not be afraid of evil tidings; his heart is fixed, trusting in the Lord. . . .' " Mr. Churchill joined the President in the annual ceremony of lighting the Christmas tree at the White House. He had a heart for Christmas, told the children of America to hang up their stockings.

In the South children were a major product. High on Gunter Mountain in North Alabama, six hundred hands were raised in salute to the flag, six hundred young voices repeated the pledge and the creed. It was a dedication program at the Kate Duncan Smith School maintained by the Daughters of the American Revolution. "I believe in the United States of America . . . it is my duty to my country . . . to love it . . . support its Constitution . . . obey its laws . . . respect its flag . . . defend it against all enemies. . . ." Children of America's most American stock, cherished on their high plateau by daughters of America's first fight for freedom, they lifted their hearts as easily as the lift had grown hard for elders. Tenant farmers, share croppers, factory workers, "poor whites," war casualties, whatever they were destined to be, they knew there on their mountain top the health of affirmation, of exalted love for the arena in which all their strivings and hopes were to be staged. Down the valleys and up other hills children were answering in the same heart. Answering in love of the great days and documents, the flag, the anthem, the oath, the "rocks and rills and templed hills." At shabby little East Lake

Negro School near Birmingham, a Star Spangled Banner was lifted. It was a new flag, gift of some white friends, presented by their four-year-old granddaughter. It tugged up the pole in the afternoon sunshine while the colored boys and girls stood in solemn ranks, singing hard, reciting original verses, loving their country in the nothing-withholding way of their youth and race. "A little child shall lead them" was the theme of the Negro superintendent. The school principal spoke of a love that put trees somehow on the treeless hilltop, grass in the grassless yard, paint on the two-room building. A race advancing from far behind was speaking its health, its hope of years to come, its title to a part in the process, a contestant's place in the great—and greatly threatened—arena.

February, 1942:   The Japanese have filtered through the jungles of Malaya, set foot on Britain's Fort of the Orient. Dying in Singapore, the English defenders say they are not dead. At Dunkirk there was a chance, but here there is none. There is only the chance not to yield. "We are not only going to fight, we are going to win" . . . that was what the Singapore radio said. It lied, and knew it lied, but it was a lie white with the magnificence of human-kind.

"I had a church. . . ." The Reverend Michael Coleman, of All Hallows Church in London, was preaching from John Turner's pulpit in the Church of the Advent at Birmingham, Alabama. . . . "The bombs burst. The church was gone. The church today is in rubble and ruins, but it lives in the air raid shelters, in the bomb-pocked streets of London and in the hearts of all our people. My church is All Hallows. It was one of the oldest in all England, built by the Druids before Caesar crossed into Britain. . . ." The people of Alabama's Birmingham thrilled to his story, knew again that England was too old to die.

In San Antonio they had the annual meeting of the Chamber of Commerce that spring. It might have been the meeting of the Third Army, the officers of Randolph and Kelly Fields, the Eighth Corps Area, and the ghosts of those who died in the Alamo across the street from the hotel. Lieutenant General Walter Kreuger sat with the mayor at the speaker's table. There were as many uniforms as sack coats, and the bounding voice of commerce was not half so loud as the voice of a Lone Star remembering its history, its battles long ago, its place in the Greatest War. Frank Huntress had a "Remember Pearl Harbor" at the foot of every news story in his *San Antonio Express*. There was hot resentment of talk that Americans were complacent. In fighting quality, a speaker said, Texas is to the American commonwealth of states what Australia is to Britain's commonwealth of nations.

MacArthur of Arkansas and Bataan arrived in Australia March 17 and took command for the United Nations. In one Southern state a candidate for governor accepted the sound advice of his manager. "You don't have to take sides on these local issues. What's the use of getting into trouble when you're in the lead. Just be for MacArthur, governor, just be for MacArthur!" The advice was good and the gentleman became governor.

March, 1942: "I came through and I will return." From Australia to Bataan goes the promise of MacArthur. Bataan has surrendered, but the fox holes remain. The rain comes down as before. The mountains look at the jungles, the jungles at the sea. The same birds wheel and cry, the same winds blow at night. Strange that these should continue after the heroes are gone, after their long story is ended in capture or dying. A multitude of trifles, odds and ends of clothing, bits of paper, campfire embers, up-turned earth, burned matches, parts of machinery, tin cans, scars on the trees, holes in the ground. It is the age-old insult of the inanimate to the animate, of the paraphernalia of man to man when he is gone, of servient survival after the master is no more. . . . The men of Bataan have gone. Why should the mountains of Bataan remain? Why indeed, except that those mountains will be unlike any others in the Orient, touched with a story that makes different forever each stone and shrub and running stream. Here stood MacArthur and his men. Here Wainwright made the last stand. Here the husband, son, brother, father of someone in far America fought, suffered, and became an American immortal. Here the spirit of man proved itself again.

On May 6 Corregidor surrendered. For all the last stands, all the lost causes and sacrificings in vain, the South had a heart. And a tradition. But the South had a new tradition for something else. It was for survival, and for victory. It had come from the football fields. It had come from those mighty afternoons in the Rose Bowl at Pasadena, when Alabama's Crimson Tide had rolled to glory, when Georgia Tech had done the razzle-dazzle, when Duke, Tennessee, and Southern Methodist had challenged while the noise of battle crackled in radios all over Dixie, in country clubs, grocery stores, lonely farm houses, homes of rich and poor. The South had come by way of football to think at last in terms of causes won, not lost.

On the campus at Texas Agricultural and Mechanical College, where fifty-two live oaks stand in memory of undergraduates dead in World War I, the night bugles played "Silver Taps." It is a ceremony performed whenever an undergraduate dies. Already there were 44 dead in military service since December. It was the evening of Memorial Day, 1942. With the student body at attention and all lights out except those leading to the Academic Building, three trumpeteers on the dome played taps slowly, three times. The trumpets were long and made a silver note. Taps for 44 gone where 52 went. The live oaks were silver, too, in moonlight. More than 6000 Texas Aggies were in service, 5592 of them officers. From the Class of 1908 Major General George F. Moore had gone to command the harbor defenses at Corregidor. Captain James T. Connally, Class of 1932, had led a flight of heavy bombers from Java to Jolo, P. I., destroyed a Jap tanker, rescued 23 pilots from Mindanao. Lieutenant Col. John A. Hilger, Class of 1932, had flown over Tokyo with Doolittle. . . .

Irvin Cobb's visit to his home town of Paducah, Kentucky, that May was interrupted by a call to join other celebrities in a war bond tour. He missed the Paducah High School Commencement on the evening of May 28 at which they sang the "Blue Danube." With no news from Vienna, it was strange to hear that song. The school chorus put in all the stops and runs, the smooth places, the swift ones, the agitations, majesties, swirls, and echoes. No news from Vienna! Where were the ones who had danced to this song so long ago? Where the shining assemblies, the glittering chandeliers, the carriages that came and went? Where the dear corners, the blonde hair, the heart-leaps, the stateliness and abandon, the million images this music made? Hitler and Vienna could not exist together in the world. But the memory of Vienna would destroy him some day and violins turn light-hearted once more, love stories would come back, gay and graceful cities exist again. The young people of Paducah loved the song. Perhaps it belonged not to a lost capital and age but to a future which our land might know in returns to grace.

June, 1942:   Tobruk has been taken, and the Germans advance into Egypt. "The Lord shall hiss for the fly that is in the uttermost parts of the rivers of Egypt." The enemies of history are in history's land. An ancient thing is threatened by the oldest thing of all—the way of brutal force. A land whose story is long is having added to it the old one that was enacted when men lived in caves and killed with clubs and sharpened stones. Hitler spreads himself in the land of the Pharaohs. Rommel takes mechanized legions where Mark Antony led the Roman ones, and there is no star-eyed Egyptian to divert him. He isn't the type.

The double life of the soldier—the stout heart for soldiering and the tender one for home. Men went to destinations unknown that summer from the Southern camps, New York men, Illinois men, ones from Iowa and from little Southern towns. They went in regiments, but each of them was something in detail, a package of experiences and exclusive possessions. At Point Clear in blue Mobile Bay, where a modern Grand Hotel had replaced the old one to which Southerners came in gayety long ago, young officers of the Navy and the Army spent dear weekends with their brides.

Here's a song to you, my dear,
Before I sail away,
Tomorrow shall be yesterday
And yesterday today.

I never knew that I could pay
For all that's in your face,
For all that you and I have known
In many a fairy place.

For Maytime on a sea-blown dune,
For autumn on a hill,
Where love would fill a golden cup
To sip or drain or spill.

But here's a song to you, my love,
Before I sail away,
To tell you that for yesterday
Tomorrow I can pay.

July 14, 1942: It is 153 years since the people of France took themselves out of jail, stormed the Bastille. This is the July Fourth of France, signal for defeat of enslavers, liberation of the enslaved. Will the millions-

at-arms in England take it for their sign as they wait untouched and strong on Germany's western fronts while
Hitler goes to total involvements in the east? The French
will be waiting. Britain's army is nearer Berlin than is
the bulk of Germany's. It is Hitler, not Churchill, who
has lost five to ten million men. It is Churchill, not Hitler, who is allied to the might of America.

In August a hero came home to Birmingham, alive
and speaking under Navy orders. He was Lieutenant
Noel A. M. Gayler, Navy flier, owner of three Navy
Crosses for successful courage in the Pacific. The Noel
in his name was for the Christmas Day on which he had
been born twenty-eight years before. The "A. M." was
for his uncle, Captain Arthur Meredyth Roberts, U.S.N.,
killed in action in the First World War. The Gayler was
for his father, Captain Ernest Gayler, U.S.N., holding
a command on the West Coast. Flying somewhere in
the same Pacific were his first cousins, William Hazzard,
Jr., and David Roberts, III, and Harold H. ("Swede")
Larsen, husband of David's sister, owner of a Navy
Cross and a Distinguished Flying Cross. His brother-in-
law, Commander Louis N. Miller, U.S.N., had come
ashore for duty in Washington. His brother, Lieutenant
Ernest Gayler, Jr., a flier too, was en route to Pensacola.
His first cousin, Lieutenant Meredyth Hazzard, was with
the forces in West Africa, destined soon to a Silver Star.
John Sharpe Roberts, another first cousin, was in training at Fort Benning, Georgia. Seventeen-year-old Rutledge Hazzard was in military school at Sewanee. At
home was Lieutenant Gayler's maternal grandmother,

Mrs. David Roberts, born in Charleston on the April day when Beauregard had opened fire, named Sumter for the fort, all sweetness and stout heart.

The Flying Fortress became a name for that summer and fall. Flying from England over Rouen, Dieppe, all Europe. Flying from Australia for MacArthur over New Guinea and New Britain. Flying in the Aleutians. Flying from the torn field on Guadalcanal. Flying over China, nearer and nearer Japan. Flying over the tight line between the Mediterranean and the Quattara Depression. Praised for the soldierly way she spoke of her son who had piloted one of the first Fortresses over Occupied France, a Southern mother wrote: "I wonder if I deserve praise for trying to be soldier-like about him, for I was reared to be dutiful and cheerful about everything, and this war is mine as well as his. I admit my instincts are first, mother; and this giving of my only son has been the hardest thing I have ever had to do. . . . I do find a peace, though, that some parents can't, and that is I know my boy is a good Christian, and his attitude and courage are my inspiration. This, and the Ninety-first Psalm, and memorizing prayers, and keeping busy, give me strength and comfort. As God wills it, I will take it, for I must deserve to be his mother. The last thing he said to me was, 'Mother, keep your chin up'—to keep his faith, I will."

A nation of mothers' sons had gone to war across the continents and seas. Men of a land which made much of its women, belonged to them, was mothered by them. A mother land.

Mothers of men!
The sea is not so wide nor the war so long,
The dead so many nor human misery grown so old
That we forget the words you did not speak
When your sons went off to war.
You did not speak, and yet
We heard you say more noble words and brave
Than any man or woman has said aloud.
We heard you tell of dear-remembered days,
Of tiny, silly fists that held your fingers tight.
You said this more-than-all-your-life you'd give—
      your son.
And yet, you did not speak.

October, 1942:   Something whose fearful symmetry
grows before the Germans is the gigantic figure traced
by the battle lines between Hitler and Timoshenko. It is
more fearful each day that Stalingrad stands and the
Russians hold or counter-attack along the line that runs
northwest to Moscow. It is a figure whose silhouette is
made by Russian guns, tanks, planes and incomparable
fighting men as they hold along the flanks and fall back
in order along the slim path between. It is the V for Victory! Written in blood on Russia's face where her men
and Hitler's go down in the war's most destructive and
deciding battle. It is the V into which the Germans are
pushing. It is the V made by Soviet armies as they receive, hold and crush in their vise the last hopes of
Schickelgruber. The longest left flank in history is under
fire. The time is coming fast now when every German
spearhead will be an exposure, when every encircling
movement ends with the encirclers inside, when every
advance is progressively more feeble like the incoming
waves of an out-going tide.

The headlines and news stories in Atlanta papers on Sunday morning, November 1st, made strange brackets for foreign reading. The biggest football game of the year was over. Georgia had beaten Alabama 21 to 10, with Frank Sinkwich starring:

Georgia's Sinkwich Sinks Tide.
Timoshenko's Men Seize Initiative Inside Stalingrad.

Mississippi State Scores over Auburn in Mud and Rain.
Fifty Nazi Bombers Knife at Britain.

Volunteers Run Riot Against L.S.U.
British Whittling Down Nazi Strength in Egypt.

Georgia Tech Trounces Duke, 26 to 7.
U. S. Loses Fourth Plane Carrier in Pacific.

Green Wave Breaks Jinx to Lick Vanderbilt.
Allied Bombers Destroy Big Jap Cruiser.

Texas Aggies Punch Arkansas Porkers Around.
Nazis Advance on Nalchik Plains.

Virginia Tech 20, Virginia 14.
Reds Gain on Black Sea Front.

All over the South, North, East and West, people listened as the broadcasters reported that Sinkwich weighed 185 pounds and was five feet, ten. There was a moment of nation-wide distress when the Georgia quarterback was hurt and had to be taken out for a while. Between halves the 100-piece Alabama band paraded in

a SINK SINKWICH formation, played "Praise the Lord and
Pass the Ammunition." Atlantans and their visitors
lived an electric day, made a night of it. Atlanta could
not be beaten. Atlanta was bound to win. Atlanta was
burning again. Was it incongruous? Did it insult the
sinking and hurting and ammunition-passing and bloody
mud across the sea? Or did it relate to what those other
young men were able to put into what they did? Did it
make examples of magnificence in the competitive spirit
when it knows rules, limits, and an arena, and is not of
the jungle or battlefield?

Eight days after the victory at Atlanta, another Anglo-
Saxon voice spoke French to the people of France. It was
the President, calling them "My Friends," as he had
called Americans for ten long years. He told them of the
American landings in North Africa, and his news was
of the war's turning. The sudden and immense ma-
neuver was like the point in a great checker game in
which all at once a square that had not been well noted
is moved into, and, presto! kings may be jumped all over
the board. It was like a cross-word puzzle, unsolved until
one five-letter word is found and, at once, all the verticals
and horizontals may be filled. It was hard to believe that
America could come so quickly to the war's strategical
front seat, that Bizerte, across from Italy, might be an
American stronghold in no time.

November 9, 1942:   Because England refused to die
in 1940, there was the chance for Russia to refuse in
1941. Because Russia refused in 1941, there was a Russian chance to refuse again in 1942 so resolutely that

Hitler's heart was broken. Because of England's refusal and Russia's, America has this moment, this gift of fate and promise of world inheritance, this chance to be the south wind and sweep the world free. That is something to remember. It may be that we shall suffer as England has, as much even—though God forbid—as Russia. But whether we do or not, we know when we are honest that we owe our shining chance to what England and Russia accomplished with their suffering and their magnificent hearts for going on.

The Russians would not let the front pages be taken, not by the American Navy in the Solomons, not by MacArthur at Buna, Montgomery in pursuit of Rommel, the Franco-American-British advances on Tunis and Bizerte. From Leningrad, Moscow, Stalingrad, and down to the Caucasian tip they moved in burning, killing, ice-covered counter-attack. The great vise was drawing together. The upper arm of the V-for-Victory was closing down. Praise the Lord and pass the ammunition! Pass the welding torch! Pass the lathe and the saw! Most of all, pass the War Bonds! Sooner than we thought—by trying harder than we knew how—this war could be won!

November 24, 1942: There is trouble between Hitler and his generals. His voices have told him wrong at last. The intuitions on which he has depended won't intuit any more. From out of the ether and the great unknown Something advised him last year to go all out for Moscow. He dismissed generals to follow the gleam, but all he has to show for it is the pair of field glasses from which a German officer was able to see the city's rounded towers just before winter and the Russians dimmed the glass. From the ether and the great unknown he was advised once more. Take Stalingrad at all cost! He listened—and let more generals go—but Stalingrad's name was steel. Another pair of field glasses— Von Bock, hiding behind a shock of alien corn, looked into the city of steel just before Hitler withdrew him and only a little while before Hitler's troops began withdrawing under orders from the other side.

November 28, 1942: They also serve who scuttle their beautiful fighting ships in the harbor of Toulon. Germans or Russians could sink their ships with ease if a situation told them to do it, but Frenchmen love their own.

At Miami Beach in December the military turmoil made more animation and moving about than had the real estate boom seventeen years before. Ninety percent of the hotel space was taken over by the army and what remained was occupied largely by army and navy officers or their families. At the Tatem the surf club scene was an island surrounded by war. Strains of "Day Dreams" and "Linger Awhile" floated across the narrow stretch of hotel sand while patrons sat in chairs under brightstriped umbrellas or stretched on rubber rafts in the sun or sipped juices at little tables. But across the street a loud drill-master put recruits through first maneuvers and along the beach next door men waited with fat blue barracks bags for trucks which would take them to parts and fates unknown.

December 23, 1942: Down from Voronezh. Down from Kursk, Velikie Luki, Rzhev, Novaya Kalitva, Kantemirovka, Monastirschina, Bokovskaya, Boguchar, Tali Radchenskoye, Mankoro-Kalitvenskaya and Serafimovich. Down from the White Sea to the Black, from Leningrad to Astrakan, down to Rostov and the mountains and shores that make a lower arm, there closes the upper arm of Russian's V for Victory. The fearful symmetry burns more fearfully each hour of the ice-cover counter-attacks. The nose thrust into the Caucasus is threatened with history's worst pinch. The armies pushed to Stalingrad are being closed in history's deadliest vise. The longest left flank ever exposed is burning, shivering, quaking, breaking, freezing by divisions, dying by regiments.

Christmas, 1942: Clear as the midnight stars over gunplay on this planet is Bethlehem's account. How extra sweet this year as its eve and day pierce all the trouble, the death, hardness and absence, the waiting and tortured trying, with an untouched and eternal message. "It came upon the midnight clear"—the message of love's surviving, beauty's truth.

New Year's Day, 1943: Alabama in the Orange Bowl, Georgia in the Rose Bowl, Tennessee in the Sugar Bowl, Georgia Tech in the Cotton Bowl—a flaming aggression to the games this year, a charging, chance-taking, victory-willing élan. It is the war. Because of the war Americans have learned how determined and robust a people they are.

The Southern rolls into Columbia, S. C., two hours late. But it rolls in. All over America trains are rolling in. Old Faithful! Pushing along through the nights, rushing forward all day, North, East, South, West, taking more mortals to more places and more mortal freight with them than was ever taken before, carrying the mails, carrying the Army, the Navy, the Air Forces, carrying the civilian population, the government people, Santa Claus. From what bottomless larder do the dining cars get the food? What vitamin do conductors, porters, trainmen and ticket agents take to make them so patient, give them such diplomacy in turmoil? What magic wand is waved over old equipment to make it serve like new? Once they said "the public be damned." Once, later, when they were losing out, they said "the public be pleased." Now they are saying nothing. They are just delivering the goods and the people in the most monumental transportation job ever done. They are just being Old Faithful, rolling along through the night, rushing on all day!

January 7, 1943:   The President speaks of an Allied air supremacy gained and increasing. He tells of 48,000 planes in 1942, promises more than 60,000 for 1943. This is changing the face of military affairs all over the world. History may say the war was won when the American automobile industry accomplished the miracle of conversion to planes.

However long or short the time might be, America knew, as March turned to April in 1943, that the war was won if the great pace could be held. Idealism was en route to its great chance—and to its great threat of destroying what it sought by overreaching itself or having no feet.

Armageddon may bring more, but the mind could not embrace it. No such scene of final battle, gathered all over the earth, had been put into the books of promise. England, bursting with armament, troops, planes, guns and tanks, its bomber output tripled in a year, ready for vast attack over a 240 degree sector of the circumferences she centered, North Africa bulging in all its bulge from Atlantic to Mediterranean, Americans, Britishers and Fighting French gathered like the south wind to blow against Berlin. Australia, with MacArthur there, sending forth streamers of planes and ships to twist the little infiltrators back through their filters. China, stronger each day in her own blood, outliving death over and over again, winning all civilization's love for honesty, courage, and brotherhood of man, about to be the grandstand for planes and troops without number that would bring Hirohito down when Hitler was no more.

And behind all the brave lines and stands and symmetries—the people of the United States of America, the homefolks of soldiers, sailors, and marines across the seas and ones in waiting here, the workers in war plants, the farmers in fields, the citizen with his War Bonds, inheritors of all that was being fought for and won—praising the Lord and passing the ammunition!

Chapter Eight

UNDER THE OXYGEN TENT

"AS A MATTER OF FACT," A BITTER SELECTEE FROM New Jersey said at Fort McClellan, Alabama, in the summer before Pearl Harbor when the draft extension bill was before Congress, "this whole draft business is just a Southern trick, and don't think we don't know it. It's something put over by Southern merchants to hold the big trade they get from the training camps." Many of his associates agreed with him. Those were the days when "morale" among selectees was without benefit of a state of war.

This book, it will be noted, does not come down from on high. It is written by a mortal who is subject to the frailties of his times, including those indicated in the comment of the soldier from New Jersey. As the two chapters preceding have been composed and a faithful report of Southern war-time attempted, there has been in the back of my mind the thought: "This is wrong. I must show something of that realism, that cynicism, that sense of social and economic misery, which distinguish the wide-eyed commentator from the moonlight-and-magnolia man. I must be suspicious. I must view with alarm. I must be careful not to sweep myself off my feet. I must bring in the tenant farmer somehow, and the Negro problem, the workingman, the barren lands. I must not seem to forget for an instant the bad health, the bigotries, the unanswered problems of the South and the sentimentalities with which they are overlooked." Such thoughts prove me a man of my period, sick with the anarchy of America's 1920's and the socialism of its 1930's, doubting every affirmation, afraid of every plus sign, a prey to so many negations and question marks that Pearl Harbor alone could have pulled him back in directions of health.

A few months before Glenn Frank died in 1940 and while he was acting as policy-maker for the Republican Party, he declared that the nation had been "under the oxygen tent of made work and government spending for the last eight years." No honest Democrat could deny it. But Democrats could raise Dr. Frank on the number of years under the tent. The number was twenty, not eight. Ever since the close of the First World War the country had been living artificially, with shots in the arm, forced respiration, local and general anaesthetics. There had been a dramatic change of doctors in 1933 but illness had continued, and even the remedies had remained much the same. In the 1930's we had saved our economic pulse with public subsidies. In the 1920's we had done it with private ones. We had paid our way with public debt in the later period but we had paid it with private debt in the earlier one, bonded and installment, corporate and individual, gambling and investment. And if in the 1930's we had engaged in what history might call a preposterous business—supporting

American purchasing power by giving away money to Americans with which to buy their own goods—in the 1920's we had done an even more preposterous thing. We had given the money to foreigners. Given it to "furriners" in floated loans that never floated back.

It is true that we had enjoyed our ill health more under Coolidge, just as it is true that the sickness under Roosevelt was anti-toxic while the other was toxic. The jazz age was gay, the jitterbug one sad. But sickness it was, in both periods, a sick economy and a sick people. Scott Fitzgerald called those 1920's the Aspirin Age. There was no other like it for ugliness and anarchy. Ugliness in manners, forswearing in the name of something thought to be forthright the little decencies that make human contact endurable. Ugliness in literature, turning out introspective, unhealthy gutter-scouring novels and plays by the ugly mile a minute. (The New York Times said of Mr. O'Hara's "Butterfield Eight" that "he calls a spade a spade and then, to be sure you heard him, he calls it a spade again.") Ugliness in music, hideous shrieks and sounds, torturing eustachian tubes in the name of jazz. Ugliness in women's wear; shaven-necked bobs, all dignity gone from the back of the neck; radically low waist lines, making the effect of a stublegged grotesque; super-knee length skirts, emphasizing the least lovely item of anatomy, the kneecap. The ugliness of it proved our incapacity for the anarchy of it, and anarchy there was. Queen Victoria paid and paid. Because the Victorians had tried to restrain the unrestrainable, the jazz age released everything. Because the

Victorians had shushed, the jazz age shouted. Because the Victorians had said things were beautiful when they were not, the 1920's made sure that all things were ugly. Ugliest was what they made of Sigmund Freud. The Victorians had been ashamed to face life's eccentricities, but the jazz age made a cult of them. Eagerly, vicariously, breathlessly, they contemplated the abnormal. Millions of good grass-root people were so impregnated that they began finding disease in every mortal relationship, something unnatural in what nature most contrives, something sinister in the very call of birds and break of dawn.

In Germany the man with the little black moustache was getting himself arrested, being laughed at, as he pushed his No-law way, called lawfulness middle class. His great ends justified every means, just as many ends were justifying means in America. Whether you were working for yourself, your crowd or your philosophy, there were no limits nor any laws. The lids were off. Moral laws, economic laws, psychological, artistic, literary laws, were cast aside. Teapot Dome, the Florida real estate boom, the Flapper, the Bootleggers, the Stock Market Players, the Installment Buyers, the Jazz Artists, all of them in one direction or another subscribed to the No-Law-No-Limit doctrine which Hitler was developing oversea.

Especially disregarded in capitalist America was capitalism's rule, the sine qua non of free enterprise. That was the rule against restraint of trade. Trade at home and abroad was restrained without restraint. Monopolists, nationalists, protectionists, price and production manipulators, invention hiders, had their field day.

For a decade the law-breakers and the unlimiteds gave nearly everybody a good time. Their system worked—in most places. But it didn't work for the Southern farmers, who were miserable through the 1920's. It didn't work for the real estate dreamers whose castles fell down in Florida and the North Carolina mountains three years before fateful 1929. Benefiting less by the anarchy, the South was troubled more about it, if not about the ugliness. The law was something about which Southerners were stern. Readier than most to break it in their own interest or righteousness, they did not like having it broken by others. It was part of their conservatism that there should be rules and that men in general should be bound by them. It was part of their social and economic system that what they conceived to be vital in the rules must be maintained at all costs. The Ku Klux Klan which rôde the South in the 1920's was a breaker of the laws, a betrayer of the rights of men, a vehicle of prejudice and lust. But its motive was the preservation of law. Wife beaters, fornicators, atheists, communists, Negroes who were uppity, labor leaders, Jews, Catholics —everyone who did not conform to what the Klansmen, in honesty and passion, thought to be the law of Southern living, was a target for attention. It was an even more hateful anarchy than existed elsewhere in that period, of course, and nearer to what Hitler was making in Germany. But its basis was a belief that people must behave properly. Respected citizens everywhere in the

South joined the Klan in the 1920's. No one could aspire to political office without belonging, even if, like Hugo Black, his real opinions would have named him for persecution rather than membership.

The most law-breaking land, the South was—and remains—the land which insists most on law, written or not. That is how it came about that Southerners were so brotherly with their bootleggers during the Experiment Noble in Purpose. The bootlegger stood well socially with his customers in the South. He was not an outlaw but a trusted confidential agent. Also, he was a man of adventure. He suited the South exactly. His existence meant that there was a law. His call or telephone number meant that the law was not to interfere with an indispensable. Hypocritical, unsocial, wrong, the Southern attitude did have the virtue of recognizing that there must be morals and law. The recognition may have a value when America comes to its post-war task of strengthening the rules, lines, and arenas in which its games are played. In the fury of playing before the war these were impaired, and there can be no productive game without them.

In October, 1929, the bottom dropped out of anarchy. A decade of socialism, pensioning and nothingwithholding hate began. The jazz artist gave way to the jitterbug. People who had been thinking there was no top decided there was no bottom. What aspirin had been to the 1920's sulpha drugs and vitamins were going to be to the 1930's. An America which had flouted all laws began to accept multitudes of laws. Liberty to vote, write, pray, and be unrestrained in one's possessions and pursuits became an academic thing. The practical liberty was to eat, be clothed, housed, free of the sheriff's hammer and the bum's rush.

For a little while the classes went down with the masses in the great depression. When recovery began in 1932-33 (partly from natural forces, partly as a result of New Deal measures, partly in psychological response to the departure of the doleful Mr. Hoover in favor of the buoyant Mr. Roosevelt) it was the classes who were first relieved and who sang loudest hallelujah's to F.D.R. But as it began to appear that the classes could be saved permanently only by some concessions to the masses, and this just as the classes began to feel the elations of Mr. Roosevelt's shots in the arm, disaffection appeared. When the Roosevelt Revolution, after the fashion of revolutions, made use of class hates and attracted crackpots, the disaffection grew. As the New Deal Administration passed from one term to another without Mr. Roosevelt's letting it be known whether he himself was a Woodrow Wilson "umpired competition" man or a Marxist, and his camp remained populated about evenly with these ultimate incompatibles, the disaffection began keeping people awake at night. Economic recovery progressed far enough for reform to seem an interference rather than a guarantee. The reformers developed bureaus and bad habits. Some who had begun as disciples of Wilson began having their heads turned in directions of Marx. The laissez faire people whose ideal was the

Republican Old Guard began looking hopefully at their ideal again.

Hate spread across the land. Not the comparatively amiable hate of the 1920's when men wanted to cut each other's throats gently because of liquor, tariff, Tammany Hall, race feelings, or religious differences, but the total hate of men whose pocketbooks and pay envelopes are involved. It was a hate born of insecurity, and it made for more insecurity, since no economic system, New Deal or old, capitalist or socialist, could succeed among a people so bitterly enemies to each other.

Especially were they enemies in the Fighting South. They were fighting enemies. Because the classes and masses lived more closely together there and because economic and social conditions tended to make the masses love the New Deal and the classes hate it more there than anywhere else, the all-American hating was compounded between the Potomac and the Rio Grande. A land of burdened agriculture, the South had suffered long, worn out both land and man. A land where three-fourths of the nation's Negroes lived, the South had America's most underprivileged group. A land of cheap industrial labor and little social legislation, the South had working people nearer the economic border, more quickly subject to distress. There was no part of America from whose masses the New Deal lifted a heavier trouble and won a greater love. Generations of Democratic loyalty were rewarded with the economic help in awful need, in a time of five-cent cotton, 25-cent wages, and Negroes with nothing to do.

But for the industrial employers and big farmers and their followers the story was as extreme in the other direction. Complain as they did that the North treated the South like a colony, many of them were colonialists themselves. A colony is a land where work is done for owners who are in large part absent and under managers who make their own laws and on terms that take more out than is ever put in. Others, who were not colonialists, were paternalists. The paternalistic system of the South, whose expression in agriculture was the tenant farmer, the share-cropper and the supply-merchant, and in industry the company union, the company house and the company commissary, came from slavery times. It came honestly and necessarily, as a result of an otherwise impossible situation when the slaves were freed. In no other way, at first, could the Negro have been put into employment. The system was abused, especially when benevolent despots had to meet the competition of those who were not benevolent or when economic conditions would be so hard that there would be a situation of every man for himself. The agricultural sweat-shop existed in the South long before the industrial one did. But industrialists and landowners were sure that their colonial-paternal way was the only possible one for the South. After the New Deal had put them on their feet again they began looking with alarm at the threat to this way when the government became the farmer's provider, educator, banker, and subsidizer, and, far worse, the industrial worker's organizer and social securer. Paternalists themselves, they did not want a paternal government.

When David Lilienthal, of the Tennessee Valley Authority, made a scornful speech in 1934 against the absentee ownership of much of industrial Birmingham and the alleged dictatorship of Northern big business over the destinies of that Southern city, Wendell Willkie, who was then president of the Commonwealth & Southern Corporation, enraptured the Birmingham Rotary Club with a reply: "The first time I see Dave Lilienthal," he declared, "I expect to say to him—'You are much fresher in the reading of the classics than I am, but if my memory serves me right, pro-consuls were not representatives of private business, but representatives of government, and, as I recall, they are classic in world history as the extravagant and wanton spenders of the tax-payers' money.'" Private capital, no matter where it came from, Mr. Willkie vowed, was better than federal capital—or no capital at all. He argued that, given the write-downs, donations, low freight rates, lesser taxes, and other advantages which, he said, made possible the Tennessee Valley Authority's retail rates, the Alabama Power Company could make rates 30 percent lower than the governmental agency's. Mr. Lilienthal's argument was that even if the TVA's low rates represented in part such subsidies they were justified in the beginning as a means of building up a volume of business, and that no matter how well the private utilities might have been able to do for the public in making low rates in the past they had notoriously failed to do so.

So it was, as in so many other instances, that the extremes of love and hate were in the South. For the masses Roosevelt was the Democratic Party, the rebel yell, Woodrow Wilson, and Robert E. Lee rolled into one present help in trouble. For the classes he came to be Satan, maker of class hates, destroyer of the Southern system, gathering place of crackpots, enemy of God and advance agent of communism. Or, as they put it more compactly, "that man."

Hate owned America—and awful fear. Fear of unemployment again, of another economic crash, of Roosevelt, of the enemies of Roosevelt. Fear of the insecurity that ruins and also of the insecurity that is normal to life and is a spur to living, the gamble that made American initiative, imagination, and contriving. Everybody began wanting to be safe, insisting on it. Not only those in such danger that they needed saving but ones subject to nothing more than the ordinary risks. The spirit of free enterprise was put to sleep. Those who hated Roosevelt and were of the classes said he had killed it by coddling the masses, trying to take economic care of everybody. Those who loved Roosevelt and were of the masses said the laissez faire crowd had destroyed it by expecting people to show aggressiveness against stone walls, be self-reliant against tidal waves. The fact that there was something in what both said did not avoid the fact of a people gone dead-hearted with hate and fear.

The sadism of the Marathon dancers, flag-pole sitters, tree-sitters, and swallowers of living gold fish was a true expression. Men were made ill, physically and mentally, by what was in their hearts. Or by what had been taken out. Strong men lost their appetites in the company of people whose views differed from their own about the New Deal.

I was a New Dealer. One of the Woodrow Wilson half who believed that the physical science which was bringing men closer together, making the world and its states smaller and smaller, calling for mass consuming to market its indispensable mass production—needed a strongly umpiring government. Not a controlling or owning government, but an umpiring one, with many new jobs for the umpire. I believed that liberty and food could both be had. In that faith I looked upon the Roosevelt Revolution as a thing necessary to assure the food, even if a little of the liberty had to be lost. Without a new deal, I thought, the free enterprise system in America could not survive.

But I was aware of the fellow travelers. I recognized the socialists and the crackpots. And in the end I was aware, too, of the awful psychological destruction. When the Second World War came and Wendell Willkie ran for the Presidency on a platform accepting most of the New Deal but proposing to put the Dealers out, I felt that the Revolution was over, successfully over. The country was needing nothing so much as an end to New Dealing. Not a repeal of what had been dealt but a consolidation of gains, an efficiency in operation, and, most of all, a healing of enough wounds to let the American people like each other again, be spiritually robust again, go adventuring again together.

Once, long ago, working men had organized themselves not only for protection and advancement, but for
quality in workmanship, character, and responsibility in
those who worked. That time must, somehow, come
back. Once business men had been truly free enter-
prisers. They had possessed the spirit of the thing, no
matter what the terms or how they might be changed
in the social marches. They had wasted no tears on what
was done with, against deals that were complete and
irrevocable. That time needed returning. Once America
was a land of adventure.

Youth will be served, but the youth called to fateful
service when Number 158 was drawn from the draft box
on a September day of 1940 was nephew, son, or little
brother to a youth served miserably in years since the
other World War. Youth had been entitled to world
peace. It had been served a pacifism that put its head in
the sand and thought to avoid war by not looking or not
liking. Youth had been entitled to the self-disciplines
without which freedom doesn't work. It had been
given instead to believe every restraint a psychological
monster called frustration. Youth had been entitled to
dreams, beauty unalloyed. It had jazz. Youth had been
entitled to shining chances. It had jitters, doles, and sick
defeats. Youth had been entitled to great truth. It had
been taught only to puncture great untruth. Youth had
needed strong conviction. It had received an open mind,
and that was excellent, but nothing to go into the open-
ing. Youth had needed God. They had taught it only
to beat the Devil.

When the war came and both life and death were offered the nation's young men, many a grieving was comforted in the thought that, if life survived death, youth might bring back to America its own lost essential. The quality of great adventuring—that was youth's right and America's way. In the grim adventure Pearl Harbor had launched the spirit of all adventure might be recalled. And what adventures together Americans had had! Adventures in the petroleum which was fueling now the engines of death. They had tapped the rocks for liquid gold. Its sparkle in bright cylinders commanded time and space, rode earth, air, and sea. Adventures in hydro-electric power. They had chained the lightnings out of falling water, set them to infinite errand-doing. Natural gas. They had made a public utility of "the wild spirit of the universe," caught the earth's own breath, given heat new names, combustion new tricks. Coal. They had dug up the time-smothered vegetables, made fuel for a million flames, by-products for a hundred industries. And that new adventure, around which were gathering the supreme commerce, industry, science, and art of our times, aviation. To ride up the heavens with the navies of the air, to cancel gravity with speed, to kiss the white shoulders of the clouds and cut the wind in two—that was to know a glory of marriage to the sky.

Adventure was coming back to America, through America's youth. Coming the hard way of trial, pain, unconscionable tax on endurance. But that had always been a part of adventure for the America that meant something, for youth that was really young. "Old Sawney" thought so, at any rate. There are many in the South and elsewhere now who can remember. "Old Sawney" ("Sonny") was William R. Webb, founder and longtime head of the famous Webb School at Bellbuckle, Tennessee. "Son," he would say, "write home and tell your folks that the food is bad and the beds are as hard as the beds of Pompeii. But add a postscript to tell them that they have a little boy who can stand it. That will make a bird sing in your mother's heart and bring a smile of joy to the face of your father. . . ."

Chapter Nine

OF ONE BLOOD

SOMETHING ABOUT WHICH THE SOUTH HAS ALWAYS
been willing to fight and whose long trouble was aggra-
vated by the war is the race problem. The fact of that
problem is so big that judgment gets nowhere without
recognizing its size. Among the sicknesses it ranks high
and has a thousand aspects. A major one is Jim Crow.

Chapter Seventeen, Verse twenty-six, of the Acts of
the Apostles reports that the Lord "hath made of one
blood all nations of men for to dwell on all the face of
the earth." Southerners who are bound by the Good
Book but are not going to give up racial segregation are
comforted by the last line of this verse. It makes the
supplementary report that God "hath determined," also,
"the bounds of their habitation." This would seem to
permit separate railway cars if not inferior quality and
service. The Southern streamliners so interpret it.

Science, like the Lord, finds distinctions if not differences in the matter of racial blood. Controversy over the
decision of the American Red Cross to keep Negro
blood bank donations separate from white at the beginning of the war brought the question much into issue.
Given a pint of Negro blood and a pint of pure Anglo-
Saxon, there is no possible way of knowing which is

which. They are the same—microscopically, chemically, immunologically. There is, however, a variation in the incidence of the four blood types in differing races and localities. The colored races are more likely to have one type, the white another. How this might be interpreted in argument for segregation (if it were only argument), I don't know, unless it relates to the fact that some Negroes and their leaders and publications get along with white people better than others.

But segregation is not an argument in the South. It is a major premise. The issue, which the South considers a thing apart from the general question of advancement for the Negro, had already been raised by Governor Eugene Talmadge, of Georgia, when the war came. It was not a genuine issue then. Talmadge was simply putting on a one-man show. But it became genuine when Negro leaders outside the South made the war an occasion for intensive campaigning against any and every differential, minor or major, between white man and black. If these leaders had been willing to confine themselves to discriminations against the Negro in war production plants and in training schools for the work of those plants, the Talmadges and all they represented in demagogy and psychopathic hate and fear would not have been given new leases. The leaders elected, however, to go crazy with their championings, looking everywhere for trouble, entering loud complaint even against the calling of Negro babies "pickaninnies." They made it plain that they intended to use the war for settling the whole, complicated, infinitely delicate racial problem.

Their point had its appeal, true. They said that America must prove the democracy for which it was asking its people to fight abroad by making it complete at home. In the circumstances, however, they might as logically have said that because America's house was on fire America must take the occasion for renovating the kitchen or putting Venetian blinds in the parlor. So little were they concerned by the fact that their all-embracing crusade meant a domestic war while their country was making supreme war abroad that they invited their followers to think in terms of a Double-V-for-Victory—victory in battle with Hitler and victory in battle at home. Victory, unhappily, didn't work that way. The battle at home began to threaten the battle against the man with the black moustache. He happened to be the greatest race-hater in history, the Jim Crow of all the ages. He had called the Negro "lower than the ape" and was prepared to treat him so if he got a chance.

These Negro leaders who insisted on appeasement as their price of full participation in the war said that Southern white liberals who opposed them in what these liberals thought the interests of the Negro and the Nation did not properly estimate the feeling among the Negro population. An answer was that these leaders themselves and their backers in high political place had brought the feeling to its intensities. A more compelling answer was that there was another feeling, the feeling of white majorities in the South where three-fourths of the Negroes lived. For grim example, Mr. Horace C. Wilkinson, Birmingham lawyer-politician, who had retired

from a career of talented gad-flying until the race ex-
citements brought him back for a speech to the Kiwanis Club of Bessemer on July 22, 1942. Mr. Wilkinson began by quoting a Birmingham bus driver who had
pointed to a group of Negroes and told him, "Right
there, mister, is where our next war will break out, and
it may start before this one is over." After a courtroom
method which practice had made perfect in him, Mr.
Wilkinson told his audience: "I regard that as an over-
statement of the situation, but I was impressed with the
man's sincerity when he detailed numerous recent instances of insolent, impudent conduct on the part of
Negro passengers that necessitated 'calling the law,' as
he expressed it. I learned that there seems to be a disposition on the part of many Negroes to disregard and
resist the Jim Crow Law and that in many instances it
had been necessary to stop and hold buses and street
cars until officers could be summoned to make unruly
Negroes occupy the part of the car reserved for them or
remove them because they refused to do so. Montgomery is having similar experiences." The speaker then
went into a list of atrocities. He told of a telephone call
to the Louisville & Nashville Railway office in Birmingham from a conductor in Anniston who was holding his
train because "a Negro was determined to ride in the
white car, the law to the contrary notwithstanding." He
told of "white men at the Republic Steel works who are
complaining about Negroes being given jobs that have
always been filled by white men—they want the situation
relieved by law, but they want it relieved." He described

a scene in a Dothan liquor store when Negroes had grown "tired of waiting in line and decided to take matters in their own hands" and "practically took over the store." He recalled "the Montevallo incident, when a number of young ladies attending the State College there were insulted by Negroes throwing kisses to them as they waited at the railroad station for a train to carry them home." He mentioned "race trouble narrowly averted at Tuskegee when there was a clash between the white civil authorities and the Negro military police in the white business section of the city," and he told how, when the Negroes had been disarmed, officials at Tuskegee had demanded that "their pistols be restored." "The situation is regarded as extremely serious by many of the most substantial people. One man in whom I have utmost confidence told me that practically every responsible male citizen in the town was a special officer of some kind." Mr. Wilkinson then spoke of a legal action "filed by a group of Negroes in the Circuit Court of Jefferson County undertaking to force the American Legion in Alabama to charter Negro posts." He quoted Wendell Willkie's address to the National Association for the Advancement of Colored People at its just concluded Los Angeles convention, declared that Willkie had "advocated a program that, in my judgment, would inevitably result in two things; namely, the destruction of segregation and the amalgamation of the races. . . . And, as I see it, the difference between Mr. Willkie and the national leadership in the opposing party is the difference between tweedle-dee and tweedle-dum." He noted the local morning paper with "an account of a demand for a racial show-down made on the President of the United States by A. Philip Randolph, International President of the Brotherhood of Sleeping Car Porters," cited Randolph for making much of "the execution of Odell Waller, a Negro share-cropper in Virginia, for cold-blooded murder."

Then, like the preacher who gives fifty-five minutes to luscious descriptions of sin and closes with a five-minute appeal against sinning, Mr. Wilkinson said: "These instances, like boils on the body, are indicative of a condition that needs attention. They are not mentioned for the purpose of arousing feeling against the Negro race but for the purpose of showing you that the time has arrived for discussion that will provoke serious consideration of the situation in Alabama and the South and bring forth suggestions for a solution of the problem within the law and under the Constitution of the United States. . . . About ten percent of the population of this country are Negroes. The whites being in the majority, it is their right and responsibility to work out the problem within the law and by a law that all whites and blacks must obey. It must be done that way. Extra-legal methods, however necessary or effective they may have been in days of yore, are not to be resorted to now."

The Wilkinson speech was quoted and passed about all over the South. Its pieties against extra-legalism were not among the popular parts. I outline it here without prejudice to questions of fact and of right-and-wrong. Its significance was in the feelings its represented and those it aroused. Set these against the ones that were being aroused among the colored people and you had your trinitrotoluol.

Alabama's United States Senator Bankhead found his state in such a fever of racial trouble and anticipation of trouble when he came home ten days later that he wrote to General Marshall, Chief of Staff, suggesting: "If you feel obliged to have Negro soldiers in the South as a result of social or political pressure, can't you place Southern Negro soldiers there and assign the other Negro soldiers in the North where their presence is not likely to lead to race wars?"

White majorities of the South were unwavering and total in determination not to have race segregation abolished. Southern liberals, who in other days had championed the Negro to the point of getting themselves mentioned adversely in Klan circles, were too well aware of this to believe that anything but harm to the Negro, the South, and the nation-at-war could come of the agitations. "The Southern Negro," said Mark Ethridge, Editor of *The Louisville Courier-Journal*, in a much discussed statement as a member of the President's Committee on Fair Labor Practices at hearings in Birmingham in the summer of 1942, "cannot afford to drive from his side, in his march to a greater fulfillment of his rights, the Southern white men of good will who have been his chief asset and his chief aid." Mr. Ethridge said this in prelude to his historic declaration that: "There is no power in the world—not even in all the mechanized armies of the earth, Allied and Axis—which could now force the Southern white people to the abandonment of the principle of social segregation. It is a cruel disillusionment, bearing the germs of strife and perhaps tragedy, for any of their [the Negroes'] leaders to tell them that they can expect it, or that they can exact it as the price of their participation in the war."

Mr. Ethridge was speaking of a fact. He was passing no judgment, simply stating a truth without recognition of which there could be no practical approach to the very real problems and needs of the Negro in the South. A New Dealer, a favorite of President Roosevelt for many posts and missions, a publicist criticized in many Southern quarters for his championings of the Negro, he found it necessary as a man accustomed to getting things accomplished to make this statement. The centripetal force that had drawn Calhoun and Grady home, had drawn him, too. Much as the statement disappointed some of his liberal friends in other parts of the country and angry as it made the national Negro leaders, it disappointed even more the reactionaries in the South. They were looking to the gathering race tensions as a shining chance for discrediting not only the New Deal but the whole liberal position. The race issue was one on which, when once hotly enough raised, anybody could beat anybody below the Potomac. To have Southern liberals like Mark Ethridge and Virginius Dabney taking forthright stands against agitation for settlement of the Negro problem in the face of an enemy across the sea, even as they led in demands for the Negro's full participation in the industrial and military tasks of the war, was confusing to the Talmadges of Dixie, to the fascists, to the Klansmen who were itching so to ride, and to the moronic gentlemen who had lately taken it upon themselves to use the club on a great Negro singer in Rome, Georgia, who had nothing but good will in his heart.

The no-compromise leadership among the Negroes would have none of this fact-facing on segregation, however. At the 33rd annual convention of the National Association for the Advancement of Colored People in Los Angeles, Assistant Secretary Roy Wilkins vowed (as quoted) that there would be no faltering in the all-or-nothing policy: "The issues are clear; the stakes are great; the path is straight; the tensions are tremendous; the pressure crushing. This is our answer to the Ethridges of Kentucky, the Dabneys of Virginia, the Graves of Alabama. This is the watchword that must go forward. We cannot give up the trust!" And A. Philip Randolph declared: "It is better to die fighting than to live begging."

What was it that made them so determined, these leaders who, in most instances, were perfectly honest in their conviction not only that their race had suffered much and was entitled to much, but also that this was the great time? There was, of course, their quite correct estimate of the differences between the democratic battle cries with which the nation had gone to war and the want-of-democracy in many of its practices, especially towards the Negro. There was their correct understanding, too, that the Roosevelt administration, both for political reasons and for genuinely humanitarian ones, was inclined to back every proposal for advancement of the Negro. More basically, there were the not-to-be-disputed facts of suppression, injustice, cheating, and denial practiced against Negroes by whites all over the land. There had been a very real need of the famous White House Executive Order 8802 against discriminations in wartime industrial jobs. There had been need of it not only as a measure for fullest employment of American manpower but also to protect the Negro against economic hardships resulting from discriminations on the part of both management and labor in war industries, especially in the North.

The issuance of Executive Order 8802 was a story. In the summer of 1941, because of nation-wide discriminations in war industry jobs and training schools, A. Philip Randolph of the Brotherhood of Sleeping Car Porters called for a "Negro March on Washington." With the support of Secretary Walter White of the National Association for the Advancement of Colored People, he arranged for buses and special trains to bring an estimated 50,000 Negroes to the capital. This proposed dramatization threatened to be too dramatic. Mrs. Roosevelt asked that the march be called off and was refused. When President Roosevelt made the same request he, too, was refused, until he agreed to issue the order banning discrimination against Negroes in war industries and setting up the Fair Employment Practice Committee, two of whose seven members were to be Negroes. Someone sent Walter White copies of my syndicated

Southern column criticizing him for the proposed march. "On numerous occasions," he wrote me on July 14, 1941, "we have pleaded with the President to break his silence and to speak out against this discrimination which not only was doing an injustice to the Negro but was definitely jeopardizing our national security through reduction of our productivity by approximately ten percent. The first time I urged him to do this was at a conference at the White House last September 25 (1940) at which were present Secretary of the Navy Knox, Under Secretary of War Patterson, A. Philip Randolph, and others. On that occasion and on several others the President gave as a reason for not taking definitive action against this discrimination that 'the South would rise up in protest.' On several occasions I have said to him 'What South are you talking about, Mr. President? The South of Bilbo and Cotton Ed Smith, or the South of Frank Graham and Mark Ethridge?' [Note: This was before Mr. Ethridge had faced the facts about segregation and incurred the displeasure of the national Negro leadership.] I assured the President that apparently I had more faith in the inherent decency of Southern white people than he did in that I was certain that at least on an issue like this far more Southerners would approve his taking an unequivocal stand than would disapprove. . . . But for five months we were given the run-around. Appeal after appeal was made to Washington with little tangible result. Conference after conference was held and nothing happened. Knudsen of OPM refused even to meet or discuss discrimination with any Negro delegation.

. . . Discontent and bitterness were growing like wildfire among Negroes all over the country. Communists were trying as usual to capitalize on this. It was only then that Mr. Randolph and several others of us planned the March as a last resort to get some consideration of the plight of the Negro. . . . We were glad that things turned out as they did, though the executive order does not go nearly as far as the circumstances warrant or the needs of the situation demand."

There was need of this federal interference in the Negro's behalf, and both the Negro and the war effort were helped. In the melee of men and goods and money which war production had brought about the Negro was losing his relative economic status quo. With peace jobs eliminated and war jobs denied, he was in danger of being worse off than before in comparison with the white man. During the boom times before 1929 he had been admitted more and more to skilled trades and the training required for them, but in the following days of depression he had lost out, as he generally does. Representing about 10 percent of the total population, he accounted for about 20 percent of the unemployment during the 1930's. After war producing began the situation grew worse rather than better. Of 29,215 employees at 10 war plants in the New York area only 142 were Negroes. In 56 plants at St. Louis there was an average of only three Negroes to each. There were practically no provisions for training. But in the year after Executive Order 8802 was issued, the situation improved, partly as a result of the increasing manpower needs and partly as a result of the order. The aviation industry, which had less than 300 Negroes in January, 1941, had 3,500 in April, 1942. The number employed in navy yards increased more than 300 percent. "In three leading East Coast shipbuilding companies today," Stanley High reported in the *Reader's Digest* for July, 1942, "Negro employment is 24 percent of the total. In Detroit nearly 1,500 Negroes have completed eight weeks training as machine-tool operators, welders, and riveters. One unit of the new U. S. Cartridge plant in St. Louis will be entirely manned by Negroes—

> These war strides have been particularly notable in the South. During 1941 the navy yard at Charleston increased the percentage of its Negro employes from 9.5 to 17.7. Negro employment in the Norfolk navy yard has been more than tripled since September, 1940, and now stands at approximately 25 percent of the total employed. . . . These "token advances," they say, are opening the door. The next job is for the Negro to make good. How well is he prepared to do so?

Liberal Southern leadership, especially the press, applauded these gains and defended against other Southerners the Executive Order and the Fair Employment Practice Committee which had contributed to them. But Southern liberals tended to draw away from the administration and from the Negro leadership when evidences multiplied of an intent to use the war for breaking down the structure of Southern race relations.

Editor Virginius Dabney wrote in *The Richmond Times-Dispatch* in April, 1942, that the National Association for the Advancement of Colored People (and its magazine, *The Crisis*) had been "responsible for many important and justifiable advances on the part of the Negroes, but the manner in which it has stirred Negro citizens, and particularly Negro soldiers, to demand the complete wiping out of all racial differentiation overnight, is one of the chief reasons why there is such inter-racial tension among us, and why some Negroes are indifferent to America's war effort. . . . So difficult and complex a problem as the race problem cannot be solved in any such abrupt and hasty fashion as the N.A.A.C.P. seems to desire. It hasn't been solved anywhere else by such means, and the efforts of those who seek an immediate revolutionary 'solution' as the price of 100 percent colored participation in our war effort, are bound to result in immeasurable strife, if not additional bloodshed."

Against this attitude of the white liberals in the South was the persisting one of Northern Negro leaders. Reciting injustices to the Negro "particularly in the Southern States," *The Crisis* declared editorially in March, 1941: "*The Crisis* leaves to its readers the question of whether there is a great deal of difference between the code for Negroes under Hitler and the code for Negroes under the United States of America—the leading democratic nation in the world." Roy Wilkins vowed in Detroit after a racial clash there that the Negroes are "fed up with this democracy stuff." And when an official of the N.A.A.C.P., William Pickens, issued a statement praising the 99th Pursuit Squadron at Tuskegee, first Negro aviation unit in history, he was dropped from the executive board for implied acceptance of segregation.

Southern Negro leaders could not make up their minds whether to follow the Southern white liberals or the Northern crusaders for all-or-nothing. But they were for the most part willing to stress the national need in wartime and the boon of this country to all of its people. "In spite of the immemorial denials of so many democratic blessings to him," wrote President James E. Shepard, of the North Carolina College for Negroes, in a letter to *The St. Louis Post-Dispatch* in the spring of 1942, "the Negro will be loyal because he knows that at our worst he has higher hopes here than any other land will offer him at its best." And President F. D. Patterson, of Tuskegee Institute, denounced Walter White and the current activities of N.A.A.C.P. as definitely harmful to his race. "Walter White's ego," he wrote a Southern Negro editor in March, 1942, "is undermining the effectiveness of the N.A.A.C.P. This organization has shown itself to be an effective instrument of protest against injustice in the courts and discriminations which have an implied state and federal sanction. The decisions it has been able to obtain from the Supreme Court in regard to these have been significant and far-reaching. But in the realm of practical adjustment of Negroes in American life, it fails miserably. The very nature of progress is a give and take affair. The extent to which White has been able to get the official ear in

Washington has accomplished little because it has been used to protest adjustments short of what he has deemed was complete democratic integration."

> It is time that thinking Negroes who are con-
> cerned about the progress of the race rather than the
> progress of individuals should ask the N.A.A.C.P.
> to stick to the phase of race pleading for which it
> has recognition and cease muddying the water by
> attempting to direct the overall strategy for the
> Negro group. If this is done there are plenty of other
> organizations and local groups that can follow up
> the far-reaching decisions which the N.A.A.C.P.
> secures and develop under them such advances and
> advantages as are possible in a given situation. This
> will, both immediately and in the long run, prove
> better than a militant stalemate which gets nothing
> for the Negro and leaves crystallized determined at-
> titudes that the future shall be equally as unproduc-
> tive of favorable results. . . .

In reference to this letter President Patterson wrote me a few weeks later: "I am hopeful that reasonable gains shall be made in a spirit of understanding on the part of those who are unselfishly working for a full ex-pression of American democracy. Certainly we want such gains to be permanent, so that when the war is over there will not be recriminations and throw-backs which will arouse hatreds with painful results."

That Northern Negro leaders were determined to use the war as their shining chance for immediate and all-inclusive elimination of racial distinctions was a matter

not in dispute, since they proclaimed it. Was the Roose-
velt Administration, too, looking in that direction?
Throughout most of the South the activities of White,
Randolph, and the others were identified with Mrs.
Roosevelt and her known positions on the race question.
What the administration itself had in mind was not
clear, but there was a growing disposition among anti-
New Dealers in the South to believe that it followed the
First Lady. Governor Frank Dixon, of Alabama, a
nephew of Author Tom Dixon ("The Clansman," "The
Leopard's Spots," etc.) intensified this point of view
when he refused to sign a contract with the Defense
Supplies Corporation for 1,750,000 yards of cloth to be
made by Alabama convicts. He gave as his reason a
clause in the contract against race discrimination in performance of the work. "Under Executive Order 8802 of
the President of the United States, which is built around
the same principle enunciated in this clause," he asserted, "the United States Employment Service Division of the Social Security Board has adopted policies,
the effect of which are to break down the principle of
segregation under which the white and Negro races have
lived in peace together in the South for all the years since
Reconstruction. . . ."

> Under cover of this particular clause contained in
> war contracts, the President's Fair Employment
> Practice Committee has been operating to break
> down this same principle of segregation of the races,
> to force Negroes and white people to work together,
> intermingle with each other, and even to bring

about the situation where white employees will have to work under Negroes. A careful study of the record of the Fair Employment Practice Committee hearing recently held in Birmingham disclosed that, however sincere the protestations of the committee members to the contrary, actually there was placed on trial the entire system of race segregation of the South, and that with the single exception of Mr. Mark Ethridge, of Louisville, Kentucky, there was no realization in the minds of any of the committee members of the basic necessity for any such system. . . . The clear intimation was that unless the Southern people changed their way of living and abandon the principle of segregation, they would be forced to do so by the federal government. Unfortunately the issue seems to be clearly drawn.

Something which the agitators against race segregation in the South overlooked was the immense difference between the Southern situation and that elsewhere. Of the 12,800,000 Negroes in the United States, more than three-fourths are in the South. The "Negro problem" in a state like New York, where Negroes are only four percent of the population, is different both in nature and in degree from the problem in Mississippi where Negroes are 49 percent of the population. And the differences are multiplied by variations in education, living standards, health, civic responsibility, law-abiding, etc. In part it is the Southern white man's fault that the Southern Negro is less qualified than he might be and should be for the full participations demanded. But the fact of that lesser qualification is sure. The advancements to which he is most entitled and of which he is most in need are the ones which will qualify him for participations. Most of the agitation for doing away with segregation and other racial distinctions comes from states where the percentage of Negroes is small. But the basic problem is in states where the percentage is large. The difference is too often overlooked:

Proportions of Negro to Total Population

Illinois .... 5 percent	Georgia .... 35 percent
Pennsylvania ...... 5 percent	Alabama .... 35 percent
New York .... 4 percent	Mississippi ...... 49 percent
California .... 2 percent	Louisiana .... 36 percent
Ohio .... 5 percent	South Carolina ... 43 percent
Indiana .... 4 percent	North Carolina .. 27 percent
New Jersey .... 5 percent	Virginia .... 25 percent
Connecticut ...... 2 percent	Florida .... 27 percent

If individuals and organizations undertaking to lead the Negro were persuaded to live where most of the Negroes live, there might be a better meeting of minds on the subject.

Chapter Ten

YOU CAN HEAR THEIR VOICES

I HAVE A PHONOGRAPH RECORD, BUT I HATE TO PLAY IT.
Indeed I would not play it if I did not think it had clin-
ical value for students of the race problem in the South.
It is a record of the bigotries, implacables, fierce arguments, dark passions, and impossibles that divide Negro
and white man in Southern states, and it comes from the
original. In course of a wartime campaign in my column
against agitators of the white man by the black and the
black man by the white, I received letters from many
people. There were enough of them and they came from
sufficiently differing places and stations to make what
I believe to be a genuine voice of race trouble below
the Potomac. But I say this before letting the voice be
heard: millions of white people and Negroes are writing
no letters about such things. They write nothing because
they have only good will for each other in their hearts
and a desire somehow to be relieved of this unhappiness
between two naturally happy peoples.

I have tried to put down passages from the letters in
a sequence which will let them be the babel, the running
noise, they represent. The general attitude of the letter
writer is often indicated by whether he spells "Negro"
with a capital "N":

An *Anderson, S. C., Negro:* "So you don't think people ought to ask for justice now, eh? Well, when in the hell should they ask for it? You have enjoyed a safe and secure place so long, never having to worry about the everyday trials and tribulations of the average man that you are only interested in preserving your own hide and lordly estate for you and your family. You never have to worry about where your next meal is coming from. You don't have to worry about anybody doing you bodily harm or taking advantage of you. . . ."

A *Birmingham white man:* "I still possess a Winchester pump gun purchased from the King Hardware Company in Atlanta on a permit issued by Mayor Jim Woodward in 1906 during the race riots there. Mrs. Roosevelt and her ilk do not realize that they are playing with fire in a hay barn. . . ."

A *Pulaski, Tenn., Negro:* "You are real worried and sorrow for the Negro, aren't you! You would do everything for him except gett off his back. . . ."

A *Danville, Va., white woman:* "I have never heard of you before and I hope I won't have to any more. The Negroes can have you because I know they are proud of you. . . ."

A *Columbia, S. C., Negro:* "You and your kind would go crazy if you did not have us to kick around and impress your superiority complex upon. I would much rather be in Africa if you white folk would stay away but the English treat the African as badly as you treat us so I don't have any choice. I am glad Hitler can make you and the British feel how it is to be the under-dog. I am glad somebody can scare you. I wish Hitler would come over here and drop bombs on every damn southern town in the United States. I would be glad to die just to see some of you dirty lowdown southerners go with me. . . ."

A *Jacksonville, Fla., white man:* "If you must attack Eugene Talmadge, a man of your own race and one of the highest ranking men in Georgia, for his views and his convictions and his actions, in all fairness to the rest of your white brethren, why not scold the average Negro who curses the white man with every breath?"

A *Negro woman college graduate:* "Equality of rights is not yours to give to any man. They belong exclusively to God. In fact you don't have social equality yourself —you are too low and too dumb to see it however. . . ."

A *white girl from Atlanta:* "I read what you had to say against Governor Talmadge. He is right about the Negroes and from personal experience when visiting Birmingham I think you need him there. Twice while out walking near the hospital grown negro men have tried to get fresh with me until I scared both groups away. One day behind me on a Birmingham bus negro boys insisted on talking nasty and telling filthy jokes among themselves for the white girls and women to hear. Down near the Greyhound Bus Station I saw a negro man slap a white boy of about 18 and run away. Down town on busy streets your negroes offend white people with their dirty language. Thank goodness I live in Georgia where white people can breath easily. . . ."

A *Negro woman from Memphis:* "You harp on protecting your women from Negro lust. Your women in the first place are too lusty, even your best women. I know how your women snare our young men and give them mistaken ideas. Rape cases involving Negro men and white women are too often trumped up cases where the Negro man attempted to withdraw his attentions and was charged by his white mistress with rape. If Negroes had an overwhelming desire to possess white women we have plenty in our own race due to the rape and enforced attentions to women of our race causing a filthy stain of white blood. I know that the white man is more lusty than any Negro no matter how ignorant. If social equality means mixing with you then the only danger is to us. . . ."

A *Birmingham white man:* "You wonder where Talmadge gets so much money for political advertisements. This money is more than likely coming from hundreds of decent and respectable people, from those mothers whose daughters have been caught in the melstrom, and from the pockets of the fathers who are now taking care of illegitimate children their daughters brought home from schools and colleges, perhaps, and from other sympathizers that understand and know what the conspirators have done for them. . . ."

A *Dallas Negro:* "It's impossible for anybody to be as prejudiced as you are. Walter White is right. Here is an example of your American democracy. In a nearby town recently two Negroes were tried for attempted rape. One was sentenced to the chair, the other to 40 years imprisonment. I don't need to mention the fact that the women involved were white because a Negro woman receives very little consideration when a Negro man rapes her and it's useless to report it when a white man is guilty. . . ."

A *Greensboro, Alabama, editor:* "We know that the Southern white man, as strong as he is today, can repeat what he did in the 70's with hardly an effort. What disturbs us is the price, and a horrible price it will be, which so many innocent Negroes will have to pay. The white man insisted on ruling the South and he will keep on insisting. If this disturbance continues there will be trouble. The night riders will be out again. There will be hangings, shootings, burnings. . . ."

A *New Orleans Negro:* "You labor under an illusion that your race is superior in spite of the fact that this has been proven untrue, and in spite of the fact that, while some of us still struggle in dense ignorance, cruel injustices, both spiritual and physical to say nothing of economically and educationally, the other part of us scale insurmountable heights. Do you think this is inferior? If you do you have even less sense than I'm giving you credit for. You could have only one consolation, there are so many in your race like you. . . ."

From a Bristol, Virginia, white woman: "Oh God what will we do if politics and money play such a part in this war that we must mix with the negro the rest of our lives. I know of a number of people who have stopped buying bonds and even hope we will not win the war because they would rather live with the Germans and Japs than for the laws of segregation to be wiped out. The negro has gotten everything from the white

man his religion his education his everything. Joe Louis
has a strong arm but what else did he have, the white
man made him. He is having too much done for him in
the army, if I were a soldier if they didn't give me half
day off for my birthday like they did that monkey faced
negro I would walk out if I were shot at sun-up. . . ."

From a Memphis Negro: "Like poetry? Everyone
does, so read this:

> Why should I flinch the white man's scorn,
> His hate, his greed? I'm American born.
> Why should I grovel and take the bones
> He throws to me as to a dog he owns?
> Should I be denied a man's full share
> Of rights and privileges to those who dared
> To make this country a lovely place
> To live in—a heaven for any creed or race?
> If I've intruded, then whose to blame?
> Who sought my services, changed my name?
> My forebears voiced no woes, no fear
> But your fathers' need. That's why I'm here.
> You opened your doors to the alien request
> For shelter, a living, when he cried in distress.
> I've proved my allegiance—isn't some merit due?
> Must I always remind you—I'm an American too?"

An Atlanta white man: "The enemies of the South at
Washington seem determined to injure this part of the
country. They are taking our men and boys away for
the war and leaving able-bodied negroes here to commit
more crimes. Is there no way to stop this draft of 18 and
19 year old boys? It is dangerous for white girls and

women to go on the streets unattended day or night. Terrible crimes have been committed by negro men. They engaged women to help keep crime down—this in Atlanta, Georgia. That devil woman hates the South. . . ."

A *Tuscumbia, Alabama, white man:* "The emphasis on Negro advancement may seem out of place in war time but let us not forget that if we white Americans only mark time at our present position of rights the Negro Americans must run to catch up with us; this despite the fact that we are asking sacrifices of others and of them equally. We must have justice, Mr. Graves, war or no war, or we shall have nothing. . . ."

A *Birmingham white man:* "Decent, law-abiding people here must take issue with the attitude you have taken toward the Ku Klux Klan. None of us believe in any group or any organization taking the law into their own hands and meting out punishment according to their own concepts. But the overwhelming majority of the white people of our city are agreed that Birmingham needs the Ku Klux Klan as never before. The decent, law-abiding Negro citizen need have no fear of the Ku Klux Klan. If the records of the Klan were known I believe there is little doubt but that they would reveal as much punishment meted out to white people as to Negroes. Do you read the Negro newspapers? Do you talk with Negroes in their own environment? Do you attend Negro lodges and listen to their lecturers? Do you attend their churches and listen to their sermons? No, you don't do that. Therefore you do not hear the opinion, you do not know the attitude, of the average Negro not only in Birmingham but in America. Let me tell you in all honesty, sincerity and truthfulness that Negroes everywhere, anytime, are attacking the white people. Word of mouth attacks, editorial attacks in their newspapers; attacks from the lecturer's platform, attacks from the pulpits. It is going on right under your very ample nose. . . ."

A Greenville, S. C., "Old Southerner": "If God wanted us to be equal He would have made us all the same color. . . ."

From J. A. Lawrence, of Greensboro, Alabama, Supreme Commander of The Thick Blood of Youth Movement For the Preservation of the Purity and Honor of the White Bloodstream: "People in the police zone of a city know little of what agony isolated rural folk suffer from fear for the safety of the women folk. None of us wants the future of our race sealed in mulatto wombs."

From an anonymous writer who tells me I would be amazed if I knew what an important person he is: "No, Mr. Graves, I will not, so long as the negro race is at its low level as it is today, help another negro. Nor would I pet a rattlesnake, and feed it so that it would have strength to attack me! Let the negro rave and rant as you would let an animal rave and rant. You would if you really knew and understood the negro, as you may know and understand an animal. When an animal is domesticated we trust it; when the negro has lifted himself from his present level, we owe it to him and to all humanity to trust and help him. . . ."

From a Columbia, S. C., white man: "If the signers

of the Constitution had known in the future history of the United States the question of race were to be brought up, would they have said we all would have equal rights? At the time of the signing were there any negroes, Japanese or Chinese in this country? Don't you think the signers meant the Constitution to be for the white race? In my opinion there should be two kinds of citizens in this country. First the white man, who is a true American, and second the colored citizen, who should do as the true American (white man) says. Such men as you should bring this question out and settle it now."

A *Birmingham white man:* "The white people feel that the negroes are armed and are arming. It is a dark outlook. The average negro lies from habit, steals of necessity, but steals nevertheless, and is cunning. In short the average negro is treacherous and must be regarded as such."

A *Montgomery official:* "I am sorry to say that a small number of citizens in Alabama are trying in every way that they can to develop or grab an incident by which they can throw this state and the so-called Solid South into an era of some sort of new 'Reconstructionism' or Ku-Klux-Klanism. . . ."

A *Meridian Negro preacher:* "I am wondering how would you feel if you were a Negro today. I wonder if it wouldn't be a bigger job than you think for, Mr. Graves, to kick out from under all the embarassments, the discouragements, the intimidations and injustices that we as a group must face because we are Negroes?

Life, liberty and freedom are sweet to us all and when we are denied all these three, any man I think, has a just cause for which to complain. I am not unmindful of the great benefits we have received at the hands of our white brother and I am not unmindful of the benefits that the white man has received from his black brother. . . ."

From a Tuskegee Institute official: "All that we have or will ever have; all that we accomplish has been made possible by white friends among whose ranks you are alligning yourself. . . ."

A Huntsville, Alabama, Negro: "Mr. Graves, the Negro doesn't want any social life with the white man, and you know that he is a kinda lazy type animal, he wants freedom to live, to sing, to sleep, to have very little responsibility. He was not born a kleptomaniac, he acquired the habit to survive. Sure I am against crime but the Negro is to be pitted more than to be punished in some cases. . . . I don't think we can force the Geyer poll tax bill and I don't think it should be attempted, but I do think that the white man in the south should give the Negro more consideration about his sufferage, if he merits it, and in forty years with the contact with the white man, and education, some have merited it. Forty years ago the Negro had his sufferage taken away from him because he was taught to abuse it through no fault of his own, but today he is better prepared. Why not give him just a little? What we want is to be proud that we are Negroes with the help of such thoughtful and considerate white men like you. I don't think I have said anything to be ashamed of, so this is my real name, and I want to apologize if I have offended you. . . ."

A *Mississippi white farmer:* "I think you are right about the race problem and I believe we and our negroes can work it out all right if left alone. It seems as if we run across this agitation in many places but look at 'Little Orphan Annie' in Sunday's paper. My little boy thinks she is the greatest heroine that has ever been and it did not occur to him but what she was right in taking George [a Negro boy] in and even promoting him. . . ."

An *Alabama Negro farmer:* "I hold nothing aganst no man, had et not been for a good set of white people I would not have had the chance to go to college so you see I have no reasons to hate. the more you write about this thing called hate the better, we need someone to teach us to stop hateing. . . ."

A *famous Georgia Democrat:* "We in the South must not allow our well-wishers and misdirected welfare workers to upset the equilibrium of our very satisfactory relationship with the colored people in our Southern states. I travel and have contacts with and see negroes in all sections of the United States, and I am absolutely sure in my own mind that they are more satisfied and are better respected in the South than any other part of the nation."

A *Meridian, Miss., Negro:* "We believe in a God that we think is loving and just. Yet we grow doubtful and need the faith such as that given us recently in the editorials of The Birmingham News. Those editorials against the acts of a high Georgia official (Talmadge) gives us assurance that the South has not gone mad with hate. It gives us assurance that men of the best blood recognize progress of both races as a needed thing for this dear southland of ours and lament any setbacks that may come. I shall renew my faith in the South and in white men of the South."

A *Winston-Salem, N. C., Negro:* "The American Negro is fighting for an opportunity to do anything he is capable of doing to earn an honest living. There are thousands of Southern white people who are willing to grant that opportunity now. When enough experience a change of heart for the majority to feel that way, the situation will change."

My phonograph record, it will be noted, is not all hate and immutable division. Some of the things said in these letters are so false, so misinformed, so blindly passionate, or so mean of spirit that I have been tempted to interrupt, to say that this or that was not so, that here was a monstrous point of view, that the writer of these words was presuming facts which did not exist, that the author of those words was blind to time and its marches. But some of the letters have in or between their lines a very great earnest, a trouble that is real, a fear that is equally real, an honest wish to get at the answer and to be free for the exercise of good will to men. Reading these I have remembered the million ties of service, memory, and common experience that bind white people and black in the South. It isn't like India, no matter what the answer. Neither is it like New York. These whites and blacks of the South have the same land. They have it together and are going to go on having it that way.

Something else that may impress those who read these letters is that there is no "The Negro." There are, instead, the 13,000,000 Negroes of the United States, the 10,000,000 living in the South. J. Saunders Redding, an exceptionally intelligent, sensitive, and objective Negro, graduate of Brown University, made this plain in a book he wrote, "No Day of Triumph," after a tour of Negro life in the South in 1940 under auspices of the Rockefeller Foundation and the University of North Carolina. He went everywhere among the Negroes, vertically and horizontally, and his book shows as many variations among them as among white people. They have color lines, class distinctions, segregations of their own. Their numbers include some of the most vicious people in America and some of the most clean-hearted and deserving. They are not to be covered under the single blanket of hate, love or indifference which their fellow Americans tend to use in thinking of them. There is no "The Negro."

Chapter Eleven

"FOR THE ADVANCEMENT OF
COLORED PEOPLE"

MORE THAN ONE HUNDRED GEORGIA NEWSPAPERS, IN-
cluding all the big ones, opposed Eugene Talmadge
when he ran for another term as Governor of Georgia in
the summer of 1942. Only three small ones were for
him. He had been guilty of the two greatest sins that can
be done against the South—the sin of laying unholy
hands on the educational system and the sin of agitating
falsely the race problem. Education is now as in the past
the South's best answer to its problems. The Negro is
now as always its most difficult problem. Talmadge was
made to pay in stinging defeat by an electorate turned
to its best lights.

But this was only one battle. And it was won against
difficulties gathering fast because of the continuing agitation of the Negro by Northern leaders who were insisting on concessions the South was overwhelmingly
unwilling to make. Within a few days after the Talmadge defeat in September an organization called "The
Vigilantes, Inc.," was organized in Georgia by his associates. Its charter recited that it should have the power
to confer "an initiative or degree ritualism, fraternal and
secret obligations, words, grips, signs and ceremonies."

Its intent was plain. A month later lynching broke out in Mississippi. Two fourteen-year-old Negro boys, charged with criminal attack upon a 13-year-old white girl, were hanged from a Quitman bridge. A Negro man, convicted of the murder of a white man, was taken from a Jones County jail and murdered by a mob of 75 to 100 whites. Murder was the name and there was enough state and common law against it without benefit of the federal government to bring 75 to 100 death sentences. Talmadge had been beaten, for the time being, but his soul was marching on—by courtesy of the National Association for the Advancement of Colored People, the Northern Negro press, the politicians and sentimentalists in high places at Washington, and the devoted but cross-eyed humanitarians.

An argument among those who proposed that the war be made an occasion for forcing Negro advancement was that promises after the other World War were not fulfilled. If the promises were of total elimination of racial distinctions they had indeed not been honored. But if they were promises of a greater progress than the race had ever made before and than any other group was making, with more in prospect, there were aspects in which they had been honored in full. There had been a striking advancement in Negro education, for example. In 1910 about 30 percent of all Negroes were illiterate. In 1942 only about eight percent were in that classification. There were 64 Negro high schools in 1915, in 1942 there were 2500. More than twice as many Negroes graduated from college in the 1930's as in the 1920's.

The number of Negro supervisors of education in the South with college degrees had increased from 15 percent to 70 percent in 10 years. Many of them had masters' degrees. There had been advancement in health. Fifty years ago the annual death rate among Negroes in the United States was approximately 33 per thousand. "Heroic improvements in health facilities and modes of living," reported President Edwin R. Embree of the Julius Rosenwald Fund, in 1942, "have cut that rate more than in half—to an estimated 14 per thousand. This is still 32 percent above the annual death rate of 10.6 for the United States as a whole, though it compares favorably with the death rates for total populations in all but a few very advanced countries." It was immensely better than the Negro death rate of approximately 25 per thousand before the last World War. In the period from 1930 to 1940 the average life expectancy for Negroes, while lower than that of whites, was increasing twice as fast as that of whites. The Negro death rate from tuberculosis had already been cut in half. There had been advancement in organization. The National Association for the Advancement of Colored People had expanded from about 50 local chapters to more than 500. Its executives were able to travel 154,761 miles in 1941 and attend 1008 meetings in 191 cities of 36 states. Seventy-one new branches were organized in 1941 alone. The circulation of its magazine, *The Crisis*, had mounted to 110,000. The National Negro Congress had 102 chapters. The ranks of organized labor had been opened. In Alabama in 1942 one-third of the

102,000 CIO members were Negroes. Reflecting the improving lot of the Negro and his developing consciousness of himself was the Negro press. There were 230 Negro papers in the country in 1942, with a total circulation of 1,406,800. Negro business organizations had prospered. The North Carolina Mutual Life Insurance Company, largest Negro business in the world, increased its assets from $476,645 in 1918 to $7,222,192 in 1942. In the period its insurance in force grew from $16,096,722 to $57,730,690.

A very great advancement was in factors represented by the decline in lynchings. In spite of efforts of the National Association for the Advancement of Colored People to keep the total impressive by counting in other forms of killing, records of Tuskegee Institute showed that the number of lynchings had dropped to only two or three a year. This compared with 80 in 1919, and 130 in 1901.

There had been advance, too, in law enforcement among Negroes themselves, and that is something of a very great importance. Most of the homicides which shift the "murder capital" of America from one Southern city to another are killings of Negroes by Negroes. In the past there has been a demoralizing tendency to think of these killings as not worth the efficient prosecution that would result if a white person were the victim. When a death sentence was executed in North Carolina in the summer of 1942 against a Buncombe County Negro convicted of capital assault upon a Negro girl, *The Asheville Citizen* commented that North Carolina was "beginning to give fuller cognizance to the principle that rights of all individuals are sacred. . . . Justice and common sense agree that the Negro who 'with malice aforethought' kills a member of his own race should receive the same kind of punishment as that received by the Negro who murders a white person. So with the crime of rape or any other legal offense against person and property."

Another important advance for the Negro in the South had been increased understanding by white people that Negroes were living as near them as their kitchens, wash-tubs, dining rooms, bedrooms and, most thought-suggesting of all, their nurseries. Syphilis is no respecter of Jim Crow, and neither is tuberculosis. Neither are the other contagions that come of poverty, uncleanliness, ignorance, malcontent, and dirty minds. The mental, physical, and moral condition of the Southern Negro touches Southern white people in many places. It touches their food, their beds, their clothes, and the minds and bodies of their children. In Montgomery an old Negro from the country was arrested for driving his jalopy through a red light. "Got anything to say, Uncle?" asked the judge. "Yasser, judge," the old man explained. "Ah see all the white people goin' on the green light and Ah knowed that wasn't for me." Traffic lights were only one of many things which the white people of the South were coming to understand that they must share on the same terms with colored people in protection of both races.

Another advance had been in the number of large

Southern daily newspapers championing the Negro. That, in some respects, was the most notable·advance of all, for the friendship of the white liberal Southerner is the Negro's basic hope there. Such papers as *The Richmond Times-Dispatch*, *The Louisville Courier-Journal*, *The Birmingham News and Age-Herald*, *The Raleigh News and Observer*, *The Montgomery Advertiser* and many others had been conspicuous in befriending the black man. An improving point of view among Southern whites towards the Negro had been illustrated in the wide outcry against Governor Talmadge when he interfered with Georgia's higher educational system and raised the race issue in excuse. The Georgia University System was dropped or suspended by the Association of American Universities, the American Association of University Women, the American Association of Law Schools, the National Association of Collegiate Schools of Business, and the American Association of Teachers Colleges—but well before most of these national organizations acted it had been dropped by the Southern Conference of Universities and the Southern Association of Colleges and Secondary Schools.

The greatest advancement for the Negro—in what it promised more than in what it had yet brought about—was his discovery by the Democratic Party. For the first time in history the Negro vote went to this party in 1932. It went again in 1936 and 1940. Insofar as it represented something near to a balance of power in pivotal states like Illinois, Indiana, and Ohio, it was possibly of more value to the Democratic Party than the vote of the white man in the South. In spite of his inability to vote in that section the Negro might actually exercise more political power in the nation than did the white Southerners who voted. That was a tremendous fact. Its implications ran in many directions and some of them were tragic. In an increasingly political and federal day the Negro was going to be competed for by both parties in years to come and on a basis of concessions that would bring unprecedented advancement.

The Negro had been discovered, too, by the Supreme Court. Over and over again that court had decided against lower court convictions of Negroes where Negroes had been excluded from the jury. The court had ruled that the pay of Negro and white school teachers must be the same, that railroad facilities must be equal in quality and service, that equal graduate schools must be made available. An interesting result of the decision for equal pay of school teachers, as Jonathan Daniels pointed out, was that the teaching profession among Negroes tended to be more than ever one of the best paid ones available to the race and to draw, therefore, the best talent of the race, while the same pay for white teachers, representing a low income according to white standards, continued in its tendency to discourage talent in school teaching among that race. Each of the Supreme Court decisions meant enormous advances and promises for the Negro.

The Negro had been discovered, too, by the New Deal. Even though some of the measures brought actual hardship on him rather than help during the first years, the target was the underprivileged American. Since the Negro was as a class the most underprivileged it was he who received most of the benefits and who would profit most from the social and economic measures as they were adapted and systematized in years to come.

Best of all for him, in the long run, the Negro had been discovered by economists and business men. There had been a time when, except for his own convenience and the conscience of white men, it made little or no economic difference whether the Negro ate anything, wore anything, was sheltered anywhere, or had the comforts and gadgets of civilization. But that was before mass production made mass consuming a practical necessity of the machine age. It was before the economy of plenty whose name is taken so much in vain by lions of laissez faire. It was before mechanical capacity for making enough of everything for everybody brought about an economic imperative of getting things distributed to everybody. More and more the great corporations and business establishments had begun to see that the final process in their integration was the manufacture of customers. And just as the South as a whole contained, because of its comparative poverty, the greatest potential customer source in America, so did the Southern Negro, whose economic lot was the lowest, represent the Southern purchasing power that offered most to development.

Much of the advancement of the Negro since the First World War had come about as a result of efforts by the very leaders and organizations that were agitating him to demand a radical and immediate more in the midst of a war which threatened him most of all Americans. The very hands that had given him so much were in danger of taking it away. For if the peace between white men and black in the South is lost there will be no advancing, nor any holding of advances. The black man must get on with the white man there, no matter what Washington orders or New York wants. The fact that Southern whites will not consent to a doing away with segregation does not preclude a constant improvement in the black man's side of Jim Crow, a constant trend, as one Negro editor in the South has put it, towards making the color line a perpendicular, not a horizontal, one. The fact that, poll tax or no, Southern Negroes are not going to be admitted to the polls in numbers threatening white majorities, does not eliminate the process under which more and more Southern Negroes are being allowed to vote.

The poll tax, an institution operating more against white voting than Negro and preserved more in the interests of those who fear union labor and the tenant farmer than of those who fear the black man, is a vicious institution. Sense, not dollars, ought to be the qualification for voting in the South and everywhere. But many Southern liberals believe the repeal should be left to the states. They are convinced that the federal government is too rough-handed to settle suffrage problems in the South. It is interesting to note—and pertinent to what has been written here—that Alabama would in likelihood have modified its poll tax in 1939 if it had not been for outside agitation against race segregation. When the

Southern Conference for Human Welfare met in Birmingham in the spring of 1938, Frank Dixon had just been elected governor on a platform calling for elimination of the cumulative poll tax in favor of one requiring only two years of back payment. With a legislature completely in his hand at that time he could have brought about the reform if he had put the power of his office into the effort. He was prepared to do so. But when some of the Northern Negro leaders, Northern federal officials, and communists who composed a part of the Southern Conference for Human Welfare made a scene over race segregation (required by Alabama state law), there resulted such a flare-up of racial and anti-communist feeling that the new governor changed face on his poll tax promise and made only the most perfunctory request when the legislature met. A real advance, even though small, which the South was about to make under its own developing impulses, was destroyed by outside agitation for the unobtainable.

There was a similar situation in the notorious Scottsboro Case of 1931 when nine Negro youths were charged with the rape of two white girls on a freight train. Initially it was the interference of Northern liberals and friends of justice which saved the Negroes from death. But when the case was taken up by radical organizations and capitalized on for their own causes and when Northern people began glorifying the probably innocent but certainly low-life defendants, a reverse effect was brought about. Several large Alabama newspapers, as well as prominent ministers and lawyers in the state, had interested themselves in having the Negroes released and could have accomplished it if the Northerners had been willing to withdraw. Especially, if Mr. Samuel Liebowitz, the distinguished Jewish attorney from New York who is now a circuit judge, had withdrawn. Every prejudice the Southern people knew was stimulated. Prejudice against Jews, against communists, against New Yorkers, along with the certain prejudice against Negroes accused of raping white women. Five of the nine Negroes are still in prison. Four were released because of special circumstances and brought to New York by Attorney Liebowitz. One of the four was arrested in July, 1942, on a charge of making advances to a white woman in the subway and following her to the street afterwards with obscene remarks.

The Negro problem is one on which the South can be stimulated into doing right things but not forced. Undoubtedly the developing liberalism of many white Southerners on the subject gets some of its inspiration from the earnest and proper concern of liberals outside. But it is to these Southerners that leadership must be left. Their on-the-spot estimates are the only practical guides.

Chapter Twelve

FORTY FEEDING LIKE ONE

CLARENCE POE, EDITOR OF *The Progressive Farmer*, IS great on cover crops. Especially ones that not only save and enrich the land but provide green stuff for the developing Southern livestock industry. A few years ago he asked me to use my syndicated daily editorial column in behalf of his campaign for more growing of lespedeza and kudsu. The two words are so pleasing and electric that it occurred to me to offer a $25 prize for the best rhyme to the longer one. The response was wonderful. Three hundred and forty-two rhymes were submitted in less than a week and I was able to fill the column with them each day in lieu of my own profundities. The editor of *The Crimson-White*, undergraduate paper at the University of Alabama, was nice enough to complain of this. He sent me a little note saying, "What we want from you, Mr. Graves, is more work and les-pedeza." It was necessary to call the contest off after ten days because the entries began to be more than could be handled. The prize went to a lady from Anniston, Alabama, whose contribution ended like this:

> Since we gave our old bossy that good lespedeza,
> Milking's made easy, we jes' hardly squeeze her.

Proving that there are many ways of helping the farmer. In the South, where most of the farmers live and most of the help has been needed, all the ways have been employed. Farm organizations, Four-H clubs, county agents, state extension services, state legislation, co-operatives, experiment stations, marketing bureaus, and a long series of federal aids, spurs, instructions, and restraints. The farmer has been coaxed, bullied, taught, enticed, organized, financed, and inspired in directions which need only to be held to make a better day for him. The great thing that has been brought to him is the lesson of self-improvement and self-help. Garet Garrett, journalist and magazine editor, who believes in letting nature take its course and the devil the hindermost, remarked a few years ago after a tour of the South that if Southern farms were operated by Japanese they would be Gardens of Eden. (That was before the unpleasantness, and he would want to speak of serpents in the garden, no doubt, if given leave to edit.) Without help I do not believe that any farmer, Jap or Jeeter, could have made garden spots of some parts of the South. But I know that the fate of the Southern farmer at last will depend on whether he has the education and vitality from which will come the constant taste to want, talent to get, and character to keep a better standard of living.

Some who have attempted to explain the belligerency of the South in months before the war have put it down to greater proportions of people engaged there in agricultural or related pursuits. Living out of doors, close to the land and the seasons, makes for something more definite in love of a threatened country. Even if the farmer lives on land that doesn't belong to him and won't support him, much less him and his landlord together, his daily business with sun, rain, and earth, his annual maneuvers against Spring, Summer, Fall, and Winter, his special knowledge of sun-up, his time to himself, and his fullness of elbow room—do things to him that come out when his country is in danger or he is called in its name.

The South has not only the nation's most impoverished farmers, it has also the wealthiest. The National Resources Committee reported in 1936 that more than 70 percent of the farm families receiving an annual cash income of $10,000 lived in the Southern States. More than 50 percent of those receiving $5,000 or more lived in those states. Since only 85,828 farm families in the United States were receiving the $5,000, there were plenty of farmers left to be poor. But they were poor in the sun, and among friends, and in circumstances which never meant a breadline even though there might be slow starving over a period of years. There was much in the often-told story of the New York banker and family driving through South Carolina to Miami and stopping at a country crossroads to ask a farmer the way. "Which is the road to Columbia, please?" The farmer didn't know. "Well, how far is it to the next filling station?" The farmer didn't know that either. "You don't seem to know anything," the exasperated banker said. "Mebbe so," the farmer agreed, "but I ain't lost."

Statistically it is hard to measure poverty in Southern

agriculture, even though it has been accepted as the Number One Sore Spot of American economy. "Nothing like it this side of the slums of New York" has been one way of putting it, but that is a qualitative comparison. The total is what counts, not the intensity. One Tobacco Road wouldn't make any sociological difference, and Southerners who resent Mr. Caldwell have claimed that there was only one, a synthesis of the worst he could find in different localities. Sam Byrd, the North Carolinian who played the part of Dude Lester in "Tobacco Road" through eleven hundred and fifty-one consecutive performances, went back to his home town in the strawberry and tobacco lands just before the war and wrote a nostalgic book. It was a very readable book, not only for good literature and passages of good South, but for the study it offered of the psychological effect of playing a part in "Tobacco Road." The effect was that Mr. Byrd was morbid, even though he is a good fellow and a trouper. Morbid, and a little conscience-stricken, so that he wanted a vindication for Tobacco Road and its implications. He gives a chapter of his book to his search for counterparts of the people in the play ("I Look for the Lesters"). And he tells how he found them. They seemed to be right there waiting to be found, for the strawberry center had moved away. The poverty, depravities, dead-heartedness, intra-family fornicators, human hookworms—Mr. Byrd was able to feel that an eleven hundred and fifty-second performance was on. A few miles away, just north of Wilmington, some of the people whom Hugh MacRae, that good philosopher and dreamer, had brought over from Poland, Italy, Czecho-Slovakia, and elsewhere and established on farms were smiling like Italy before the war. Mr. MacRae would tell you as he passed each farm house, "They are happy there"—"they enjoy life in this one"—"the family living there is very domestic and healthy." These farms were exceptions, of course, but Sam Byrd's were not the rule. The truth was somewhere between.

The extent of farm poverty in the South is not to be measured in cash income. There are so many offsets to cash. And the way of life is so different that there are differences in the cost of living. To me a more convincingly dramatic picture of distress in the agricultural South than all the eleven hundred and fifty-one consecutive performances of "Tobacco Road" is the Hillman Clinic in Birmingham, where Dr. Tom Douglas Spies is treating thousands of sufferers from nutritional deficiency diseases. In 1939 he was awarded the John Phillips Memorial Award of the American College of Physicians and Surgeons for this work and for research which is taking it into many new fields. He is able to cure a case of pellagra now with twenty-five cents' worth of nicotinic acid. Heretofore the prescribed cure has been better food, a grim paradox since the disease comes usually from economic inability to have better food (although there are many cases of simple ignorance regarding the right foods to eat) . A thickset, soft-voiced, forty-year-old Texan, Dr. Spies is informal to the point of being startling at times. He has a forever straying black forelock like Wendell Willkie's. For the red-tongued, sore-mouthed, dead-eyed people who flock to his clinic, he is a miracle man. Anyone who is unable to engage a regular physician and who can get himself to the clinic may be sure of free treatment. But when a Hollywood moving picture star, who believed himself to be a sufferer from failure of his food to nourish him, flew to Birmingham from California for a treatment, he was refused. You have to be poor to be treated by Tom Spies.

Some of the money with which the Spies Clinic is financed comes from philanthropic institutions and individuals outside the South. In March, 1942, there was criticism in Texas of an alleged use of University of Texas money for this work in Alabama. Dr. Spies appeared before a committee of the Texas State Legislature to deny that any money from Texas was so employed. "But even if it were, gentlemen," he said, "it is a fact of science that discoveries made in Alabama will work here in Texas."

In the summer of 1942, while the wartime "farm parity" debate was on, Senator John H. Bankhead, of Alabama, who has been party to more national legislation for the farmer than any other legislator in the country's history, made a speech in Dallas in which he justified his stand for higher cotton prices not only on grounds of existing conditions of supply and demand but with an overall picture of the farmer's inferior economic status through the years, especially the cotton farmer's. In spite of all that he and other legislators had accomplished, the total income of farmers in 1941 was only about 10 percent of the national income, he said, while farm population amounted to 22.5 percent of the national total. The average net income of cotton farmers for 1941 was $380 a family, or about $85 for each individual. The senator was right, and his championship of the farmer has made history, but on the same day I had a letter from a woman who was working at wartime wages in a cotton mill. Once she had worked on a farm, and she was homesick. I had led my column the day before with some bucolic lines from Wordsworth:

> The cattle are grazing,
> Their heads never raising,
> There are forty feeding like one. . . .

She wanted to be back where there were forty feeding like one. "It keeps running in my head all day," she wrote. "The girl next to me wanted to know what it was I kept saying and it was 'the cattle are grazing—the cattle are grazing.' And it seems so peaceful and quiet where there is that part about 'forty feeding like one.' It helps me stand the noise."

The scene this mill worker was remembering was not a cotton farm but a dairy and livestock one in Alabama's Black Belt from which she came. Ancient aristocracies of cotton had been driven from there to the highlands by the boll weevil and a new nobility of herds and hay established. In the Black Belt and all over the South a developing livestock industry represents the healthiest of all limitations on the monarchy of cotton. Annual in-

come from livestock and dairying is as great now as
from cotton. Wheat is coming back, too. And in areas of
eastern North Carolina not far from where Sam Byrd
looked for his proof of Tobacco Road there has come a
new prosperity from poultry. Agricultural diversification,
already on the way, was speeded in many directions by
war demands. The Southern farmer is beginning at last
to grow the right things—and in right ways and amounts
—and to find markets for what he grows. But the markets
he is able to find at home depend very considerably on
the industrial progress national policy permits the South
to make. In peace times the Southern farmer needs nothing so much as industry to absorb the surplus products
and populations of the farm, to keep more money in the
South by processing more Southern things, and to save
transportation costs. What industry can do for him and
he for industry are eloquent in the farm marketing work
of the Tennessee Coal, Iron and Railroad Company,
United States Steel subsidiary in Birmingham. Finding
and identifying farm markets, encouraging farmers to
grow what markets require, persuading industrial communities to use what farmers grow—is a work in which
agricultural extension services at colleges like Clemson
in South Carolina and Auburn in Alabama have engaged
with notable success. But a pioneer with them in the
work has been the Tennessee Company. Its Dr. M. F.
Jackson was given the job some years ago of making
the company's large purchases for its commissaries a tool
for aid to farmers by persuading them to grow what the
commissaries needed and making sure that the com-

missaries bought what they grew. Confined at first to Alabama, the work has been extended now into eight Southern states. The basis is enlightened self-interest. Leroy Holt, who has general supervision of this activity for the Tennessee Company, has his own ways of measuring improvements accomplished or to come. When he speaks of livestock, sweet potatoes, strawberries, pecans, they add up in his mind to the fencing and barbed wire his company makes, to roofing and siding sheets he expects farmers to be buying from him in greater numbers. He thinks, too, of the hardware, household appliances, farm tools and equipment and hundreds of small items which neither his company nor any other makes in the South now but which will come to be made if the farmers go on improving their lot.

In the little town of Enterprise, Alabama, there is a monument to a boll weevil. It was there long before the spinach people in Texas put up their monument to Popeye. The boll weevil is honored for having forced the farm people of that area to give up cotton and go in for peanuts, just as it forced other middle Alabama farmers into livestock and dairying. But cotton has not disappeared. It has only moved away to the higher lands. When all the farm aids and instructions have succeeded, when man and land have both been saved, when the red rivers are turned back to clear and the red tongues are pink again, when the statesmen are immortal in marble, and the chemurgists have gone through their last erg, when Tobacco Road is an avenue through Eden, and Erskine Caldwell is president of the Augusta, Ga.,

Chamber of Commerce—there will still be cotton. The rest of the country should rejoice at that and resolve on it. If the South could be driven totally from its white staple, Southern competition in many other things, and on sub-standard terms initially, could bring much trouble to other regions. "You dare not make war on cotton," Hammond told the United States Senate in 1859. "No power on earth dares make war on it. Cotton is king." The gentleman from South Carolina was mistaken. Grant and Sherman made war immediately. The Radicals of Reconstruction made foul war. The tax and tariff policies of the nation have never ceased to make war on cotton. The boll weevil made war. The butter interests of Wisconsin have made war on the oleomargarine that comes of cotton's oil. Hitler has made global war on it. That cotton should have survived all the war-making and still be so great an item of our national economy that American consumption in 1942 was more than 10,000,000 bales, proves it as perpetual as two and two. The centuries are on its side, gone and to come. "Tree wool" it was called when Herodotus wrote of it 2400 years ago—"trees of India bearing as their fruit fleeces more delicate and beautiful than those of sheep." Caesar covered the Roman Forum with its fabrics, Verres used it for his tents in Sicily. Columbus found it growing when he came to America, and Cortez quilted the jackets of his Spaniards with it against the arrows of Indians. Jackson's men had its bales for breastworks against Pakenham's artillery at New Orleans. Fabrics made by the ancient Hindoos without benefit of machine were so

fine that only now are they beginning to be matched—
but they will be more than matched in magics developing for post-war use. In ancient Calicut they made a
cloth they called "calico" for the city, sometimes of a
quality so delicate you could hardly feel the material in
your fingers and the spun thread was almost invisible.
A single pound was spun out to a length of 115 miles.
They made airy muslins, "webs of woven wind," so fine
that four months were needed to finish a single piece
and when it was laid on the grass and the dew fell it
could not be seen at all.

So deeply is cotton stamped on the face of the South
that its ranking servitors wear its first letter if not its
livery. The "C" which is for cotton is for the Cannons,
Cones and Cramers, great cotton manufacturing families
of North Carolina. It is for Coker, of South Carolina,
who educated the South to longer staples, and for Carver, of Tuskegee, who put chemistry to work. It is for
Comers of Alabama and Callaways of Georgia, dominant
manufacturers in those states. It is for David L. Cohn,
author of cotton's Mississippi Delta epic. It is for Clayton, of Texas, cotton factor extraordinary and possessor
by choice of the shortest biography in Who's Who in
America ("Clayton, William L., cotton factor; head of
Anderson, Clayton & Co. Address: Houston, Texas").

The centuries to come are on cotton's side, too, because of its multiplying uses, its promised economies,
its limitless supply. In California, where cotton growing
is new and where there is no natural irrigation, the ability to apply artificial irrigation as needed is making mir-

acles of growth. Machinery will come, too, for more and more of the planting, growing, and harvesting. And economies of large scale production. At Tuskegee Institute George Washington Carver, born a slave, gave his genius to agricultural chemistries that promise cotton new worlds. The farm chemurgists have followed, and the federal laboratories, and the National Cotton Council, whose mother, father, sister, and aunt is Oscar Johnston. There are food qualities in cotton, and they are being developed far beyond cottonseed meal and oil. There are wonders in plastic and cellulose. Cotton will feed and house as well as clothe people in years to come, and make highways and automobiles for them, too, and perhaps shoe soles for the hitch-hikers.

"Literally tens of thousands of articles and manufactured parts now made from metals will be made plastically from materials grown on the farm," Henry Ford has predicted. That is as it should be. Metals are exhaustible, coal seams are worked out, trees need long years for growing, petroleum wells go dry, but the annual product of the farm is infinite. The common sense of raw material economy in years to come will prefer the annual things like cotton, wheat, and sweet potatoes over things limited or slow of supply. The crop is mightier than the seam, deposit, well, or stand. That is the principle which, if other things were as equal as they were said to be, should have guided the development of our wartime synthetic rubber industry. Perhaps it will be had in mind if that industry survives the war. "I certainly feel," Secretary of Agriculture Claude R. Wickard wrote me in June, 1942, "that in the present situation our abundance of grain should be used to the greatest possible extent as raw material for the making of synthetic rubber. I do not know that I can endorse the flat statement that 'the crop is mightier than the seam or deposit or stand or well.' It seems to me that you have got to qualify according to the circumstances of the times. But certainly wherever the annual crop is the best source, all things considered, of raw material, then it ought to be used. . . ." The Secretary of Agriculture, it seemed to me, was being polite to the Secretary of the Interior and careful in presence of the grain-petroleum-cotton-rayon controversies over synthetic tires. The Secretary of Cotton, Wheat, Potatoes, and Corn knew in his heart that he had things possessed of eternities not known to those of the Secretary of Iron, Petroleum, Wood, and Coal.

Concern for Southern agriculture, and for all agriculture, in days to come need not be for its economic improvement, it seems to me. That is being arranged. What should concern us is whether this basic American way and point of view are going to go on being a base. Are there going to be enough of us close to the land and loving it, enough of us meeting life in terms of its individualism and health, living in terms of seasons and infinites? There is sickness on the farms, but it is never the incurable sickness of cities. If better economic rewards are being prepared for American agriculture after the war, including that major and least rewarded sector called the South, will our farmers know themselves

enough in the new dispensations to be strong? Will the
agrarian tradition survive an agriculture turned large-
scale and mechanical and so joined to industry that the
smoke is in its eyes? It seems to me that it might—if we
keep or restore our taste for it. As industry and agriculture are joined and as machines and chemistries alter
both, we might hope to keep the smell of outdoors and
the love of that God whose laws are mostly writ in
nature's book. Cordial choice might advertise these
things enough for survival among a people whose majorities through all generations have been kin to the
farm. If Henry Ford, maker of more industrial history
than any other American, has managed somehow to have
a climate of new mown hay about him, there is hope for
his fellow citizens. Especially now that the sciences and
machines which were taking people and things from the
country to the city have begun taking them back, spread-
ing industries, shopping centers, moving pictures, radios,
and good clothes all over outdoors by grace of electricity
and gasoline.

Eugene Talmadge told me once—he was defending
Georgia's notorious county-unit voting system which
gives small agrarian counties relatively more voting
power than big city ones like Atlanta's Fulton—that he
believed in letting the country people rule. City folks,
he said, were not to be trusted. They were too much
alike and too accustomed to having things done for
them. In the country were real people, he said, people
who were different from each other and who knew how
to work and pray and wait and manage for themselves.

People of character. He would have had a better case if there had not been himself and others like him in the picture. Take away the demagogs, bigotries, poverties, and sometime depravities, or, rather, forget about that side of Southern agriculture and remember the ideal and approachable way of which the Nashville "Fugitives" wrote in their immortal volume ("I'll Take My Stand") —and you have the hope and need of America's years to come. They are fallen apart now, those twelve who wrote "I'll Take My Stand." Some have turned socialist, some have gone sour, some sentimental, some have lost themselves in purest art, some have been overtaken by the sicknesses of the South, while some are holding fast. But the book they wrote together, with all its bad economics and kicks against bricks, is a thing for the future out of the past.

Chapter Thirteen

THE LAND IS BRIGHT

IS IT UNSOCIAL TO SAY THIS COUNTRY IS GOOD LOOKING? Some of our earnest workers think so, but even they are likely to go to the devil in May. In May the shabbiest parts are pretty, and the beautiful ones are beautiful indeed. Sun-magic gets into the slums, there are silhouettes in tree boughs and bricks, pitiful things turned picturesque, economic hungers lost a little in hungers of spring, honeysuckle, and other cheap, free-and-easy things, an animation on all rivers, dirty or clean, a gleam about all window panes.

Is it a sin to feel affirmative when such things happen to you? I think it is a virtue. The Victorians who wouldn't look at anything if it was ugly were no more stilted than moderns who think it immoral to look at anything if it is good. Keats may have been only half right when he said beauty was truth and that that was all you needed to know, but he was half, anyhow. And there is no law that you must always make a bow to ugliness before doing business with beauty, even though some of our pre-war Social Minds go on thinking so. Reviewing Samuel Chamberlain's "Fair Is Our Land" in the summer of 1941, *The New Republic's* Malcolm Cowley was shocked at a volume devoted, according to its advertise-

ment, to "the incalculable beauty which is America . . .
portrayed in infinite variety by eighty outstanding American etchers and photographers." Mr. Cowley found in
the very existence of such a book a proposal that "in this
deepest crisis of our history as a nation, we should close
our eyes to every feature of the American landscape that
suggests injustice or sufferings or even vulgarity." Reason
shivered. Why shouldn't Mr. Chamberlain have put
pretty pictures in a book? And why shouldn't we-the-
people have enjoyed looking at them? It was a sick point
of view. I call it that in no disrespect of Mr. Cowley's
fine health and talent. He was reflecting a trouble into
which all of us fell in the days of hate, doubt, and dreary
pensioning. He was making the great American minus
sign of the 1930's.

Beauty and grace were confined to your party line
then. Appreciations were subordinate to passions political. Art was for a purpose or not art. There were the
leading leftist magazines, for example, edited by scholarly people with names for literary judgment as well as
social mind. In the 1930's they let the judgment be
clouded by anyone who wrote from the left. They sacri-
ficed their literary reputations by calling literature what
was only leftist. Books whose grammar might otherwise
have outraged them were praised because they took the
party line. Equally on the right the party line was a cloud
to judgment. The adoration which big business men
gave stuffy conventionalists who were on their side in
politics and economics would have been laughable if it
had not been tragic. The tragedy was that, pleased with

their pleasing and eager to please more, the politicians, lawyers, publicity directors, writers, and association managers who served Big Business became more pious than their Pope, committing their principals to policies more rightist than these would have chosen for themselves. Second-string politicians who yelled "states' rights" when all they meant was "leave my employers alone" became Thomas Jeffersons in the fatuous sight of the business men who owned them. Publicity directors who developed a loud love for "the right to work" and meant only "to hell with union labor" became Horace Greeleys. Lawyers were listened to as respectfully as if they had been John Marshall when they passed out legal opinions in favor of their clients to the tune of a vast love for the Constitution. Paid directors of business associations built up great issues on which to take a stand, snapping at trifles until the trifles grew, setting up a cause and championing it, or a bugaboo and opposing it, while their admiring bosses followed and paid.

Judgment was so party-bound that wishes were horses, and a picture tended to be nothing but the eye of its beholder. In 1937 Erskine Caldwell and Margaret Bourke-White published "You Have Seen Their Faces," photographs of human wreckage in the South. Afterwards, in answer, the cotton mills published "Faces You See," pictures of the brighter side, mostly smiling, well-fed mill hands. Neither book proved anything about the South, since each was extreme. But the odd thing was that you could see faces in both books which were much the same. Looked at in the one book they were pinched, poverty-stricken, depraved. Looked at in the other they were clean-swept, noble. The Scotch-Irish-angel type of Southern farm woman looks starved if you are looking for starvation, spiritual if you are looking for that. Just as the same cabin in the country may be an example of ugly poverty for the sociologist and a picturesque event in the life of an artist.

At Gee's Bend, Alabama, on a plateau above a bend in the wriggling, yellow Alabama River, there is a Negro community whose members all bear the name "Pettway" for the white master who owned their ancestors in slavery times. The Pettway Negroes had to be helped by the Resettlement Administration in 1937 when the price of cotton fell to five cents. Visiting the place with Mrs. Graves for a story The New York Times had asked me to write, we could not decide whether the scene was a pity or a delight. Although the Gee's Benders had managed to live in happiness and economic self-sufficiency for generations before the depression, they were poor indeed when we came. But they were beautiful, too. Half a hundred little cabins around a vast cotton patch, the big house of the one-time master looming apart, guarded by two pecan trees, an elm, and an ancient water oak. The Big House was a ghost, paintless, dilapidated, but the fanlights over front and rear entrances, the well-proportioned rooms, the high ceilings, the fine detail of cornice, woodwork, and plaster, spoke of a day that was. The Negro cabins made tattered tops above the cotton rows, but the logs that walled them were hand-hewn, the hand-split shingles were weathered

to a gray so silvery that Eastern architects would have
loved the sight, the bare yards were clean and sandy-
white under their chinaberry trees, and the picket fences
were all in place. From front to rear of each cabin, divid-
ing it after a superstition that no two rooms shall have
a common wall, was the "dog-run"—an open hallway
through which not only dogs but pigs and chickens—
and pickaninnies—ran. The Pettways of Gee's Bend
needed the help the government gave but, luckily for
them, Pete Hudgens, the government's man, was so free
of the malady of the times that he was willing to confess
beauty and did much to keep it in the reconstructions
there.

In course of much lecturing and free lancing, I traveled the South during the ten years before the war. Usually my wife was with me. Her name is Rose. The
majestic way to enter the region is to step down from
the Alleghenies into Mr. Jefferson's Virginia. On the
156-mile drive from Elkins, West Virginia, to Charlottesville, you come in at an elevation of 4300 feet and
at once are out of forests and spinning across plateau
lands of grass and grain. The mountains step down to
Thomas Jefferson, the highway bears his name. The
Shenandoah Mountains are 1200 feet below the Alleghenies, the Blue Ridge is lower still, and in Albemarle
there are only the rolling hills. On one of them is the
Rotunda of the University of Virginia. Some prefer the
Grand Canyon, others the Taj Mahal, the Pyramids, the
skyline of New York or the stately pleasure dome which
Kubla Khan decreed, but Rose and I vote for the Ro-

tunda, Lawns, and Ranges of Mr. Jefferson's University. At twilight they put Alfred Noyes' "temporal into relation with the eternal." Age, history, and promise do as much for them then as the architects have done. There are the detachments of eternity gone and to come. The undergraduates speak of "George Washington," "Robert E. Lee," and "James Madison," but when they have reference to their designer they say "Mister Jefferson." He is not a man in history but their neighbor and associate. He is the free spirit, the "good life."

Albemarle, where Charlottesville and the University and Monticello and the ghost of Jefferson live, is a "good life" county. Some call it the finest in the land for beauty, government, and gentilities of spirit. Virginians prefer to say what they consider to be the same thing. They say it is the finest in Virginia. That is acceptable language to other Americans, I believe. To come into Virginia's heart of grace by way of her down-stepping mountains is to know something good that men and God have made together. If the Nazis had overrun the world with their armies and philosophy, the souls of men would have gone searching and complaining until another Albemarle, somehow, was made with another three centuries.

Fair is our land! Before our tires were taken away Rose and I had driven over so much of it that we found our past tires rushing before us when war made us stay at home. We remember the face of the land and we mean to see it again someday, North, West, East, and South.

We'll begin at those factories on the coast of Maine where ocean sand is put through raw and semi-finished process. It is a sight-and-a-sound—along that rock-held, saw-toothed, cove-and-cape-run coast. You can see it and hear it in every stage. The rocks are the raw material, resisting the white foams and green swells. Centuries of tides are needed to break them, and there are many miles unbroken. Along other miles the initial break has come, and others the second, third, and further process of nature's rolling mill. Big rocks have been beaten into smaller ones, jagged ones have been made smooth and then round as geometry, smooth and rounded ones have been rolled until they are egg-sized, pea-sized, pebble-sized, no-size-at-all, grains of sand, indivisible on a bright beach.

The brightest beach will be several thousand miles away. It will be on the Gulf Coasts of the South where Columbus first touched America. Moving waters have washed the sand whiter there than anywhere else in the world, I think, and without taking the cream out. At Pensacola and Fort Walton, the dunes make charmed mountain ranges, the sea-blown trees are twisted in art, the mullet are flashlights as they jump out of the water and the sand-pipers are merry-legged. At Pass Christian the Lord has put a sleeping potion into the air—you go to sleep without trying. Woodrow Wilson was able to sleep there when he couldn't anywhere else. Point Clear, Dauphin Island, and below them Clearwater Beach where the grass reaches down to high tide and the seagulls are so sure of benignity in men that they hover to eat from their hands. No flying ship in the world, not the best that has come out of the war, compares with these fliers at Clearwater. No Lockheed or Boeing can match the wing spreads and textures, fuselage, power-drives, speeds, and maneuverabilities. They are the most efficient things in the air. They soar, hover, poise, wheel, dip, coast, climb, bank, turn, and make helicopter landings on the beach. They are beautiful, too, and so is the sea there, and it matters not from what party line you come.

We'll ride out to Texas when we get our tires back, too, be there when it's sundown on some universe of treeless plains and you can watch the planet curving as you do on the sea. The lonely farm building may be ten miles away for all its near-appearing. We'll go down to San Antonio, the military city, where Mexican tiles make such bright walls and the little river goes shopping downtown. Back through the Teche country of salt and pepper, sugar and calm bayous. We'll come to New Orleans at Christmas time. Candy, paper, popcorn, hard liquor, drug stores, automobiles, perfume, and street cars on Canal Street at Christmas time. People living in no moment to come, not even the moment of Christmas morning, but the mathematical present. Happy errands, the climate of holiday. They knew about Hitler, but Hitler didn't know about them. He didn't know about Vienna either. Eternity is the moment, the gay moment when New Orleans is doing its Christmas shopping, celebrating its Mardi Gras, going to its races, restaurants, weddings.

We'll go up to Tontitown again one summer for some wine, where grandchildren of those who made it in

Italy make it on a sunny plateau in the Ozarks near Fayetteville. There is no wrath in the grapes of Tonti-town. The smell is heavy over two thousand acres in August. Making and selling wine, growing things to eat, going to their Catholic Church, having a good time together, the Italian people of Tontitown are happy, or-derly, united. God is their Father. They could make bet-ter wine if the countryside wanted it. "But they just want something sweet with a big kick in it," the Tontitowns-men say.

We'll take a plane from Shreveport, let it drop, climb and shiver as it crosses the Delta lands. The river will be wriggling below like a water moccasin and the great squares of "dollar-cotton" land will make checkerboards where the gray cyprus was. The Mississippi does almost as much to the air above it as it has done to the soil beside it, and the levees which have saved the soil at a price of some of its fertilities have done nothing to the pocket-making moistures above. We'll visit the Hands, the Fields, Percys, Scotts, on their plantations, be depos-ited for the night train to Birmingham in that railroad station at Vicksburg where they have rocking chairs. In all the world are there rocking chairs in any other rail-road station? In all the world, if there are to be rocking chairs, where could they better be than in Vicksburg?

We'll go over to Alabama through the north forests of Mississippi, carpets of green grass beneath the pines. In the Black Belt the cattle will be grazing on rolling acres, with big oaks for shade. There will be forty feeding like one. Up to Tuscaloosa where the gleaming University is, where gracious timber and stone are preserved from old days and richly employed, and where Hudson and Theresa Strode have put all their travel, talent and good taste into a modern home in the woods. We'll sit an hour in one of those classes of his which have made so many novelists and short story writers. We'll come to Birmingham at night on the Montgomery Highway, look down on a million lights as we cross Red Mountain, an inverted sky of stars with Sloss-Sheffield furnace a comet. We'll go over to Anniston one afternoon and out to Alexandria Valley where the Lord and the government are giving Adam his Eden back. A garden spot until erosion and one-crop farming ruined it, the valley is being a garden again. Fields whose wealth had been washed or eaten away are growing rich under kudzu and lespedeza. Hillsides scarred with gullies, grassless, treeless, ugly with the forsaken ugliness of beauty gone, are green again with planted things. Rainwaters caught and controlled, refreshing the land again. Cattle grazing where cotton was, cotton growing in self-respecting limit and rote, vegetable gardens and small grain, hay, poultry, and little pigs. And County Agent Guy Wood preaching farm organization, science, believing the farmer should be the balance between capital and labor because he includes both.

Into Alabama's northeast corner the Appalachians push their last arrows from Lookout. The Tennessee River rolls to the west, green-banked and strong except where two impedimenta of concrete and steel have driven the waters back to the valleys, hidden them behind the mountains, made them fill up the fields and push harbors into the hills. These lakes which the Tennessee Valley Authority dams have made are deep and blue. They are bluest around Scottsboro, the beautiful little hill town which won so bad a name because a train stopped there once. (None of the parties to the Case came from there, only one of the many trials was held there, and less than five percent of the population is Negro.)

We'll go over to Rome, Georgia, where they had to put away for the duration the Romulus and Remus statue Mussolini gave them. They have nine hills there to old Rome's seven and the Tiber is outclassed in waterway by noises of the Etowah and Oostanala making the Coosa. We'll drive around the palaces in Atlanta and out for another look at Atlanta's one lost cause, the Confederate carvings which have never been completed on Stone Mountain's face. The editorial that started them was my father's, years ago.

We'll go with the river along the rich Republican plains of eastern Tennessee, leave it at Norris Dam, cross into Kentucky through Daniel Boone's Gap. "Bloody Harlan" it has been but Harlan doesn't look it. It is run with clear streams, knobbed with green hills. From it to Pikeville along the Cumberland River goes the Rhododendron Highway, a sight for the miners' sore eyes. In Pikeville the county's one publication advertises that "The News is the only newspaper in the world working for the best interests of Pike County." Mr. Hatcher has a hotel. He began building it when

Wilson was President but stopped when Harding came, swore never to resume until there was a Democrat. Opened for business in the first year of Franklin Roosevelt, the lobby walls are covered with big printed bits of verse, historical information, and such sound philosophies as "The Only Known Substitute for Brains is Silence—Quiet Please."

We'll go over again to Virginia, dropping down from Bluefield to that charming inn-by-the-railroad at Roanoke and on from there to Lexington. Lexington, where a man could spend the rest of his life. A high place circled by hills that are higher, a place apart but belonging to all and not far off. Francis Pendleton Gaines is a gentleman and a lover. He presides over Washington and Lee University with intuition for all that has gone before, faith in all to come. The modern mind for Robert Edward Lee is Douglas Freeman's but the heart for him is Francis Gaines'. His house is the one in which Lee lived. His automobile is in Traveler's stable. He has deciphered most of the initials scratched on the great horse's skeleton by students of other days (including John W. Davis). Beside the recumbent statue in Lee Chapel he speaks softly as if he were in presence of a living pulse, and when he shows you from his dining room window the vista upon which Lee looked out during his last illness you feel that the great Confederate is gone no further than the blue rim of mountains there. It has been good for the world to have so active and modern a college president living at Lexington with Robert E. Lee beside him. It will be even better for the world to come.

Lee meant duty, loyalty, discipline, rules of living—and we know now that democracy won't work without them. In the entrance hall of the administration building Dr. Gaines has placed a portrait of Lee as Superintendent at West Point before the Confederate War. He is not the grand old beard there but a vital and very human being with a black moustache and a magnetic eye. The portrait, somehow, takes him forward, not back, makes him stand for things to come. Perhaps that is why Francis Gaines and the students at Washington and Lee like it.

We'll go up to Mountain Lake. Up and up and up, straight as a predestined Presbyterian to heaven the highway goes, which is to say, with some curves but not many, and easily managed. Rarely a tree or bank obstructs the giant Appalachian view. The eardrums lift, and lift some more until they settle down. Even if there were nothing at the journey's end there, four thousand Virginia feet above the sea, the road is enough. But when you are up, there is the immense blue, deep lake. How the Lord got it up there no one knows. Dean Ivey Lewis' University of Virginia biologists who have a station near-by say it is done with springs. Others, pointing to the surface, say mirrors.

If he has survived the war, that light-hearted mountain-scenery lad, Lynn Harris, who was landscape architect for the Blue Ridge parkway when the war came, may take us over some of the construction again. The pathway spirals from crest to crest. Mica gleams where the rocks are cut and the quartz is white on wide embank-

ments. The Spanish stone-cutters love the sun, laugh
their greetings when addressed. Big rocks turn to smaller
ones, smaller ones to gravel. The mountain tops quiver
with high explosive. There are slides to dodge and mend,
fills and cuts to make, under-passes, viaducts, bridges,
mountain streams to be covered and let go. Through
rocky tunnels the sky is framed. Down walled embank-
ments are pools of rhododendron and mountain laurel.
Familiar skylines are strange in new places, ancient
domes come to sight again. Twisting, climbing, dropping, rising, the great highway goes, the parts complete
no more engaging than the parts in process, God and
science on the job. From Roanoke to the Smokies this
highest highway extends, via Linville and Asheville.

We'll spend a week, or sixteen, in Asheville, acropolis
of the Southern Appalachians and the Blue Ridge.
When Mr. Webb or Hiden Ramsey writes an editorial
for their newspapers there they are writing to the South.
For happy meeting, Asheville is the South's capital city.
In its tall vicinities Southerners meet Southerners on
terms of holiday. When Dr. Howard Odum wrote his
monumental book on Southern Regions, he mentioned
the long thrust of mountains from Pennsylvania into the
South's heart as something holding all together and
identifying the region as a region, but he left out the so-
lidifying effect of the annual sociability (this is the first
time Dr. Odum has ever been accused of leaving out
anything, so I say it with fingers crossed. I may be
wrong). To have Birmingham and Charlotte meeting at
Roaring Gap and Linville, Atlanta and Richmond at

Highlands and High Hampton, Charleston, Montgomery and Columbia at Flat Rock, and all in Asheville, is to have a legislature. The automobile, which has done several other old-fashioned things in its up-to-date life, has done this. On the stone gate-post of a Charleston estate at Flat Rock is a placard which has been there since the early days of automobiling. The first machine had been a nine-day wonder and then a scourge for the dust it made and the horses it frightened. "The automobile is not allowed in here," reads the placard.

We'll end our round-and-around trip at no war speed but in high—and on high—at the top of the South. Newfound Gap is as high as you can take an automobile in Eastern America. At one point you are 6300 feet up, higher than the tops of Mt. Washington in New Hampshire and Mt. Mansfield in Vermont. You can go up from Asheville or Knoxville. If you go the Tennessee way the 15-mile journey from Gatlinburg, 1292 feet above the sea, to the 5045-foot Gap is a trip from Tennessee to Canada, botanically, arboreally, and meteorologically speaking. On lower levels you pass the sycamores, elms, gums, willows, and cinquapins of the South. On upper ones will be the black spruce, balsam, striped maple, aspen, and red cherries of Canada. The thermometer may have been near 100 in the valley but you will be in an area where overhangs of ice are found the year around. Below, North Carolina and Tennessee are lands of dream. In these high vicinities there flies the raven, most sagacious of winged creatures, the first bird made free out of the Ark after the flood. That is as

it should be. You can't stand at Newfound Gap and
have a party line. You can't be a Democrat there or a
Republican or a New Dealer or an anti. You can't even
be a Southerner. All you can be is an American, singing
—"I love thy rocks and rills—Thy woods and templed
hills. . . ."

Chapter Fourteen

FAR LIGHT

THERE WAS SOMETHING IN HER EYE, BUT SHE SANG IN the church choir and was a well-reputed lady. As she was our hostess at the little country inn and we were the only guests, we came to know her rather well in the three days we were there. The night before our early morning departure she had a "date" with the organist; so we asked for our bill and arranged to put an envelope with the check under her bedroom door. I stuck it half way under before we went to bed. In the half-light of early morning, as we tiptoed out, the envelope was still there. She had not come in. Rose went over and pushed the note under the door—out of our sight. I called that chivalry. And from woman to woman! Mr. Funk and Wagnalls defines chivalry as "disinterested courtesy." I will not say that Rose was disinterested, for she talked about it all morning. But she was courteous and with nothing to gain for her trouble. The chivalry was in that.

There was chivalry, too, in what I once saw Dr. Harper do with his hat. Dr. Harper was a country doctor in the part of North Alabama where there are rich woodlands and clean streams and picnicking was once a great fashion with people from Birmingham. Ross Smith invited me to a big one he gave. The star of it was a plump and beautiful cousin of his. Dr. Harper, an old friend of my host's, joined us and made himself popular with his quaint courtesies and speech. After lunch we walked through the fields and when a high fence interfered, all undertook to climb it. The beautiful-and-plump cousin got herself caught at the top of the wire and her tangled skirts made a beautiful-and-plump, and very extensive, exposure. To the rescue came Dr. Harper, all efficiency and courtesy. The efficiency was in the way he disentangled the skirt. The courtesy was in the way he first removed his hat and held it before his eyes while he worked. That was courtesy against intensive interest. Ross Smith, himself a man of much chivalry, remarked that Cyrano had used his hat to sweep the floor of heaven but that Dr. Harper used his to hide from a lady's legs.

When I asked President Henry Noble MacCracken, of Vassar College, for a theory on the greater willingness of the South to go into the war, he said chivalry. It was interesting to know that he believed such a thing existed any more, in the South or elsewhere. But he was sure of it. Lynching is not chivalrous, of course, even though the lynchers think so. Scarlett O'Hara had no chivalry, nor did the Little Foxes of Southern industry's first days. Sweatshops, drunken killings, the passing around of venereal disease, the farm diets that make pellagra, the demagogs, Negro-cheaters, sentimentalists, haters—there is no chivalry in these. Maybe Dr. MacCracken meant only something done with hats. Millions of male Southerners today, even at war, are taking their hats off in elevators. Millions are getting up and giving their seats in buses and street cars to members of the other sex. Civilization has not brought such herding in the South that there is no elbow room for baring one's head or such vitamin deficiency that there is no energy for getting up and letting a poor-weak-woman, no matter how well vitamined, sit down. There was more getting-up-and-seat-giving than ever when the war made bus and street car riders of so many Southern gentlemen. Seat-giving is a more useful thing to do for a lady than hat-lifting but the latter is the more important chivalry, I think. It has to do with élan, the sort of thing for which the army and navy invented the salute to the flag and the superior officer. In the old Half-World War I was in, I remember how humiliating it was at first to salute some little whippersnapper lieutenant. But when I became accustomed to it and got the big idea, saluting was a definite little pleasure, a sign not that I was anybody's inferior but that I was a soldier. It was an exercise in being a man, and so, in another sense, is hat-removing in elevators. There is in it the manly exercise of recognizing women as women still, after all the years from Eden. The pity is that some such gesture of biologic respect is not available to women too. As a feminist, I hope one will be invented. Perhaps a slight, perfectly invitationless bow when a gentleman removes his hat. Or, in street cars, a "thank you so much" in lieu of the customary graceless acceptance.

Removing hats in elevators, some of my fellow feminists say, is a thing of false meanings. It hands down from days when women were on pedestals and neglected, when their capacities for the work-a-day world were denied and when hypocrisy and artificiality were the rule. Removing hats in elevators, some of the futurists might say, is nothing worth discussing, for there will be neither hats nor elevators in the brave new world. But it seems to me that until the hats and elevators are indeed done away with the gesture is good and has nothing to do with "woman's place." Scientists of the perfect day may value it or its equivalent as a salute to the co-operation which manufactures the human race in an Image, a recognition of every mortal's debt to sacred differentials.

I have forgotten his name, but I heard a psychologist talk once in New York on the need of giving expression to emotions when something has aroused them. Otherwise, he said, there is not only a frustration but a deterioration of social capacity. If you go to a cinema or a play which moves you deeply, he said, you should do something about it even if it is nothing more than getting up and giving your seat to a woman or an old man in the subway as you go home. He added that if the woman happened to be pretty you should not try to pick her up after you had given her the seat, for that wasn't the point. It was good to know that chivalry's place in science was recognized in New York even if they made no provision for it in the subway.

A name for one subdivision of chivalry is hospitality, whether it be the Southern, Western, or New England kind. In the South they are hospitable because they are sociable, enjoy having company in homes they love and of which they are proud. In the West they are hospitable because they accept people as friends, have warm hearts for them. In New England the hospitality has an element of conscience. The New Englander takes you in because God is your father, the Westerner because he likes you, the Southerner because there is something he wants to tell you. But once you are taken in, whatever the reasons, South, West, or New England,—chivalry is what happens to you. The surrender to your will and pleasure, the grant of an immense claim on your host, the day-long code in your favor, the fee simples to whatever comes up, make you a king for as many days as you stay—which is likely to be longest in the South. The exercise is good for both host and guest, but I think it does the greater good to the host. It is one of the spiritual equivalents for the socialism which has its good points but which most of us don't want.

Good manners are an aspect of chivalry, too, and like hospitality, will have their use in years to come. They can cover so many bad situations, add to so many happy ones. When the atom is split and we have more time on our hands we shall need to give some of it to the amenities which make human contacts endurable. That will be true not only of the so-called polite world but of the world in mass. The manners will be nothing written down but an inner grace which tells you to consider your fellow being when you meet him, to cherish a pleasant relationship with him on a basis of cordial trifles. Especially the good manners which persuade people to say thank you. Of all the petty failures in grace the most unattractive is the failure to thank, whether it comes of an unwillingness to recognize a debt, a fear of having to pay, or a thick insensibility. Some of the most mannerless people I have ever known are Southerners who have put away grace as a thing too soft for these times, too identified with a South against which they have emancipated themselves. But manners exist in the South, and, what is more important, a tradition of manners. The tradition will need circulation when the crowding on this planet makes it necessary either to be polite or get off.

A name for another denomination of chivalry is sportsmanship. Long before the perfect day we are going to need all we can get of that. We are going to need it among our young people below draft age if the war is not to be followed by a decade more ugly and anarchic than the one after the other war. It wasn't the men who came back from that war who invented the jazz age. It was their little brothers who had been too young to go but who had learned to say "c'est la guerre." And their little sisters. Within a few months of Pearl Harbor there were indications that unless something changed their minds, the 16-year-olds might destroy what the 20-year-olds were risking their lives for.

Since 1924 the Birmingham public schools have had courses in what their originator, Ex-Superintendent Charles B. Glenn, calls "character building." There has been especial emphasis on sportsmanship. A $500 trophy, given by Erskine Ramsay, Alabama's most giving philanthropist, goes annually to the school judged to have shown the most sportsmanship in athletics, classrooms, or elsewhere. Sportsmanship, as Dr. Glenn sees it, makes a man not only just but generous. It persuades him to go easy on the weak ones. It makes him decent even to those he fears or of whom he is jealous. It tells him there are more important things than winning. It makes him courteous and law-abiding. Until the war came Dr. Glenn was proud of the sportsmanship developed among his students. But with the war something happened to them there and everywhere. The excitement, the news of wild adventure, the prospect of being called, the sense of rules suspended, made 16-year-old vandals, rowdies, and worse all over the country. Public buildings and unoccupied private homes were broken into by night, furniture destroyed, nuisances committed on floors and walls, lead pencils used to scratch every handy surface, dirt brought in and spilled about, valuables removed. Sometimes when the vandals were caught they would be sons of "best families." In a Southern city one night a group of boys and girls rode in an open car shooting out street lights with small rifles. It was the war. It was also the makings of another post-war jazz age unless someone did something old-fashioned about a wantonness that was more than wild oats. Juvenile delinquency in 1942 increased 15 to 20 percent. By 1943 school teachers in New York were asking police protection against violent pupils.

Dr. MacCracken, of course, had in mind the major rather than the minor notes of chivalry. The thing that sent the Eagle Squadron to England so long before

Pearl Harbor. The heart for other people's troubles when they are dramatic and there is a dramatic way to serve them. The ability to identify yourself not with something large or dear which includes you, but with something alien which catches your dramatic imagination. Disinterested heart-giving, life-risking. Insofar as it is sacrifice in terms of drama, large or small, and offers a man a gallant picture of himself, Southerners do, perhaps, respond more than others to the chivalric impulse. But whether they do or not, the impulse is worth attention. Unless there is a drama about unselfishness it tends to fail as a mass operation. Unless there is color in the social mind not enough of us are likely to be of such a mind. And unless there is gay disregard of the main chance sometimes in favor of the tilt, the business of reform is going to be unattractive, identified with long-faced piety and a certain gracelessness in doing good. It may be that there were few Cavaliers in America but there has been a legend of Cavaliers. There has been a tradition of light-hearted, dramatic, nothingwithholding disinterestedness. It is a tradition which means something to many Americans, whether they live in Boston, San Antonio, or the suburbs of Seattle. And the meaning has a democratic value.

Even though he would not in these days let himself be called one and I hesitate to use a term so trifled with, there is such a thing as a Southern gentleman. He may live in Chicago. He may wear overalls. But he exists and his tribe must increase if we are to get anywhere in years to come. Not the gentleman who is a smelly compound of Little Lord Fauntleroy, the Southern-veranda-father in "Kiss the Boys Goodbye" and Mr. Dickens' Uriah Heep. Not that, but the individual anywhere and always who is willing to go out on a limb with his eyes open and his heart beating. The individual who can be imposed on for a principle, who holds the rules above the winning, the thing of grace above the gainful one. The individual who admits nothing so deadly or dark that it turns the world's light out.

My father was a Southern gentleman. But not because he was born in South Carolina, had ancestors and enough to eat. He was one because his imagination was caught always by the magnificent, his heart was won every day by something outside, and his thinking was in terms of a world all human and alive. People took money away from him, but he had the talent always to make some more, to keep his five children well fed and offer them educations. His political, social, and economic theories were not of a nature to have many people remembering them now and saying how right he was, but he came on them all in a way so right that it counts more than the theories. It was the way of chivalry, of high-hearted, disinterested, colorful willingness to go out on a limb. When he died, in August, 1925, William Cole Jones wrote an editorial in *The Atlanta Journal*:

> Of John Temple Graves it may be said as truly as he himself said of Henry Grady that the "fires of his genius were kindled in his boyhood from the gleam that died on his father's sword." All his life long that knightly touch attended him—a glow from his

page, an inner and lovable light of his personality. Whether he wrote or spoke or mingled with his host of friends, there was ever about him a something reminiscent of "brave days of old," as if a song from Camelot were echoed back to earth, or a far light were flashing from the plume of Navarre. . . .

. . . He saw life in terms of chivalry and he so reflected it, kindling the imagination of his readers and hearers alike to a more vivid, more colorful sense of the world about them. As an editor and author alone he would have won wide distinction. As an orator alone he would have been nationally famed. But for his potent and charming command of both the written and the spoken word he will be remembered as one of the rarely achieving spirits of his generation. Especially will he be remembered in this state to whose upbuilding was given his heart's golden prime and in whose bosom will rest the dust that bore his gallant spirit's image. Home he comes from mortality's last adventure; home he has gone to the God he loved.

They are going to need some far lights when the world is put together again after the war. There will be a call for gentlemen when the atom is split. When our only problems are how to treat each other and our driving power comes all of our own bright eyes and tempers, the scientists are going to prescribe chivalry. They are going to tell us it is social-mindedness with a kick in it.

Chapter Fifteen

THE ARISTOCRATIC TRADITION

WHICH IS TO SAY, THE TRADITION OF COMING FROM somebody and going somewhere. Much as I love my friend Jonathan Daniels and the South he discovered, he makes me uncomfortable with his talk of "little people." He is forever having it that the War of 1861 was fought on the Southern side by "little people," and that everything of moment before or since is to be credited to the same people, including the Southern impulse to get into the Second World War. I have not his sharp sight nor his literature but I have traveled the South as he has and never yet have I met a little person. Not anyone who admitted it, or liked being called it. Everyone in the South, let it be known, is descended from somebody, and on the way to becoming an ancestor. Everyone has in him, too, the makings of a king. This goes for Tobacco Road and Peachtree Street, the share-cropper and the country clubman. With none of Jonathan's virtue or light, Huey Long had the better idea about this. He said every man could be a king, and that is what every man likes to think. Especially every one who lives below the Potomac. It is a part of the Southerner's defense complex. The picture of himself as what he would like to be and is persuaded he could be differs so from what he knows himself to be that he uses boastfulness to escape the contrast. He hates being a little person.

Sometimes when I hear Jonathan and others whom I have been wont to call fellow liberals making us all out so little I wonder if they have not forgotten what the war is about. We liberals were beginning to forget even before the war came. The Hitler idea is that men must be very little people, servants to their government and slaves to their need of food. We of the democracies think every man is a king, entitled to dignities and privacies untold. We even think he is made in an Image. We think it because we enjoy thinking it. And it is good for us to think. Neither our democracy nor our machinery will work without it. Unless there exist or are developed certain excellencies in individual human being which fit us to vote and consume, our democracy will be destroyed at last by our shabbinesses and our machines will lack the mass consuming for which their mass productions call. Jonathan knows this, of course. No one has paid a more poignant tribute to human excellence than he did in his comments on the Petigru gravestone in "A Southerner Discovers the South."

Privately, but not for publication, I am willing to confess to Jonathan the littleness and downright commonness of us all. W. J. Cash convinced me of that in the first chapter of "The Mind of the South," and indeed I had suspected it before. "During the last twenty-five years," Mr. Cash wrote, "the historians, grown more sober since the days when John Fiske could dispense with discretion and import whole fleets packed to the

bowsprites with Prince Rupert's men, have been stead-
ily heaping up a mass evidence that actual Cavaliers
or even near-Cavaliers were rare among Southern settlers. . . ." It was nice of Mr. Cash not to mention
that embarrassing thing about the founding of Georgia
in 1733. General Oglethorpe did it with debtor prison
people from England. We natives claim that being
troubled and even jailed by creditors is a very aristocratic failing and that anyhow the people who landed at
Yamacraw Bluff did not stay long but moved on to
South Carolina. It is even asserted that one of them
reached Charleston (where the Atlantic Ocean forms).

Let it be said that we Southerners have not come
down from English lords, dukes, earls, and Cavaliers
at all. But we have come down. And the people from
whom we came down were good people, generally speaking. They were good enough to survive the stresses of
their days, play a part in their times. And some of them,
no matter where they got it, had a fine way about them.
If this gives us a sense of being part of a process, so
much the better for us. In the little graveyard on the
place out in the country where Rose's people live there
is a stone which reads: "Audley Hamilton—Born July 9,
1780—Married February 1810—Died March 13, 1838—
'He Died in the Faith.'" Audley Hamilton was Rose's
maternal great, great grandfather. She and her mother
love having him there with his beautiful name and his
105-year-old gravestone. It means a very great deal to
them, but I am sure they do not think better of themselves because they had an ancestor. They feel only that

they are parts of a going concern. It keeps them going. They feel that the temporal is related to the eternal. They feel profoundly and loyally at home in the world. My father felt that way about John C. Calhoun, who was his great grand uncle. Great grand uncle is not a very close relationship, it always seemed to me, but my father said that made it all the better because we could enjoy it without being tempted to depend on it. And how he did enjoy it! Being Calhoun's great grand nephew made him feel kin, somehow, to all history, and to nearly everybody living or dead. When he read a book once discussing the several theories about the paternity of Abraham Lincoln, he was enthusiastically partial to the one that Calhoun was the man. On the morality of the Immortal Misconduct he had no judgment. "The point is," he would tell me, "that it makes Abraham Lincoln our cousin." My father bored me in those days with his talk of family histories and people gone before. Once when I showed it he warned me sorrowfully that I would regret my inattention someday when I grew older and such things came to have a meaning. I regret it now.

There are critics who say that the Southern people of whom William Alexander Percy wrote were too limited in numbers and too unsoundly based in economics to have been worth his beautiful "Lanterns on the Levee." I do not think so. "What that class despised as vulgar and treasured as excellent is still despised and treasured by individuals scattered thickly from one end of the South to the other. Those individuals, born into a world of tradesfolk, are still aristocrats, with an uncanny ability to recognize their kind. Their distinguishing characteristic probably is that their hearts are set, not on the virtues which make surviving possible, but on those which make it worth while." The tragedy of Will Percy, it seems to me, is that he surrendered when it wasn't necessary. He never was able to believe that the "tradesfolk" could become the aristocrats for whom he was saying good-bye. Perhaps that is because he thought of aristocrats rather than of the aristocratic tradition. The reality is the tradition. So long as it survives there will be people learning to despise what Will Percy despised, love what he loved.

The only present-day Southerner I know who has been hurt by accents on ancestry is William Faulkner. The harm to Mr. Faulkner is literary, not personal. His obsession makes him such hard reading. Flashing back with his genealogical flash-backs, running up and down family trees with him, computing and accounting for the percentages of white, black, and Indian blood in each character, holding one chapter's unintelligible hint in mind until it appears more broadly in another and finally interrupts with full detail a far-away situation which has absorbed you—is too intensive an exercise, and too irritating. The Faulkner genius is great enough to make you wish his stories unwound but not quite so great that you have energy for unwinding them.

Only a few Southerners have been so puncture-proof to the deflations of the 1930's, to all the debunkings, fact-facings and social and economic rakings-over, that they see any future in the business of living on ancestors. So few are left now that, if their cousins will support them, they should be preserved for the amusing stories that can be written or told about them. But there are many, many Southerners who, when there isn't a war on, take time out for family trees, who have history made intimate for them by cherishing some grandfather's existence in it, who think of the future as a time in which grandchildren of their flesh will be taking a part, and who get a social-mindedness from a sense of belonging to a generation-after-generation process.

Take the case of Judge James E. Horton. He is the judge who, in 1933, set aside the jury sentence in the so-called Scottsboro Case on grounds that the conviction of the Negroes for rape of two white girls on a freight train in North Alabama was not justified by the evidence. His act so defied a local feeling inflamed with every prejudice known to the South—against Negroes, Jews, New Yorkers, and Communists—that he was beaten for re-election and had to retire. The name Judge Horton made with Northern liberals for this act of courage was no solace to him. His own liberalism was confined to the strict business of fair playing, and his social-mind was fixed on the dead and the yet unborn. The social-minded *New Republic* found that out when it asked me to write a story about him. In my newspaper column I had been advocating the release of the Negroes on the grounds of innocence. The evidence was unprintable, but I had read it and it satisfied me as it did Judge Horton that the defendants were not guilty. I had

no such hopes of a flaming social ideal in the Judge as
The New Republic had. When I asked him about the
decision, his explanation was simple. "Fiat justitia, ruat
coelum"—was a precept he had learned at his "mother's
knee." He believed in letting the heavens fall on you for
justice's sake, for the rules' sake, and he was reconciled
to the fall of his political heavens as a result of doing
what he deemed to be justice in the Scottsboro Case.
He was under no illusions about the Negro defendants.
They were a vicious, degenerate lot. We all knew that
and resented the ridiculous glorification of them outside
the South. But they just happened not to be guilty as
charged. So Judge Horton had set aside the verdict and
accepted a sentence of retirement for himself in consequence. But this seemed too simple a story to tell *The
New Republic*. I asked Judge Horton if he wouldn't
write me a letter about himself, hoping to find in it
or between its lines something of more interest and
significance for a social-minded magazine. He did write
me a letter. It was in long-hand and there were twenty-
six pages. It was given in toto to a recital of his immediate and remote ancestors, with special reference
to General Daniel S. Donelson, of Tennessee, an in-law
of Andrew Jackson's. In closing Judge Horton spoke
briefly of his own sons. That was his way of "telling me
something" about himself. I could only report to *The
New Republic* that the Scottsboro decision had been set
aside because the presiding judge was a man who was
descended from General Donelson and who had sons
through whom he, too, expected to be an ancestor, and

who thought he owed it to the past and the future to be
just although the heavens fell.

The social-mindedness of James E. Horton, in other
words, was vertical, not horizontal. It ran up and down
the genealogical tree rather than around the contemporary lot. He wanted to do right because he came of good
people and because he meant good people to come of
him. That is not the only way of arriving at a social-
mind but it is one way, and we are going to need all the
ways we can get in the years to come. A place on a family
tree, an estimate of kingly chance in yourself, a sense of
the dignity and importance of being a human being—
these are not to be disallowed merely because Southerners have used them sometimes for kibitzing and con-
ceit. As between the social-mindedness which is a purely
objective losing of one's self in the oppressions of mankind and the one which is subjectively aware of one's
dignity as an individual and place in a biology, it may be
that the latter is the more to be counted on.

There is no Santa Claus, Virginia—you are a 51-year-
old little girl now and it is time you should know. It is
better that you be told by me than have to learn from
that unsympathetic Mr. Jonathan Daniels. There are
hardly any aristocrats in the country either, Virginia—
South, North, East, or West. There are no kings at all.
And the institution of chivalry is extinct. But there are
things in people's minds and hearts, Virginia, and they
are real. They have to do with the Image in which we
all have been told we are made. They have to do with the
quality we are going to have to give our quantities in this

country if democracy is to work. They have to do with the sort of world our liberals, progressives, and reformers have been breaking their necks to get a chance to make —even though some of them forget what it is they want to do with the chance.

Chapter Sixteen

WOMAN IS PLEASING

FIGHTING IS ONE OF MANY THINGS SOUTHERNERS DO because of their fondness for women. They are fond in the old way of the original invention. Their sensitiveness in this respect is a thing whose social, economic and biological aspects have had the attention of the South's most distinguished and complete sociologist, Dr. Howard Odum, of the University of North Carolina. He believes it one of the items which identify and preserve the South as a region.

"The perfect ankle," announced the toastmaster at a War Bond Luncheon in Birmingham in September, 1942, introducing Vera Zorina, star of stage, screen, and the Russian ballet, "is the one not too small to suggest substance or to support the burden it bears, but the ankle of smooth and slender sufficiency, the charming focus of the upper foot. . . ." Applause, and Zorina, beautiful as running water, pays attention . . . "the lovely isthmus, linking gracious lands. . . ." More applause, and Zorina blushes . . . "the tender introduction to the fullness of a limb. . . ." Zorina is alert. "The Lord has given Vera Zorina an introduction. Mlle. Zorina, will you stand up!"

A few miles away in the shipyards of Mobile, women welders were sweating hard.

The loving and punctilious analysis by the Birmingham toastmaster came of no old-fashioned limitations on experience. The feminine ankle is as lost in the plethora of other items in the South as elsewhere. Indeed, more so. It came rather of a sensibility that leaves nothing out. Put it down to living at "ninety degrees in the shade," or the Latin touch, or a circumstance making for kinship with nature, or for immortal longings—the Southern male is a totalitarian about the female of his species. And because of that, nearly always he is her master or slave, rarely her comrade. Generally he is her slave. Sometimes the relationship is a shifting one. I know a male slave in Jacksonville who, by a psychology all his own but worth study, becomes the loud master when he finds himself partner to his wife at a bridge table. And she, in turn, who ordinarily speaks for herself, becomes a mouse. It is not that he is the better player. She is much his superior. Neither talent nor virtue make the relationship of Southern men and women. It results from the Southern man's extra knowledge that women are pleasing, that they are not like men and that attitudes which pretend a sameness are impractical and involve a net loss. The more successful the man the more subordinate he is likely to be to his wife or daughter or some other woman. I am told that this is a good thing. Races survive best where women are dominant.

The situation is not confined to the South. It is American. The South is only the exaggeration again, the cartoon of a nation. Compared with Europeans, all American men are subject to their wives. Some of them became effeminate about it in the years between the two World Wars, but not the Southerners. Their subordination, coming more directly of their sensitiveness to woman as woman, keeps them masculine.

While Miss Zorina's ankle was receiving progressive consideration in Birmingham women welders on the Gulf Coast were doing their union day's work in the shipyards, overalled against any sign of ankles. Husky, matter-of-fact young women engaged in the war's most important American job up to that time. "Next thing you know," said a veteran of days when shipbuilding was a man's job, "they'll be chewin' terbaccy and spittin' like they was born in a hull."

In the aircraft assembly plants of the country more than 24,000 women were at work. By the end of 1942 more than 200,000 women were in munitions plants, and the total employed in all factories was more than 3,000,000. In some instances their children were cared for in nursery schools or by neighbors, in others not. A California State Senate investigating committee reported on children living in boarding houses and trailer camps whose mothers were in west coast defense industries: "Small children were caged like animals, some even chained in outdoor stalls, undernourished, filthy, and wretched. Fifteen children were fed soup made from one pound of weiners. A year-old child was found whose ears were so full of wax that his hearing may be permanently impaired. Children too young to be sent to school are locked all day in cars while their mothers and fathers are at work. Little children play all day long around the wheels of cars, on the highways, and wherever else their fancy and their short legs can carry them."

A shipbuilding plant at Pascagoula, Mississippi, obtained a $15,000 grant from the government in the fall of 1942 for an addition to its infirmary. The money was to be used for the equipment and maintenance of a "miscarriage room." Similar rooms were set aside for women welders in other plants throughout the country.

Women were going into industrial and business offices, taking major and minor positions formerly held by men. The WAACS, the WAVES, the WFSC, were training for special military services. To Washington while Vera Zorina was in Birmingham came the last word in war women. She was Junior Lieutenant Liudmila Pavlichenko, Russian army girl sniper. She had killed 309 Germans. She expressed amazement at the "silly questions" asked her by the press correspondents at the capital. "Don't they know there is a war? They ask me do I use powder and rouge and nail polish and do I curl my hair? One reporter criticized the length of the skirt on my uniform, saying that it made me look fat. This made me angry. I wear my uniform with honor. It has the order of Lenin on it. It has been covered with blood in battle. It is plain to see that with American women what is important is whether they wear silk underwear under their uniforms. What the uniform stands for they have yet to learn. . . ."

But Lieutenant Pavlichenko was speaking against

frivolity, not femininity. She added that even though she was a sniper she was "a womanly one." In Northampton, Massachusetts, the same week, Commander Gene Tunney, former heavyweight boxing champion, quoted Shakespeare to a WAVE training class at Smith College. From "Henry the Sixth" he warned:

> "A maid—a maid and so martial.
> Pray God, not too martial ere long."

In Detroit Henry Ford said he had found women in war industry "just as good as men and in many instances possessing a little better brain capacity" but he was certain that "after the war they'll resume their place in the home."

At the Gulf Coast plant of the Ingalls Shipbuilding Corporation, male welders on the night shift complained that they did not have as many women welders as the day shift had. Nature was still on the job, and the original invention still working. Indeed the same tempest that was giving women jobs theretofore limited to men was calling both sexes to be their biological selves. War, most masculine of operations, was creating extra tastes for femininity. If women were no longer a part of the booty of war among civilized peoples they were still a part of the warrior's dream. In the fall of 1942 excerpts were published from the diary of an American engineer who had salvaged a $500,000 bomber forced down in the Amazon jungles—

> July 28—Left 1:30 p.m. on Beechcraft No. 2 and scouted jungle for three hours. No success.

July 31—Located plane in small clearing.

August 6—Arrived at Turiassu. Continued to Santa Anna. Arrived 9 p.m.

Aug. 7—Stream forks. . . . Left canoes to continue on foot . . . decided to cut trail to try and locate plane. Bearings S. 72° E. . . . Put under observation by native Indians. They actually believe we are crazy for doing this. . . . Jungle night studded with an incredible concentration of stars per square light-year. A hammock strung between two trees at the edge of the clearing. The hut is quiet. Voices recede and stop. The jungle night takes over . . . a big cat prowls around looking for something to kill. . . . Presently she materializes out of the night. Instead of reaching for the coffee cup she presents to me, I take her hand—dawn would reveal a rather bulging hammock with a hastily dropped coffee cup under it.

Aug. 12—Four days of sweat, bad food and virgin jungle. A bushmaster bit me in the left index finger —had to shoot the end of the finger off to avoid dying.

Aug. 13—It must be luck or the patronizing hand of an angel. Trail broke out under the left wing of B-24 bomber. For the scouting planes that are checking on us we wrote a large three dots and one dash for victory and success.

Aug. 14—Feel like a gentleman of leisure. Would like a tall, sleek, beautiful brunette to bring me my coffee. . . . Scouted clearing and ran set of levels for a proposed take-off strip.

Aug. 15—If women knew how beautiful they look

in the semi-darkness of a bedroom they would become exclusively night prowlers. The day a woman
forgets her vanity and realizes the power of unin-
hibited surrender, the day of the prowling male is
finished and the period of man the domesticated
animal begins. Total length of take-off strip—5,000
feet.

Aug. 19—Finger doing fine. Monkey meat is
plenty tough but ah!—the spareribs. Man is a four-
dimensional animal because he can project his personality into space by his creative powers. Woman
is three-dimensional.

Aug. 26—It feels like Saturday. Two thousand five
hundred feet of take-off strip cleared. Food delivered
by parachute.

Sept. 8—Civilization is the great birth-control
agent—nature in the raw, a baby every year.

Sept. 12—Bomber take-off successful. Delivered
same at Army base.

In the South men and women are always their biological selves, war or no. In December, 1939, when the
motion picture of "Gone With the Wind" had its pre-
mière in Atlanta I printed in my column the Ernest
Dowson verses, written in the 1890's, from which Margaret Mitchell had taken her title. One of the greatest
lyric poems of our time, Arthur Symons called it—

Last night, ah, yesternight, betwixt her lips and mine,
There fell thy shadow, Cynara! thy breath was shed
Upon my soul between the kisses and the wine;
And I was desolate and sick of an old passion.

Yea, I was desolate and bowed my head:
I have been faithful to thee, Cynara! in my fashion.

All night upon mine heart I felt her warm heart beat,
Night-long within mine arms in love and sleep she lay;
Surely the kisses of her bought red mouth were sweet;
But I was desolate and sick of an old passion.
When I awoke and found the dawn was gray:
I have been faithful to thee, Cynara! in my fashion.

I have forgot much, Cynara! gone with the wind—
Flung roses, roses riotously with the throng
Dancing to put thy pale lost lilies out of mind:
But I was desolate and sick of an old passion.
Yea, all the time, because the dance was long;
I have been faithful to thee, Cynara! in my fashion.

I cried for madder music and for stronger wine,
But when the feast was finished and the lamps expire,
Then falls thy shadow, Cynara! the night is thine;
And I am desolate and sick of an old passion,
Yea, hungry for the lips of my desire:
I have been faithful to thee, Cynara! in my fashion.

Why so beautiful and exotic a poem had not been
better known I do not understand. When I printed it
I was besieged with requests for copies of the paper in
which it had appeared. I printed it again when there
were no more copies. The requests poured in again. Five
times I have printed this poem, and each time with this
response. Interest runs to all ages. A sweet old lady wrote
to ask for a copy of the paper, but called my attention to
what she said was a misprint. "In the third line of the

second verse," she wrote, "you made a rather unfortunate mistake. It should be 'bright' not 'bought.' "

Woman is pleasing. The fact accounts for a Southern birth rate which has alarmed Sociologist Oliver Edwin Baker, of the United States Bureau of Agricultural Economics. Asserting that a quarter of the nation's people —in the South—is producing nearly half the nation's increases in population, he warned that "unless the disparity is greatly diminished most of the citizens of the nation a century hence seem likely to be descendants of the rural people of the South today." What a task for the tenant farmer and share-cropper! What a job for Tobacco Road! The birth of a nation! Organized contraceptionists are at work on this problem but even with limitation made uniform throughout the country there would be factors tending to preserve the Southern percentage. The only real insurance against the "threat" to the nation would seem to be in production of better Southerners, even at cost of economic concessions from the nation and from an element of landlords and employers in the South. Given a more generous environment after birth, Southerners would do very well. Even with pellagra and other troubles they may be better physical specimens than people in any other part of the country. This will surprise many, as it did me when I found it indicated in recruiting statistics of the Navy for the fiscal year 1941. In Southern recruiting districts rejections for physical defects were 38 percent of total applications. In Northeastern ones rejections averaged 55.7 percent, in Central ones 45.8 percent, and Western ones 45.3. Comparing with rejections of 66.8 percent in the Albany, N. Y. district and 60.7 in Salt Lake City were—

Richmond	22.6
Nashville	27.8
Raleigh	30.0
Dallas	32.0
Birmingham	34.7
Houston	40.1
New Orleans	42.2

Woman is pleasing. Because of that in the South there is much local fighting. There are vanities, boasts, hates, illegal lusts, and blood-lettings. There is, or has been, lynching. And there is the racial barrier. "This caste system," wrote Dr. Odum in an interpretive review of Allison Howard's "Deep South" for The Saturday Review of Literature, "is not based upon economic factors but is organized around the control of sex, in which there is an unbridgeable chasm for all time, past, present, and future between the white woman and the Negro man."

A virtue in the pleasing which is worth the attention of years to come, it seems to me, is that it makes for recognition of varieties and inequalities which our regimentalists and sentimentalists tend to ignore in their estimates of democracy's meaning. It may be that Herbert Agar's cherished "egalitarianism" admits of mortal differences, as he says it does, but the practical effect of it as he plans it would be to make the differences more painful and unfair than they are. Human beings who are not equal in fact simply cannot be treated exactly alike. And human beings who are not the same are robbed of something invaluable to civilization if they are regimented. The real "revolt against civilization" (Mr. Agar's term) is a revolt against individualism. I think Mr. Agar really wants only a floor to inequalities above which men will act as the brothers they are, not the equals they can never be. But what he is in danger of getting if he is too much heard is a stamp upon all living, a seal on precious energies which come of the desire to get ahead. Because woman is pleasing in the South and because that results in knowledge there of mortal differences and inequalities, the war against the regiment in favor of the social-minded but intact individual, which is going to go on long after Hitler's regiments are liquidated, may hope for strong recruits. But to have the Southern recruits strong, as Mr. Agar would point out, there will need to be enough limits on individualism and inequality to make a floor against economic and social miseries which have crippled the South in other days.

Woman is pleasing. Another virtue in the Southern male's sensitiveness to woman is that it makes for masculinity in a nation which went into this war sick, psychopathic—and effeminate. No matter what the degree of civilization, nature meant men to be male, women female. This does not mean the hair-chested-he or the simpering-she. But it means men and women differing from and complementing each other and not swapping sides. It does not mean the hair-chest but neither does it mean the crooners, the tenors turned soprano, the lightly

chattering radio men, the effeminate soul-searchers of
the 1930's. It does not mean the males who were too
educated and nice to take sides, or the ones who were
so sweet about perpetual peace that they thought to
avoid war by not looking. Among women it does not
mean lavender and lace, but neither does it mean the
contraltos turned baritone, the torch-singers whose flame
was only a sticky place in the throat, the slap-stick ladies
who failed to notice how funny Irene Dunne was, the
earnest workers in the vineyard who forgot that both
Mary and Martha were gentle, and the lady politicians
who thought it all a matter of being quarrelsome, suspicious, and loud. Just before the First World War the
woman suffrage movement began, and needed to begin.
We needed to learn that women were more like men
than we had let them be for the prior ten thousand years.
Just before the present World War we were needing to
learn that women are less like men than we had pre-
tended for the prior twenty years.

The need will continue, whether the post-war woman
is to be "in the home" or still out a-welding. Where she
will be no one knows. My guess is that she will not be
so down-town and afield as some of her champions suppose. There are thirteen people at the economic table.
Someone is going to have to drop out. Perhaps it should
be the too young or the too old but there are arguments
that it should be the people to whom the Lord gave the
more delicate hair, skin, muscles, and sensibilities. Technology has brought us to a place (even without atom
splitting) where the work of the world can be done with

so much less human labor that in ordinary times (if they come!) there will not be enough work to go around. The war has multiplied progress in this direction to startling extents. A surplus of human labor can do more harm than that surplus of little pigs which, in the dark of the 1930's, inspired anti-New Dealers to poetries of protest against the atrocities of New Dealing.

When the men have all come back from war, when the immensities of reconstruction tasks have been leveled and when the developed and waiting science of producing enough of everything for everybody is applied with all the gadgets war invented, somebody is going to be a clog on the labor market. No hard rule will be applicable, of course, for women are at large now and few doors will be closed to them. But there will be influences tending to eliminate them as an economic class. "Are women to be used by selfish employers as a reservoir of cheap labor competition to lower men's labor price and make worse the conditions of work, to smash their trade unions while they are away fighting?" Richard Frankensteen, of the United Auto Workers, asked a Town Meeting of the Air in September, 1942. Mr. Frankensteen proposed to make room for women if they wanted to come into his and other industries, and to guard men workers against their competition by taking all into a bundling party under the trade union blanket. But he predicted, and hoped, that "the vast majority of women, if economic conditions at home are proper when this war is over, will return to the home." The vast majority, of course, was already there. Mr. Frankensteen estimated that

5,000,000 women would be working in factories by the end of 1943 if the war went on, but he spoke of 22,000,000 who would still be engaged in the ancient and honorable business of housewifery. Post-war housewifery may not be enough, but there will be other things. There will be the million things of that leisure time the machine age has promised.

Whatever happens we may be sure that in the South woman will continue to be pleasing, whether she is afield, down-town, or at home. The sun shines bright.

Chapter Seventeen

HERE WE REST!

SOUTHERN READINESS TO FIGHT COMES IN PART, NO doubt, of an unreadiness to take the harder way of negotiation and counter-plan. Southerners are lazy. Some of the laziness is the plain kind, some comes of nutritional deficiency. The Southerners who are energetic are much ashamed of this regional torpor. They try to hide it or disprove it. Anne O'Hare McCormick, of *The New York Times*, told me she had never seen a place in which business men worked harder proving to themselves and the world that they work hard than in Birmingham. She thought they should take more time for lunch.

It was in Alabama that the most vigorous of all moves against the Southern name for laziness was made. A few months before the war the Great Seal of the state was changed by act of the legislature to eliminate the words "Here We Rest!" which had featured it since Reconstruction. In substitute for an American eagle with the words on a streamer in his beak there was put an outline map of the state and the words: "We Dare Defend Our Rights." The change ended years of mortification on the part of Chamber of Commerce officials and business men who felt that such a motto as "Here We Rest" exposed them to a suspicion of relaxing. They had tried to make

the world believe that the word "rest" did not refer to
a taking of one's ease but rather to a taking of one's
stand. They had passed around a story that the Indian
chieftain who was first to come with his roving band into
the area of what is now Alabama had been so won with
the looks of things that he had thrust his spear trium-
phantly into the soil and cried: "This is a goodly land.
We have found no better. Here we shall make our home.
This shall be our abiding place. Here we rest!" Carrying
the chieftain forward as the first Alabama real estate
booster, they had imagined him saying of the modern
state: "Here we rest upon six million acres of cotton,
corn, and hay. Here we rest above billions of tons of coal
and iron ore, beneath billions of board feet of standing
timber, beside 1400 miles of navigable streams. Here we
rest where two million textile spindles turn, where two
million annual tons of pig iron are poured, where a million hydroelectric horsepower run. It is a goodly land.
We have found no better. Here we rest!"

Some Alabamians, even without benefit of pellagra,
were able to believe in rest. These radicals claimed the
future as well as the past. They said that in days to come
when science would have made the earning of a living
easy and the art of living intricate, a capacity for being
leisurely would be a boon. Just as in days past the slow
paces of the South and the fine relaxations had marked a
civilization. There is a restfulness, they agreed, which is
a mere going to sleep, a stupor, by-produced from malaria, hookworm, or the like. But there is another restfulness which is better named serenity and which may be

the last secret of life, answer to all the nervous fatigues and multiplying jumpinesses. They, too, carried the Indian chieftain forward. They carried him as far as the atom's splitting, and translated him thus: "Here we rest enough between the businesses of life to know life's art. Here we rest enough to sense the days, hours, and moments as they pass, for they pass but once. Here we are not so absorbed in saving time and making money that we have no zeal for the time saved, no imagination for good use of the money. Here we anticipate with our arts the leisure which the machine age has promised and must give. Here we labor with all our might, but when labor is done, here we converse, sing, smile, remember, and make an occasion of our meals. Here we work hard, and, after work, here we really—really—rest!"

They might have carried a philosophy of rest to still another interpretation. Noting how the South was torn with hates then and tortured with a sense of problems, how "realism" and social-mindedness were being denied their rewards because of what they had done to the imaginations and tempers of men, they might have spoken up for rest from revolution, reform, and problem-finding. Important still as it was to know whether Southerners were hell-bound or heaven-bent, they might have suggested nevertheless that life had its moments here on the earth which is so far above the one and below the other. They might have proposed remembering art for art's sake, entertainment for entertainment's sake, and an old-fashioned thing called the joy of being alive.

Not against Southerners en masse did this point need

making, but against some of the leaders of Southerners, and of other peoples. In spite of all the literature and legislation that have been poured over them, the people of the South, especially the colored ones, are extravert, able to laugh from the stomach even if it is empty, to be absorbed in something foreign, excited over matters that neither put nor answer a question. It is the leaders of the South, and of the world, who so often threaten the results of their own work by failing to rest on them. Especially when they are paid or political leaders. They conceive their task as a championship which must be content with no achievement but forever find new causes if their pay or office is to be justified. Demanding things in the name of their group is an activity which has no end in their sight, a daily business, a daily bread. The American Legion took official note of this practice when it met at Boston in 1930, and rebuked it. Wisely the Legionnaires saw in it a menace to things already achieved for them. "Be it resolved," they declared, "that the American Legion call upon its members to oppose all such veteran legislation that may jeopardize the support of our citizens in the continuance of our hospitalization and rehabilitation program; and

"FURTHER, we do declare that we condemn the practice of proposals of legislation primarily designed to attract our votes."

It was a great idea even if it didn't work. Offering the Legion something was so easy, refusing the offer so inhumanly hard, that the demanded restraints were not imposed. A few years later some bright young men at

Princeton organized themselves facetiously into what they called the "Veterans of Future Wars" and asked immediate advance payment of bonuses that would be demanded for them if another war should come and they should serve it through. Little did the young men know that Corregidor, Tunisia, and Guadalcanal would be names for some of them a few years thence.

In the months before and after Pearl Harbor the unwillingness of American domestic leadership to stop leading threatened the war effort. Some of the unwillingness came of honest belief that evils or inadequacies at home must be adjusted before we could face the world as champions of right. Some of it came of an estimate that the war was a shining chance to force a cherished advantage. There was belief that the war was a time for extending the New Deal, other belief that it was time for having done with the New Deal. There was belief that it was a time for putting labor up, a time for putting labor down, a time for making sure of free enterprise, a time for collectivism, for extending democracy, and for discontinuing the gift of it to so many disreputable people, for making the Negro behave and for elimination of all discriminations against him, including segregation in the South. There was belief that it was a time for obtaining justice for the South in such matters as freight rates and distribution of industries. There was equal belief that it was a time for forcing the South to do justice in the matter of poll taxes and other things. In each case the shining chance or bitter need involved a quarrel, usually an irreconcilable one, and the forcing of it meant division in the face of the enemy. That was the unanswerable argument against the domestic crusaders, in my opinion, and it applied without regard to the merits of the crusade. Some of the leaders refused to stop because they were caught that way and couldn't. Force of long habit had given them a blind conception of their jobs as calling for campaigns without ceasing and at any cost. Paid secretaries, managers, and lobbyists, who had made the business of demanding things the whole climate of their existence, carried on. In one way or another they managed to identify the advancement of their group with the proper conduct of the war—just as some of the gentlemen of the advertising fraternity were able to discover that patriotism and the products of their clients were parts of each other. For winning the war it was important to invest in somebody's custom-made clothes or pills for the pallid—and in some pressure group's great wrong to be righted.

With leadership become so basic to representative government, and with the radio, loudspeaker, airplane, and press services implementing it with more power than it ever had before, a better science of it is going to be needed. A science of exercise and a science of being still. Long before the war there were examples of leadership that spoiled itself by not knowing when to stop or by insisting on itself at a wrong time or in too great a hurry. It is a tenable proposition that if Hitler had been willing to stop forcing issues on the world somewhere short of the final forcing that brought war he might have won much for Germany, and the remaining issues would in time have settled themselves. It is, to my thinking, an even more tenable proposition that American leaders who saved the capitalist system with the Roosevelt revolution threaten all they achieved when they fail to recognize their revolution as a thing accomplished and are unwilling to settle down with their New Deal. A body in motion tends to stay in motion, and so does a crusader. It is the principle of inertia. The menace of it will grow in years to come as pressure groups multiply in organization and power of approach. Lobbyists at Washington, group leaders in Congress, executive directors of business associations, labor leaders, farm leaders, regional leaders, representatives of veterans' organizations, and their counterparts in clubs and cities everywhere, will be "leading" with all their might when the war is over and the scramble for places in the new dispensation is on. They will be leading with benefit of sciences of communication, organization, and psychology which will arm them as never before. Much of the leading will be called for, much will lead in right directions or offset leadership in bad directions. But much will go into action at wrong times or for wrong causes, and much will carry on after the need for it has passed.

Here we rest! The slothful motto which the South has rejected in shame is going to need recalling. The tradition of the South in which people and things come eventually to rest will have post-war mandates. A hundred years ago, out of the burning intellectual energy which never let him be still, the gaunt-eyed South Carolinian spoke for being still. Debating the Oregon Question in 1846, Calhoun suggested that "a wise and masterly inactivity" would be a better foreign policy than war. "I venture to say 'a wise and masterly inactivity' in spite of the attempt to cast ridicule upon the expression. Those who have made the attempt would seem to confound such inactivity with mere inaction. Nothing can be more unlike. They are as wide apart as the poles. . . . The one is the offspring of indolence, or ignorance, or indifference. The other is the result of the profoundest sagacity and wisdom. A sagacity which looks into the operations of the great causes in the physical, moral, and political world which by their incessant operation are ever changing the conditions of nations for good or evil. And a wisdom which knows how to use and direct them when acting favorably by slight touches to facilitate their progress and by removing impediments which might thwart or impede their course and, not least, to wait patiently for the fruits of their operation. . . . He who does not understand the difference between such inactivity and mere inaction—the doing of nothing—is still in the hornbook of politics, without a glimpse of those higher elements of statesmanship by which a country is elevated to greatness and prosperity."

Infinite go-getting, no matter what fine impulse is behind it, will not be practicable in the increasingly small and related world to which we are destined. There was notable example against it during the first months of America's war effort. Every branch of the armed service, and of the arming one, and of the service of economic supply, was so imbued with the spirit that each became a menace to the other, and it was necessary at last to set up co-ordinators to limit the go-getting. It became necessary to tell the army it could not take any more doctors from civil life, to make industry give up to the military its younger men and take older ones, to stop the manpower drain from farm to factory, and in many other fields to make leaders stop leading. By the fall of 1942 the go-getting of doctors from civilian life for the army had been carried so far in the South that, with the exception of Florida and Arkansas, every Southern state had had dangerously more than its quota taken. While such states as New York, Pennsylvania, California, Massachusetts, and Illinois had provided less than 65 percent of assigned quotas, Alabama had furnished 155 percent and had only one physician left for each 2000 of population (the accepted minimum is one for each 1500). When asked how many doctors he wanted from Alabama one official replied, "All we can get, by God!" But total war doesn't work like that any more than will the world we are going to live in when the total war is won. Alabama's fighting men at the fronts could not have been very happy in victory if they had come home to find their loved ones all more or less dead, diseased, or toothless because an enterprising official had wanted all the doctors he could get, by God.

Here we rest! In sorrow I report that the agency most responsible for removal of the motto was not the Chamber of Commerce but the Alabama Branch of the United Daughters of the Confederacy. The words spoke of serenities which belonged to the very tradition the Daugh-

ters served and which they might well have given themselves to carrying forward. But they had them stricken
from the Great Seal. One count against the motto was
that it suggested laziness in Alabama, but another and
even more serious one was that it had been put into the
Great Seal in the seventies by a carpet-bag governor
from the North. It might have come from the devil himself and been no less precious. Sectionalism was at its
worst in this argument, the same which, elsewhere in the
South, wanted the "Battle Hymn of the Republic" taken
from Southern song books for children because the
battle of which Julia Ward Howe had written was
against the South. The same which, in years after Appomattox made bitter issue against calling that war a "rebellion," insisting the proper term was "Civil War," and
later when the crusade had been won attacked its own
victory, outlawed "Civil War" in favor of "War Between
the States." A few years ago when the Southern controversy over the proper name for the War of 1861-5
came to the attention of a writer for *The Boston Tran-
script*, he commented that, as the son of a Union soldier, he had been taught that the correct name was
"War of Rebellion" but that he was broad-minded and
didn't care what they called it. His only objection to
"War Between the States," he said, was one of grammar. "Between" had reference to two things only, and
since there were many states, the term should be "War
Among the States." He was wrong about that, I think.
"Among" implies a free-for-all. There were only two in
the fight. Perhaps the finally accredited title (if another

crusade is indicated) will be "War Between the Groups of States." Meanwhile, we newspaper people, afraid of the Daughters but not able to find room for so long an expression as "War Between the States," have hit on calling it "The Confederate War." For the time being, that seems to be satisfactory.

Sectionalism in the South, happily on the way out now, is a silly thing, sentimental always and looking backward. It is very different from regionalism. Regionalism, is a recognition of facts of geography, economics, history, etc., which distinguish parts of the nation and give each a set of problems, opportunities, interests, and expressions, with resulting contribution to national variety. Regionalism in the South is concerned with freight rate discriminations, tariffs, the existence of two races in great number side by side, the long dependency on a single crop, the preponderance of agriculture, the need of more industry, etc.

In defense of the Daughters—and there are more than sentimental reasons for wanting them defended and preserved—it should be said that the action against "Here We Rest" came from no wide demand among them. It was merely a response to leadership which was looking for a target, which wanted to make a record and happened on this particular crusade in all honesty and error.

I dreamed of the United Daughters of the Confederacy the other night. It was a dream of fair women. I dreamed that they had carried on, won a new significance in a post-war era three wars after the one they remembered. I dreamed that something defeated at

Appomattox had come back to victory in an atom's splitting, that a dignity and balance in living which were the Old South's tradition had become the order of a New World's day and that the Daughters of the Confederacy had turned themselves into first agents of that order. And I dreamed that the stone rejected by one of the Daughters' builders had become a corner one for building in years after the Total War. I dreamed that "Here We Rest" was not only restored to the Great Seal of Alabama but made the message of the Daughters. I dreamed that, partly by grace of these women and the memory that first brought them together, America learned a lesson for its new days out of its old, learned to rest in bright affirmation and love of its land, learned to rest its case for the rules and the free way, learned to rest in competitive balance under a faithful umpire, and, when major causes turned to minor, learned the fine art of stopping.

Chapter Eighteen

"—AND THE DEMOCRATIC PARTY"

Two weeks after the mid-war Republican victory in November, 1942, Senator Barkley of Kentucky had Senator McKellar of Tennessee arrested. As Democratic Majority Leader he asked that the sergeant-at-arms be instructed to arrest Democratic Senators Hill of Alabama, Maybank of South Carolina, Doxey of Mississippi, O'Daniel of Texas, McKellar of Tennessee, Russell of Georgia, Overton of Louisiana, and Bunker of Nevada.

It was one of several measures against efforts on the part of the Southern Senators to prevent a vote on the bill outlawing the Southern poll tax. A majority for the bill was assured if a vote could be taken, and a similar bill had already passed the House. So determined were the Southerners against federal interference with their election laws that they were using every means to avoid the vote, including the device of staying away from the Senate in enough numbers to leave less than a quorum present. It was to obtain a quorum that Mr. Barkley had asked the arrests. Mr. McKellar professed himself so angry at the indignity that he had his name withdrawn from a petition asking the President to appoint Mr. Barkley to the place on the Supreme Court made vacant by the resignation of Justice Byrnes, who had become war-time Director of Economic Stabilization. The principal weapon of the Southerners was the filibuster. Endlessly they filled the Senate's time with talk, demands for a calling of the roll, meticulosities of Parliamentary law, elaborate snappings at senatorial trifles. Mr. Bilbo of Mississippi announced that matters he wished to discuss would need at least a month of the Senate's time. Southerners like Maybank of South Carolina and Hill of Alabama, who had been one hundred percent New Dealers, were joined with anti-New Dealers like Byrd of Virginia and George of Georgia.

The centripetal force had brought them all home at once and lined them up together. What put it into play this time was what had done so most often in the days before—the Negro problem. The unshakable belief of Southern whites that the problem was peculiarly their own and that attempts to force a settlement from outside were hateful and incompetent. The absolute determination that the blood of the two races should not be confused and a mulatto population emerge. The rest of the country might rail as it pleased against provincial obstructionism in the midst of a great war and against attempts to defeat majority will. This was something as vital to white Southerners as the war itself. They believed it to be that, at any rate, and without regard to the merits of the quarrel I think the impartial historian will place the greater blame for the disgraceful scene on the incorrigible domestic crusaders who forced the poll tax issue, with all the bitter irreconcilables it involved, at a time of greatest war.

What would have made the situation comic if it had not been tragic was that no matter how the controversy might end there would be no effect upon Negro voting in the South as an immediate result, except that the feeling aroused would discourage an existing Southern tendency to permit more Negroes, even if not nearly a majority, to vote. Poll tax or no, the South knew a score of ways to keep the Negro from voting. Tricky ways, violent, cajoling, intimidating ways and honest ways of educational qualification. In counties where the Negro outnumbered the white man eight to one he was not going to be allowed to vote no matter what was done about the poll tax. In other counties where the whites were in large majority, Negroes who qualified in education and responsibility were already voting and in increasing numbers. The poll tax had nothing much to do with the case. In Alabama, with the worst tax of all, a cumulative one of $1.50 a year for all years since voting age was reached, thousands of Negroes were exempt as veterans of the First World War, but they did not vote. In the winter of 1940-41 controversy arose between New Dealers and antis over a discovery that Farm Security Administration officials were including sums for payment of poll taxes in loans to white tenant farmers and share-croppers. When, as an aside to complaints against this alleged federal interfering with Southern elections, someone asked why the FSA discriminated against Negroes in the loans, the reply was that lending money to them for poll taxes would be a waste because they would not be allowed to vote even if their tax was paid.

Those of us who had fought the poll tax in our Southern states for years, damned it for the undemocratic, vicious thing it is, and demanded its abolition by state action, knew that much of the opposition to its elimination came not from anti-Negro elements but from anti-populists. It is the vote of working people and of poor whites on the farms which would be increased if the poll tax were abolished.

On the side lines until the filibuster succeeded at last sat the Republicans. Most of them were committed in their recent election campaigns to support the bill but many of them were no longer enthusiastic, and all were willing to have the Democrats left to fight each other about it. They could see the outlines of fundamental revolt against the Democratic Party in its greatest stronghold.

Before ever the atom is split and its energies released, there is promised this political split in the Solid South. Whether it will release productive energy or be only a gaseous division between white and black remains to be seen. Efforts to take the South from the Democratic Party on other issues than the Negro had been without success. The Populists broke away for a little while in the 1890's but returned. Teddy Roosevelt had some following for his Bull Moose Party in the South in 1912 but carried only Louisiana. Hoover in 1928 won North Carolina, Virginia, Florida, Tennessee, and was so near to winning Alabama that many believe he did, but the remainder of the South held fast in spite of Al Smith's rum, Romanism, Tammany Hall, and sidewalks, and by 1932 the faltering states were safely back. Strenuous and amazingly hopeful efforts were made for Willkie in 1940, without success. But the situation which the anti-poll tax bill reflected and made intense was something different. It was the one thing which could split the South because it was the one thing that had made the South solid. Meaningless as regarded actual voting by the Negro but full of meaning for indications of the Democratic Party's new sympathies and alliance, it made a focus. The thing that had held the South since Appomattox existed no longer. A culmination was coming to the process which had begun in 1932 when, for the first time in history, the national Negro vote went Democratic and became a thing to be competed for by both parties thereafter. The vote of the Negro in pivotal states like Ohio, Indiana, Illinois, Pennsylvania, New Jersey, and New York had become in plain mathematics more valuable than that of the white man in the South. The era of Southern political solidarity was approaching its close.

A side light was that throughout the years the machinery of national politics had given the Southern white man less voice than the Southern Negro in naming Presidents of the United States. That was because of the composition of the party conventions. In Democratic conventions, with representation from states and districts based on total rather than party population, large states like Pennsylvania which rarely went Democratic were able nevertheless to outvote any three Southern states. From this it resulted that the Southern white man was under-represented in his party. The rule requiring a two-thirds majority for presidential and vice presidential nominations was deemed an offset to this under-representation but at best it was only a veto. It was abolished in 1936 in favor of a simple majority. In the following convention of 1940 an organized effort was made by Southern delegates to obtain a delegate apportionment system similar to the Republican one which based representation in larger part on actual party population within the districts and states and on loyalty in preceding elections. Gilchrist Stockton of Florida, Gordon Gray of North Carolina, Robert Anderson (son of Sherwood) of Virginia, Senator Burnet Rhett Maybank of South Carolina, Marion Rushton of Alabama, were among the leaders in this. It resulted in a concession so minor that some of them called it a "tip." The convention voted to give one extra delegate to each state going Democratic in a previous general election. This meant that the delegate strength of Virginia, North Carolina, and Alabama combined was increased from 68 to 71. It was still not quite equal to the 72 delegates of the Republican state of Pennsylvania. Contrasting with the under-representation of the Southern white man in the Democratic Party was an over-representation of the Southern Negro in the Republican Party. Time and again Southern Negro delegations were used to make a balance of power in Republican conventions. Since the Republicans had been in office during most of the years since Appomattox it was a tenable proposition that the

Southern Negroes, or those who controlled them, had been given more voice than Southern whites in the choice of our Presidents.

When I pointed this out to Walter Lippmann in 1929 while he was editor of *The New York World* he commented editorially that "if the influence of the Southern Negro at Washington makes itself felt through the Republican Party rather than the Democratic Party, it is because the Democratic Party has so effectively closed its doors to him and so successfully driven him over to the Republican side." Time marches on.

Aggravating the threat of final revolt in the South against the party of its long choice was a disgruntlement among the group most populous there—the farmers. Ingratitude it may have been, for no element in America had received more attention, but there it was. The farmers resented the unwillingness of the administration to let their greatly increased labor costs be considered in estimating "farm parity" prices. Equally they resented being held up to the country as unpatriotic gougers in wartime. They listened to those who told them Franklin Roosevelt was not an agrarian but a laborite. They began calling dangerously leftist certain Presidential gestures in behalf of union labor which, if made in their own directions, would not have been thought so. Southern textile interests came forward, against economic but not political interest, as champions of the cotton farmer in the parity price dispute. The Alabama Cotton Manufacturers' Association issued a statement in behalf of the farmer's right to have his labor costs represented in his price ceiling. The association's very able young president, Craig Smith, pointed out that this was done in spite of the fact that "the ceiling prices of cotton cloth are fixed, and, therefore, any increase in the price of cotton narrows the manufacturing margin of the mills." "How any fair-minded person could have objected to the farmer having his labor cost included in the parity formula is impossible for me to understand," he declared in an address to the Talladega Kiwanis Club in October, 1942. "The successful efforts of part of the metropolitan press and of certain professional labor leaders of this country to portray the farm group as war profiteers, to my mind, established a new high in unscrupulous misrepresentation. . . ." Other Southern industrialists were open in expressions of sympathy. With a preponderant balance of political power in the South, the farmer was apparently swinging it against his New Deal patrons and being encouraged by the industrialists, most of whom were long-standing anti-New Dealers. But this situation was not like the racial one. A change of party leadership or policy could eliminate the farm grudge. But no change could take away the epochal new fact that the national Negro vote was going to be competed for thereafter by the Democratic Party and that in this competition the race attitude of the Southern white man was destined to less and less consideration. That, and that alone, was the rock on which the party in the South could at last be split.

In other days it had been said that the three things which dominated the South were "hell, calomel, and the Democratic Party." Hell and calomel were holding fast in 1943 but there was trouble about the party. If the one-party system was about to go, historians would be able to speak of its good points along with its bad ones. It has been bad for the South to have its loyalty so certain that no concessions or recognitions were needed to hold it. It has been bad for the country to have the South a dead weight in favor of one party no matter what the national issues. And it has been bad for both the South and the country to have the South made even more separatist than its regional circumstances required. But there have been good points, too. The one party arrangement was a "moral equivalent for war" every election day. Every two years the South has had the moral benefit of putting aside its hot domestic quarrels and coming to the aid of the Party. That is a good exercise, whether it happens to a nation at war or to Southern states upon the advent of a national election. The one-party system in the South has been no agency of a total state as in Germany, Italy, and Russia, where the party is continually controlling and the control comes down from above. In the South the Democratic Party has had within itself divisions as sharp as any that have separated Democrats and Republicans elsewhere. Democratic primaries in the South close periods of political competition so fierce that there is nothing like them anywhere else. It is only that once each election time Southerners have had to recognize the party as a thing more important than all their contests within the party. The effect is like a whole nation's recognition of itself when war comes. Perhaps that is another reason why it was easier for the South to picture the country joined in war against Hitler.

What will come to a South no longer politically solid, I do not know. There is talk again—as there was in 1940 —of a Southern Party to deliver the white South's vote on a bargain and concession basis. But that, I think, will get nowhere. It would be too hatefully a separatist and one-issue organization. Nicholas Murray Butler has proposed changing the Republican Party's name to have it accepted in Southern states. Whatever comes, unless it be hideous division along race lines, will mean a new competition nationally for the South's vote and a clarification of many issues within the South. Good Woodrow Wilson Democrat that I try always to be, I think competition is the life of trade. But I hope it will not be a competition with no holds barred and nothing superior.

The Southern approach to revolt had not come far enough to be a factor in the Democratic Party's mid-term losses in November, 1942. Those losses came in part of simple weariness after ten years of the same faces, voices, and philosophies. They came in part of objection to social reform continued too long to let itself work. They came of a fear that federal centralizations which had been in progress for eight years before Pearl Harbor and were necessarily multiplied thereafter might be carried into the peace and make socialism or a total state. They came in part, too, I think, of much talk among elements of the Administration that the war was a revolution and that what the New Deal had been would be as conservative as the horse-and-buggy regime in comparison with what would be thereafter. People did not want another revolution. They wanted only to save the revolutions gone before, the one of 1776, the one of 1865, and the Roosevelt one of 1933. By the President's own mathematics two-thirds of them were not ill-fed, ill-housed, or ill-clothed (he had said that one-third were), and even though they wanted no going back and knew that one-third of a nation or world could ruin the two-thirds unless provided for, they wanted no more revolution. They had had theirs. They did not thrill to talk that things would never be the same again. To have many things the same was one of their objectives in the war. They wanted a world which would have learned its lesson, be more social-minded at home and international-minded abroad, but they wanted a world, too, in which a man could find his bedroom slippers. The message of the 1942 vote was not that the Republicans could win in 1944 with isolationism and domestic reaction. But neither was it that Democrats could win with talk of revolutions just beginning and of New Deals from Greenland's ice to India's coral.

It was noted, or seemed to be, that the leader of the Party did not participate in the revolutionary never-the-same-again talk of his associates. While some of them were making it out that the Democratic defeat had come not of too much New Dealing but of too little, Mr. Roosevelt said nothing. While some cited the anti-poll tax bill as a burning example of the New Deal's unfinished business, the President refused to be identified with it. Asked what he thought of the filibuster, he said he had been too busy to give the debate any attention. Asked if he thought the bill should pass he said he had not studied it and, therefore, was not in a position to form an opinion. Carroll Kilpatrick, one of the best informed of the Southern correspondents in Washington, reported that Leader Barkley had consulted "neither the President nor the party leaders" when he had called the bill up. Was the New Dealer himself coming to look upon it as dealt? Had great events put something new into that open mind? Was he, like Mr. Willkie, in flux?

When the first Democratic convention met in Baltimore in 1832 it adopted a rule that "two-thirds of the whole number of votes given be required for nomination." In the debate before adoption, Mr. Pollard of Virginia opposed this as "inconsistent with the fundamental principles upon which our Government is founded, which provide that the rule of the majority shall prevail, and because it might possibly be found to be impracticable to unite the votes of so large a proportion in favor of any one individual." But W. R. King, of Alabama, supporting the rule, argued that "a nomination made by two-thirds of the whole body would show a more general concurrence of sentiment in favor of a particular individual, would carry with it a greater moral weight and would be more favorably received than one made by a smaller number." In the institution of the famous two-thirds rule the South was not a consideration. There was no thought of the veto power it was destined to give that region in theory if not in fact. What did have this first convention's thought, however, was the conception of a national rather than a sectional party, one required by its own rules to reach a certain unanimity of sentiment before going to the nation with its candidates. The philosophers of the party believed then, as many have believed since, that it was good for Americans to have a quadrennial subordination of intra-party differences in favor of the whole. The same thought animated a fine address over the America's Town Meeting of the Air program on November 19, 1942, by that good philosopher and Democrat, Professor T. V. Smith, of the University of Chicago. He held it a virtue that the two parties should differ not nearly so much with each other as within themselves. It tended to make differences less bitter and explosive, he thought, since there was the necessity of forgetting them period-ically in aid of the party. I have always been impressed with that point of view. It amounts to a little of what England gets with her institution of monarchy, a king who is above parties and to whom all men owe allegiance no matter how they differ under the sovereignty. Car-lyle proposed once, I believe, that since the upkeep of a king was expensive and little was required of him beyond his mere being, England do away with living kings and set up a cast iron one. There might be advantage in a cast iron Democratic Donkey and Republican Elephant, making emphatic the symbolism of unity in difference. With cast iron, Americans might be the better per-suaded that there must be a permanence beyond all challenge and change, that there must be lines, rules, umpires, and an arena strictly preserved as the great games proceed.

Chapter Nineteen

LORD GOD ALMIGHTY

THEY SANG LIKE TOTALITARIANS AT THE BAY VIEW Assembly on Lake Michigan in the summer of 1942. "Oh
God, our help in ages past—Our hope for years to come—
Our shelter from the stormy blast—" They sang in a worship not even the most consecrated of those good Methodists had known before Pearl Harbor. The war made
them full-voiced. Trouble gave them whole hearts for
their God. Into the last verse, though it was not so familiar, they poured their best—

> "Before the hills in order stood,
>   Or earth received her frame,
>   From everlasting Thou art God,
>   Through endless years the same."

There was comfort in the presumption of order and
a frame, changeless through the years. Comfort against
the gathered threat to order, frame, and endlessness.
Those people from the middle classes of Michigan, Illinois, the West, and South, were not rich but neither
were they poor. Life was not perfect but it was precious
enough in sum total to be saved. They wanted no world
made over. Rather they wanted one in which they might
enjoy and use better what they had, the things not ap-

preciated before they were threatened so. These singers at Bay View were members of the nation's two-thirds, not the one-third officially reported ill fed, ill clothed, ill housed. Two-thirds is a majority.

Listening in that land of maple, birch, and rolling hills, beside the cool blue waters of that Great Lake, I thought of Plymouth Rock. The Pilgrim Fathers, landing beside great waters on a shore of rocks and trees, coming, they said, to worship God in their own way. The important thing was that they came to worship God. In the years since their coming we descendants have put such emphasis on the "in their own way" that we have overlooked the "to worship." The Pilgrims wanted God. That was the great point of their arrival, not that the way they preferred was denied them across the sea. The way was important only because the desire to worship was sure.

We have been so intent on ways that we have forgotten what they were for. That has been true in all our living, not in religion alone. Some of us have been fighting so hard for democracy that we have failed to use democracy. Some have been so bent upon the rights of labor that we have not remembered how the rights should be employed for quality in workmanship, character, and responsibility in those who work. Some of us have so feared for free enterprise that we have ourselves taken away some of the freedom or been wanting in enterprise. In the South we have denounced so bitterly a discrimination and lack of understanding on the part of the rest of the country that we have failed sometimes in attention to our proper exercises as a region, in expression of our best with the material at hand. Especially in the matter of our race problem. Some of the attention given to racial threats or injustices might better have gone to making ourselves individually more excellent human beings, white and black.

Mrs. Thomas W. Marshall was at Bay View. The widow of Wilson's Vice President had come back for the first time since a summer with her husband years ago. She told me how sad it was that of all the things he had said in his life-time the one most remembered should be "What this country needs is a good five-cent cigar." She told me the Wendell Willkies had spent the summer of 1937 there. Little could Mr. Willkie have foreseen, as he joined the singing, that five years later he would be the defeated Republican candidate, riding a bomber plane around a world-at-war as emissary for Franklin Delano Roosevelt serving a third term. Little could he have guessed as he joined, perhaps, in "How Firm a Foundation," that when he would reach China on his mission the adoring people would give him a name which, being translated, meant "Powerful Foundation."

At Bay View I met Dr. Frank Buchman, founder of the Oxford Group, leader of the crusade for "Moral Rearmament." He had come to see his young people stage their patriotic pageant "You Can Defend America." When he told me how pleased he had been with the response to him and those personable young lieutenants of his on a recent visit to Atlanta, I asked him if he did not think the South the most religious part of the country. He said he did but that this could be a bad thing as well as a good. A trouble there, he said, was that "when we make an appeal the response is likely to be an old-fashioned revival, and what we want is a revolution." Since Dr. Buchman is so quick and devoted a gentleman and is interested in having people armed again, it seems to me that he might have accepted the revivals and considered making something of them. Reviving and rearming have similar connotations, after all. And while there is no hope of religious revolution in the South there is hope of cleaning and carrying forward the great sum total of religious organization and influence already there. For better or worse (it has been both) religion is an immense thing in the South. It is religion with a Lord God Almighty in capital letters. Perhaps that, rather than a lack of revolution, is Dr. Buchman's case against it. It is a religion in which goodness and greatness have God's capital "G." A Goodness which triumphs over evil at last and is worth while for its good sake whether it wins or not. And a Greatness with the same capital "G" to which failing ones may turn for things that do not fail, for supernatural powers within them that may be unlocked. Robbed of the capital letters, religion would have no such force in the South.

There is the cold authority of George Bernard Shaw and other mentalists that capital letters are needed elsewhere, too, in this still immature world. After the First World War, when, as will be the case after this one, there was a hope and need that religious impulses the

war had revived might hold against the materialistic reaction, Mr. Shaw obligingly wrote "Back to Methuselah
—A Metabiological Pentateuch." He described it as "a
Bible for Creative Evolution" and his last really great
work ("My powers are waning; but so much the better
for those who found me unbearably brilliant when I was
in my prime"). Believing that Creative Evolution (he
was careful about the capital letters) was "unmistakably
the religion of the Twentieth Century," he argued that
no religion could amount to anything with the masses
unless "it has its legends, its parables, its miracles." And
that was where he was to come in. His book was to provide the legends, parables, and miracles. He warned of
danger in taking them literally, but that was rather by
way of a Shavian footnote to his fellow mentalists, we
must believe. He was sure that religion could be no force
without what he called its fables—and its capital letters.

Another mentalist in whose science I believe and who
has testified not only to men's need of religious exercise
but to the dependence on capital letters—is Mr. Walter
Lippmann. He did it in his "Preface to Morals." Testi-
mony to the same point came from Dr. Foster Kennedy,
neurologist for Bellevue and General Memorial Hospi-
tals, when he addressed the County Medical Society in
Birmingham in October, 1941, on "Science, Civilization and Faith." "For two hundred years," he said, "we
have drained out of our religion and out of our literal
opinions the magic of emotion. We believe in kindness
but hardly in the Immaculate Conception; and the Holy
Ghost seems more like a J. M. Barrie whimsy than a

Tongue of Fire. And that a citizen is a free man we take to be a natural law. But the innate need to draw strength from the level of Mystery and Magic must be served in us all." Faith, he said, "gives civilization force." In his philosophy faith involved (1) a making up of one's mind, and (2) an expression of that mind with emotional force. Educated Americans were losing both capacities when the war came, he thought. "We have allowed ourselves and are constantly encouraged to become so pliable, so flexible, so 'relative' to all things, in a current phrase so 'broad-minded,' that we are in danger of having no ethic, no vision, no hope. Through our lowered power of personal judgment we have vacillated for years on the knife-edge of indecision. Indecision locks up energy. It stabs the heart. But decision, clearly taken, brings calmness, strength, the quiet mind, and a flow of power."

The artificialities of the oxygen tent, under which America had lived in years between the World Wars, were in this distinguished neurologist's memory as he spoke: "We have in Freudian psychology beaten the drum of the Subconscious to drown the still small voice of intellect. In painting, the discipline of drawing has been jettisoned for meaningless crazed abstractions. . . . Modern music is either cacophony of fire-irons descending a nude staircase, or sentimental crooned aphrodisiacs to impotent youth. . . . The impertinent idiocies of Gertrude Stein, e. e. cummings and James Joyce, are less important than the lack of judgment, lack of independent personal opinion, lack of reverence for the great traditions of language, present in their half-educated and wholly uninstructed admirers. . . ."

In the South the Holy Ghost is a Tongue of Fire. Millions of Methodists and Baptists, hundreds of thousands of Presbyterians, thousands of Episcopalians, hundreds of Roman Catholics and Jews—believe in the Lord God Almighty. The One in the Bible. He is a Force, a Personality, a Love, a Wrath, a Justness. He is beyond mere morality, ethics, and altruism, although He endorses them. The South has more than its share of the long-nosed, thin-browed ones who meddle in the name of the Lord and are so graduated in goodness that they can give their time to making snoopingly sure that others are undergraduates. It has, too, the gasping, babbling, heavy-breathing evangelist with his public fits in the name of God. And the professional finders of things that are "against the Bible," the ones who put laws against teaching evolution on the books of Southern States and invited the disgraceful monkey-doings at Dayton in 1925. It has pious politicians who hang on to the Lord's coat-tail. And people with suffocating odors of sanctity, and ones whose religion is in the offensive style of dandruff on a coat. And the lunatics in robes, hoods, shirts, or feathers, who associate God and country with their bigotries in the nastiest concoction of all. But there is warm, sweet, lifting religion, too, and a capacity for infinitely more because what there is is based on the eternal stories, the great literature, and the capital letters. I think the South was willing to fight this war partly because it believed in a God in Heaven who had to be served and who attended His servitors. It was willing to fight because Good was being threatened by Evil in dimensions and circumstances that commanded even the most sinful of Southerners. It was willing to fight because it believed God would help and would bring its sons home again. All over the Southern States in the summer of 1942 there was reading and quoting of the Ninety-first Psalm: "Surely He shall deliver thee from the snare of the fowler, and from the noisome pestilence. . . . Thou shalt not be afraid for the terror by night; nor for the arrow that flieth by day. . . . Nor for the pestilence that walketh in darkness, nor for the destruction that wasteth at noonday. . . . A thousand shall fall at thy side, and ten thousand at thy right hand; but it shall not come nigh thee. . . . For He shall give His angels charge over thee, to keep thee in all thy ways. . . . They shall bear thee up in their hands, lest thou dash thy foot against a stone. . . ."

On December 7, 1938, three years exactly before Pearl Harbor, William Alexander Percy wrote me from his home in Greenville, Mississippi: "We need a Peter the Hermit, or a St. Francis. The right person, I believe, could kindle a great religious revival. Something of the kind must happen to the democracies if they are to be saved." When I suggested that the leadership must come from many, not one alone, he wrote: "Perhaps you are right . . . I don't believe St. Francis could talk over the radio, and these days a great leader must have that ability. It is a pretty sick world." Illustrating the sickness was the willingness of the Honorable Eugene

Talmadge to be St. Francis. In his race for re-election to the Georgia governorship in 1942 he announced that the issues were "white supremacy, Jeffersonian democracy, and the 'old time religion.'" He wasn't the type. No more than Huey Long was the type to make every man a king. But, as in the Kingfish's case, Talmadge knew his South and its psychology. In a time of war and appalling turnover the old time religion had its sure appeal, just as the talk of being made a king attracted all that was most human in human nature.

With or without benefit of another St. Francis there is in the South this immense pool of religion. Since our mentalists and neurologists have been joined by our economist, Mr. Roger Babson, in asserting a need of religion in our American business, the Southern pool is worth consideration. Whatever else may be said against the religious manner in the South, the churches there may no longer be called "tools of the mill owners." There has been much swinging in the other direction, in the South and elsewhere. The humanitarianism which goes naturally with a worship of God has turned many of God's ministers collectivist. They do not look upon this for what it is, a taking of sides on an economic question in which they are not qualified and by which they impeach their spiritual estate.

Whether we have a system of free enterprise in the years to come or a socialism we shall be needing a Lord God Almighty. Great things can be done with the people of the South in His name. Sociologists and atom-splitters must not forget that the capacity for believing things which Mr. Mencken calls fatuity is precious. The value is in the intransitive verb. The psychology of faith is what carries us forward, not the science of being doubtful and rejecting all. Faith may not yet move a mountain but it gave the giraffe a long neck. Darwin said the neck was an economic accident, implied that all other progressions were too. He said the lower leaves of the trees were eaten away and only the longer-necked giraffes could reach anything to eat. But LaMark knew better. He said it was aspiration. He said there were plenty of leaves on the lower limbs but that tenderer leaves were at the top. The giraffe aspired to them, had faith through the aeons that he would reach them. This yearning, with perhaps a little stretching, resulted at last in the long neck which is so much admired in the jungles and zoos. There is report, too, that the first monkey who slid down the limb of a tree in the primeval forest and stood erect was fatuous to an extent worth Mr. Mencken's hearty despising. The other monkeys hung by their tails from the topmost limbs and told him so. They said he had no sense of the scientific orders. They said he had been listening to propaganda. They said it was written in all the books of light that a stand upon hind legs was backwardness. And they said that only a sentimentalist would wish to walk without four feet solidly beneath him. But the fatuous monkey, full of his believing, lifted his face to heaven, and stood erect, and walked. And in the process of time the monkey who had faith became a man and the one who hung doubting by his tail remained a monkey.

When I remember Will Percy I do not think of the aristocrats who may never have existed in enough bulk to deserve a book nor of the social and economic orders that are going with the wind. I think of what he loved, how worth loving it was, and how surely it can be held for loving hereafter. I think how he wanted to be still and know there was God—

> I have need of silence and of stars,
> Too much is said too loudly. I am dazed. . . .

Here on the little Solomon Island of infinity we call the earth, here in the clock-tick of time we call the Second World War, all of us are wanting to be still, whether we know it or not. And many who were dazed begin to see. There is a clairvoyance in crisis and danger, in dying and hard denials, in sudden multiplications of human misery. Those who love the light begin to find it then. And that is as it should be. The dark and bigoted ones are not confused. The ignorant know what to think. The cruel and the unjust are clear in all their seeing and believing, and the hearts that swell with hate are strong. Unless those who want the light can match hateful clarities with benign ones the hope of years will fail. Unless there is that robust thing that seems to come only of the religion whose Lord God is Almighty, we shall not be strong enough for the challenges. We were so full of negation and weak solution and broken things. We had lost so much of that power to adventure and believe, on which health and forward-march depend. We had disqualified ourselves in spirit for the great controls even as we set about controlling more than men ever had before. We confused humanitarianism with socialism. We neglected our great games in one moment, and in the next played so furiously to win that we broke the rules, smeared the lines, endangered the arena. We organized ourselves up, down, and in all directions but forgot to be joined. We won freedoms and didn't use them. We called our brothers equals but failed to call them what they were more surely—brothers. We looked for God in silly places without seeing Him kind and mighty in the sky.

Not science, economics, machinery, natural resources, geography, nor possession of the earth's remaining instrument of war and peace will let our American people be what destiny says they can be—unless there is a still place and they know God.

Chapter Twenty

FREE FOR ALL

Its variety goes to America's spice. Its extremes cartoon a nation. Its highlights advertise, its low ones warn. Its poverties and racial troubles ask for answers that must be made for a world entire. Its tradition, lodged in fact or Southern fancy, has ideals for our future if the future is to be brave. Its sicknesses are the mendable ones of the immature. Its health is a stone from which may be chiseled something near the heart's desire. And its fighting, for the good thing or the bad, speaks of nature's law and the dream of enterprise. That is why I say this book about the South is a book about the United States and its years to come.

The Fighting South! Until we confess that fighting is the world's way, and, having confessed, concentrate on making contests fair, we shall come to nothing. From the molecules of basic matter, pounding, colliding, bouncing, with never a loss of kinetic force, to the battle tanks of Eisenhower and the peace-time offerings of Ford and Chevrolet, competition is the law of life and the life of trade. When I was in college there would come evenings when we could find nothing better to do than sit about in someone's room, discussing things-in-general. "Bicker sessions," we called them. The problems of a day and of forever were our themes, and, being sophomores, we knew the answers. Early on those evenings while our brains were fresh we would talk of the important problems—the football team, the club elections, and that perpetual matter of the blonde and the brunette. When our minds would dull a little, we would talk of heavier things—the tariff, the income tax, woman suffrage. Later would come problems which had concerned philosophers, whether "everything flows on"; whether change or permanence was the great illusion; how many incorporeal angels could stand on the point of a needle; whether a tree, falling in a forest, made a noise if no ear was there to hear it; what lay behind the "baths of all the western stars." And always when the hour was latest and our brains weighted past capacity, we would talk of the Problem of Problems, the one to which all others relate and from which all others derive. Could life be thought out or must it be fought out? Thought out or fought out? Could men, by taking thought together, run their world aright? Could they assemble in some great committee, bureau, parliament, or board and, with maximum intelligence and socialmind, fix the conditions of mortal living? Or, failing, must there be a dependence on the play of forces, on the outputs of competition, with concert only against such play-endings as come when the tiger eats a lion or a nation at war destroys another? All-wise, we would decide in the last smoke of those evenings that life must be fought out. There was not in all the world, we said, enough wisdom, data, character and clairvoyance to fix satisfactorily by fiat the price of a single pair of shoes, the wage of one day's work, the rent of a room there in Holder Hall, or the content of a mind. And even if there were, mortal degeneration would set in. Human beings were not intended to be told what to do about everything. If they consented to be they would become, in one way or another, by exterior force or inner corruption, slaves and peas in a pod. In addition, they would be bored to death.

We sophomores were right, as usual. In all our lives to follow, never more so. We were recognizing the case for what the songs, speeches, poems and great documents were about—liberty. We were identifying the American system. Without the competitive principle, without arrivals that result from a play of opposing forces, without the variety for which competition calls and the enterprise which results from it, freedom could have neither existence nor use. The province of thought is wide, but its world must be fought out. That is the American belief. That is the American system. War suspended the system but it made an object lesson against the alternative. Leon Henderson testified to that when he spoke in Birmingham in the fall of 1942. As director then of the Office of Price Administration, he was the nation's foremost Thinker-Out, and he testified that it couldn't be done. In post-war days he would be able to tell out of his experience, he agreed, a heart-rending tale of controlled economy, of delicate balances each move upsets, of a thousand controls gone wrong.

A tree is one of many things God alone can make.

Some of the others have to be attempted by governments in wartime. Only God can interfere fairly to the multiple parties concerned with the prices of things, the rents, wages, but our government in wartime had to try. Only God can make rationings and priorities without injustice and much wreckage, but Washington had to attempt it. Only God can tell economic laws to stand still, but Washington had to give the order. Only God can arrive at the exact line between the maximum a people can give to total war and the too much that will cripple them and their war—but Washington had to seek it. To know this was to forgive many mistakes and inadequacies. To know it was, also, to be advised again that God-playing by government, the total state to which Americans were submitting proudly while the war went on, was the thing they were fighting the war to be spared thereafter.

Life cannot be thought out. Not the free, various, and democratic living in which we Americans believe. A world thought out is necessarily a world controlled by the thinkers and those who apply their thoughts. That has been so in Russia, Germany, Italy. Whether the controllers act initially in the name of the masses or classes, whether they call themselves communists or fascists, they come bringing a regiment, a dictatorship, and a slavery.

Life must be fought out. That makes a hateful sound, but it need not be so. It need not mean the "darkling plain" of Matthew Arnold, "swept with confused alarms of struggle and flight—where ignorant armies clash by night." With thought, with character, science, justice and good will, competition can be productive, not the tooth-and-claw of jungles or the thing of battlefields. But unless we accept this competition as the law we fail to civilize it, and then, indeed, the darkling plain will take us. Civilize the plays, put a just umpire over them, educate the players, respect the rules, set limits in decency, and the fighting world becomes the free world, the various world, the democratic one. That is the American notion, at any rate, and it is no more laissez faire than collectivism. The name is Umpired Competition.

When the American automobile industry added one more to its miracles by making the transfer to plane manufacture which turned the war's tide of arms, there were many to point out this industry as the example in perfection of the American system. This was the same industry which, after the other World War, had come with its mass production and appeal to give America a life-saving job. It did not win that war but it won the economic peace that followed for a time. Won it by giving more jobs than had ever been given at once before, jobs in steel, textiles, petroleum, rubber, highway building, salesmanship. It was this industry, too, which gave first recognition through Henry Ford to the corollary of mass producing, the rule that there must be mass consuming, too, and that for this mass consuming there must be high wages. Ford's $5 a day was as much a victory for economic law as his flivvers were a victory for the common man over time and space. Out of the automobile industry's experience had come, too, a les-

son which some of those who are more loud than enlightened in their championing of private enterprise
overlook. It was the lesson that, if technology is to give
men employment rather than take it away, one of the
implications that must be respected is the public-works
nature of some of the new work a technological advance
creates. The automobile put the horse-and-buggy people
out of business, but it put many more people into business—steel, rubber, textile, petroleum, selling, servicing,
etc. And the biggest business it created was public business, the business of building the highways which lace
this land. These could not have been built by private industry. There wasn't enough money. There were too
many public interests involved. But unless they had been
built, unless this immense public work had been under-
taken, the automobile could not have developed and
served as it has. This was the biggest and best example
of the fact that while private enterprise is still the basic
way for America, it needs supplementing with public enterprise.

The automobile spells America's century, too, for a
little device it has put at every busy street intersection
of the land, a thing that flashes red and yellow and green,
interfering with our liberties in order that we may not
ruin them through exercise at the wrong time. The traffic lights are a message to reactionaries at all the cross-
roads of America that the liberty for which our country
stands and has been fighting, the political and the economic liberty, is a liberty under social law, a liberty

which can be preserved in essence only if sections of it are given up for the sum total.

But it is America's way of umpired competition which the automobile industry illustrates most. The competition of Ford, Chevrolet, Plymouth, and the rest has produced the greatest value known to man, the modern low-priced car. Competition has forced a price so low that profit has had to be sought out of volume rather than margin over cost. Because the automobile has passed on to the public in low prices and to the workers in high wages a great share of its economic returns, those returns have multiplied—to the glory and enjoyment of us all and the proof of our American system.

"This," said Vice President Wallace in the spring of 1942, "is to be the century of the common man." Ever since 1776 we Americans have been trying to make a century of the common man. We are able to report progress, against all odds and back-slippings. Much is left, and we are sure to go on doing it. We must be equally sure that we go with the instrument we have been using and the ideal we have had in mind. The instrument has been competition, the ideal has been freedom. How shall we know the common man's century when it comes, by what sign, what achieving? A decent standard of living will be an indispensable, but not enough. It is true that unless economic misery is removed nothing else will matter but if, when it is removed, there is slavery, nothing will matter either. Hitler promised economic survival, but you had to be his goose-stepper to get it. The sign of the common man's century will be a two-in-one—bread and liberty. It is the American sign. Our faith has been and must be that liberty and ham and eggs can be had together. This means umpired competition. It means a free enterprise more free and enterprising than some of those who talk it have in mind.

Not by the National Association of Manufacturers was Free Enterprise invented. Some of the members need to know that, and so do those who suspect whatever the members talk. Free enterprise was invented by God. It was discovered for America by Thomas Jefferson, saved with America by Abraham Lincoln, and identified with America's day of mass and machinery by Woodrow Wilson. This should entitle them at last to honorary membership. And not from government bureaucracy alone does Free Enterprise need to be made free. It needs to be free of things the members of the National Association of Manufacturers do, things the members of the American Federation of Labor, the Congress for Industrial Organization, the American Farm Bureau Federation do, things all of us do. We are sinners all against our American way of competition, our liberties of enterprise. That enterprise needs freeing from the progressive federal interfering which the Marxian half of the New Deal desires, many of us who were in the other half begin to see. But we do not overlook the need of freeing from other interferings, too. Enterprise needs freedom from all the walls and restraints that limit the flow of goods to market, of raw materials to manufacture, production to demand, prices to competitive levels, economies to bear, capital to investment,

and inventions to use. It needs freedom from all inter-
ferences—whether collectivist or laissez faire—with that
umpired play which is the only promise of liberty and
abundance together.

Going into the war with an administration which had
been engaged for eight years in New Dealing had advantages and disadvantages. The advantages were (1)
a practical experience in operations and controls similar
to ones the war would require, and (2) a certain knowledge in the American people that the government which
was asking them to spend their blood and treasure had'
their mass interests at heart, was a people's government.
Disadvantages were (1) domestic hate so psychopathic
that not even the war was able to remove it; (2) a me-
dicinal point of view in which the public was subjected
throughout the war to psychological doctoring, sedatives
against good news, stimulants against bad, when plain
truth would have been healthier; (3) a paternal habit
which made unnecessary delays because of a belief that
the public must be waited for when, quite often, the
public was well ahead; and (4) a habit of Great-and-
Good-God-playing which (a) encouraged divisive domestic crusades throughout the war, (b) tempted government
officials to do more organizing, controlling, rationing,
etc. than was necessary or wise, and (c) became planet-
sized when talk of peace began.

After the American landings in North Africa, and
the launching of the Russian counter-offensive, the God-
players in America began to go astronomical in plans
for taking care of every sparrow that might be falling or

flying wrong. This in spite of the fact that reaction in America against God-playing was so developing that trouble was in sight.

For America once again to lead the world to a high place and let it fall back to confusion and darkness would compound a monstrous sin. For America once again, as after 1918, to turn cynical and self-centered, refusing participations upon which the world's hope and its own depended, would be tragedy past comparing. But the threat was there, and it came not from the resurging isolationists alone. It came, too, from the God-players. They were making new isolationists by persistently associating the cause of international participation with the different one of universal control and reform. Americans had learned their lesson well enough not to wish another withdrawing and time of "normalcy." It was beyond belief that they would listen again to talk of leaving the world alone after being drawn twice in a quarter century into an appallingly destructive world war. They were ready, surely, for great association with other nations in behalf of peace and of the just and productive relations among nations that would give no germ of war a new inception. They were ready, too, no doubt, for sacrifices to put the torn and bleeding lands together and assure a world in order. But they were not ready for planetary regulation. They were not ready for a controlled economy between and within all nations. Not when they were turning against the very thing at home for having been carried too far. They were for international umpires and policemen, and they had indulgent hearts even for the sentimentalists who were dreaming a peace all love and white wonder, but they were not for God-playing. They were not for looking on the victory as one for collectivism over free enterprise when all the circumstances said it was the other way. Without employing the term or perhaps even liking it, they were for umpired competition—among nations and men.

Out of this war the advertising will go to Russia. Out of this war the great remainders of wealth and power, the commands over instruments of war and peace, will belong to America. What will have been advertised in Russia, I think, is not communism but human being. The spirit of man has made its bravest survival in bulk there. But it is in America that the spirit is offered its loftiest altitude in years to come. Comparatively unhurt, we close the war advantaged as never before for making our dream of economic and political liberty come true, and for leading into our light the community of mankind. For the first time in history enduring peace is possible. That is because, for history's first time, universal plenty is possible. Heretofore men have not had a power of making enough for everyone, but now they have. Technology made it so even before the war began, and when the curtain is lifted on technological advances that have been made under war's impulsion, this making of enough will be more possible than ever. Since the want of enough has been the basis of wars before, the existence of enough, if we achieve and distribute it, will be assurance against wars to come. The achievement is not yet. There is a trick in it, a knack not quite acquired. But we know that it can be, and in that is the hope of the world and the challenge to America. The challenge is to employ the supreme position that will be ours at the peace tables and for years thereafter to make this plenty and this peace, and to do it, not in the Hitler way of slavery or the Stalin way of a collectivism that turns to slavery, but in the American way of liberty under the law, political liberty and economic liberty.

The free way will call for uttermosts in civilization, self-discipline and human excellence. It will call for those umpires, rules, lines, and arenas we were destroying in the furies of play before the war. It will call for men more excellent in their expression and human being than they have been. It will call for accents on quality in all the exercises of democracy. Before the war and in its course some of our leaders have concerned themselves for this qualitative element. George Denny, Moderator of America's Town Meeting of the Air, who has made his radio program the instrument of more free speaking than any other agency in the world, has never thought free speech enough. He would not limit it, but he would have better speech, more honest, informed, objective. Men have a right to speak, he knows, but they have also a duty to speak truly. I wish I could persuade him that they have a duty, also, to make up their minds, even if only tentatively, for it seems to me that this is what open minds are for and that unless our honest and well-informed have a vitality of opinion the dishonest and illiterate who always know what to think may take us over. But as a moderator, Mr. Denny's interest is in the openness of minds and in the quality rather than the content, and I agree that those are the more important. Unless there is quality with quantity in our democracy, and unless there is duty with rights in our free system, we shall not play our game of umpired competition well enough to win. That will be the immense point for a return to liberal arts in colleges and universities after the war's call for technologists is over, and to general as against exclusively vocational education in lower schools. Without excellent human beings, who know not only their work-day tasks but the fore and aft of them and who are possessed of the character, taste, and intelligence to be citizens and consumers as well as craftsmen, the free way will surely fail.

In the ever so dark and bright corner room which fronts on the Atlantic and the Gulf I have written this book about the United States. Because it is my own room, the one where I was born, I may be over-inclined to think it holds all the examples of what I have wanted to say about the United States, and that the examples are more large and clear. Be this as it may, they are the examples of which I know most. And I think they make my points, with their good things and bad, their problems and chances, their accentuations of what is base and best in human being, their sociabilities and their drawings apart. A weapon against the slaveries of collectivism after the war will be the persisting demand of the South for "states' rights" and all this connotes of individualism and local governing in the world as well as the nation. Possessed of more than its share of peculiar and separate problems, the South knows you cannot step into a people's midst or an individual's life from afar and play God. You can only see to it that nations and regions and individuals do not play the devil with each other in their mutual relations and that there is a just umpire over their competings. But what some Southerners, like some Americans, overlook is that "states' rights," "local self-government," and "American individualism" are terms often profaned. As often as are those other terms—"free enterprise," "the right to work," and "freedom of the press." They are enemies, not friends to states' rights who mean only the right of the strong against the weak, the backward-looking against the forward-looking, the chain-gang step of prejudice against the march of time. They are enemies, not friends, to the free way who cry "down with federal bureaucracy" when all they mean is "up with the right of a few to kill liberty for all," "up with the right of the unsocial to destroy our free society." The freedom for which we have won this war is a freedom to be preserved by a law and a light and in which we shall adventure as individuals who have been made in an Image and are members of a world.

For the sins of my book and my corner room and my country—and for the promises mercifully open to all of us still, I close these pages on my knees. I exercise my democratic right to lead in prayer—and for this I pray—

One more chance, O Lord, to know that the world is round, and wondrous small. As round as our Columbus proved it, as small as our science is making it the more each day. Too round and small for any of us, or any region or nation of us, to escape the others by putting up a wall, looking in the other direction or walking away. One more chance to give liberty the virtue and the vigilance which are its prices and which we forgot to pay. One more chance to know that only the affirmative, hopeful, generous, and brave can be truly free. One more chance to make faith our climate, believing our habit, and Thou, God, the deep heart of our believing. One more chance to be young as we failed to be in the anarchy of our 1920's and the socialism of our 1930's. One more chance to be beautiful—and American—and alive—O God, our strength and our redeemer!

INDEX

Adams, James Truslow, 11
Adams, John Quincy, 49
Adventure, 116, 117
Agar, Herbert, 221
Alabama Cotton Manufacturers' Association, 244
Alabama Polytechnic Institute, 169
Alabama Power Company, 113
Alabama, University of, 162
Alexander, Will, 66
American Legion, 123, 229
American Red Cross, 119
American System, 265, 269
Anderson, Robert, 243
Angel, death is an, 73
Armageddon, 102
Army enlistments, 82
"Arp, Bill," 27
Ashe, Frieda, 32
Asheville Citizen, 154
Aspirin Age, 106
Atlanta, 40, 98, 253
Atlanta Constitution, 8, 27
Atlanta News, 30
Atlanta and West Point Railroad, 22
Automobile Industry, 267, 269
Aviation, 117
Babson, Roger, 259
Baker, Oliver Edwin, 220
Bankhead, John H., 125, 167
Bataan, 90
"Battle Hymn of the Republic," 235
Bay State Club, 55
Bay View Assembly, 251
Beale, Sir Louis, 73
"Bicker Sessions," 263
Birmingham, 40
Birmingham News-Age-Herald, 9, 148, 156
Birmingham Rotary Club, 65, 113
Black Belt, 168, 185
Black, Hugo L., 45, 109
Blood Bank Donations, 119
"Blue" Army, 73

"Blue Danube Waltz," 71, 91
Blue Ridge Parkway, 189
Boll weevil, 170
Bootlegger, 109
Bourke-White, Margaret, 179
Bryan, William Jennings, 21
Buckman, Dr. Frank, 253
Butler, Nicholas Murray, 247
Byrd, Sam, 165, 169
Byrnes, James F., 45
Caldwell, Erskine, 5, 66, 170, 179
Calhoun, John C., 49, 206, 233
Carmichael, Oliver Cromwell, 10
Carnegie-Illinois Corporation, 61
Carver, George Washington, 163
Cash, W. J., 66
Cason, Clarence, 12, 66, 71
Centripetal force, 126, 239
Century of the common man, 269
Chamberlain, Samuel, 177
Chappell, James E., 9
Chivalry, 193
Church of the Advent, 88
Civil War, 235
Clayton, William L., 172
Clearwater Beach, 183
Clemson College, 169
Cleveland, Grover, 25
Coal, 117
Cobb, Irvin, 91
Cohn, David, 66, 172
Coleman, Rev. Michael, 88
College Park, 20, 29
College Park News, 24
Commonwealth & Southern Corporation, 113
Confederate War, 236
Connally, Captain James T., 91
Corregidor, 90
Cotton Bowl, 101
"Cotton is King," 171
Cowley, Malcolm, 177
Cox College, 27
Crackpots, 115

Creative Evolution, 255
Dabney, Virginius, 8, 66, 126, 127, 132
Dairying and Livestock Industry, 62, 168
Daniels, Jonathan, 6, 63, 66, 157, 203, 210
Daniels, Josephus, 44
Darktown, 30
Daughters of the American Revolution, 87
Dauphin Island, 183
Death is an angel, 73
Democratic convention representation, 242
Democratic National Convention, 76
Denny, George, 274
Dixon, Frank, 9, 135, 160
Double-V-for-Victory, 121
Dowson, Ernest, 218
Duke University, 90
Dukes, Miss Kitty, 30
Dunkirk, 72, 75
Dunne, Irene, 223
Eagle Squadron, 199
East Lake Negro School, 87
Eleaser, R. B., 66
Embree, Edwin R., 153
England, 74
Enterprise, Ala., 170
Ethridge, Mark, 8, 58, 125, 126, 127, 129, 136
Evangeline Oak, 47
Evening star, 75
Executive Order 8802, 128, 130, 135
"Faces You See," 179
Fair Employment Practices Committee, 58, 125, 128, 131, 135, 136
"Fair Is Our Land," 177
Farm Security Administration, 240
Faulkner, William, 71, 207
Fearful symmetry, 96
Federal Trade Commission, 60
Feminine ankle, 213
Fitzgerald, Scott, 106
Force Bill, 54
Ford, Henry, 173, 175, 216
Forgy, Chaplain Howell, 84
Fort Jackson, 80
Fort McClellan, 104
France, 78

Frank, Glenn, 105
Frankensteen, Richard, 224
Free enterprise, 107, 114, 115, 270
Free Speech, 274
Freeman, Douglas, 8, 188
Freight Rates, 59
Freud, Sigmund, 107
Gaines, Francis Pendleton, 188
Gallup Poll, 4, 12
Garrett, Garet, 163
Gayler, Captain Ernest, 94
Gayler, Lieutenant Ernest, Jr., 94
Gayler, Lieutenant Noel A. M., 94
Gee, Wilson, 66
Gee's Bend, 180, 181
Geopolitics, 3
Georgia Tech, 90, 97
Georgia University System, 156
Glass, Carter, 4, 7, 15, 44
Glenn, Charles B., 198, 199
God-playing, 271, 272, 273
"Gone With the Wind," 218
Grady, Henry, 21, 25, 51, 53, 126
Graham, Frank, 46, 66, 129
Grand Hotel, 93
Graves, Cothran Calhoun Carter Smith, 25
Graves, General James Porterfield, 26
Graves, John Temple, 201
Gray, Gordon, 243
Green Wave, 97
Gulf Coasts of the South, 183
Gulf of Mexico, 83
Hamilton, Audley, 205
Harlan, "Bloody," 187
Harris, Lynn, 189
Haskell, Joseph, 12
Hazzard, Lieutenant Meredyth, 94
Hazzard, Rutledge, 94
Hazzard, William, Jr., 94
Heflin, Tom, 43
Henderson, Leon, 265
"Here We Rest!," 226
High, Stanley, 131
Hilger, Lieutenant Colonel John A., 91
Hill, Lister, 9, 77
Hillman Clinic, 166
Holt, Leroy, 170
Horton, Judge James E., 208, 210
Hospitality, 196

Howell, Clark, 8
Hudgens, Pete, 181
Hull, Cordell, 45
Huntress, Frank, 89
Hydro-electric power, 117
"I Have Been Faithful to Thee, Cynara!," 219
"I'll Take My Stand," 176
Ingalls Shipbuilding Corp., 216
Jackson, George Pullen, 47
Jackson, Dr. M. F., 169
Jazz age, 106, 107
Jim Crow, 119, 121
Johnson, Charles S., 66
Johnson, Oscar, 173
Jones, William Cole, 201
Joyce, James, 256
Juvenile delinquency, 199
Kelly, Colin P., Jr., 86
Kennedy, Dr. Foster, 255
Kilpatrick, Carroll, 249
Konoye, Prince, 77
Kreuger, Lieutenant General Walter, 89
Ku Klux Klan, 44, 46, 108, 144
Laissez Faire, 110, 114
"Lanterns on the Levee," 206
Larson, Harold H. ("Swede"), 94
Lawrence, J. A., 145
Lee, Robert E., 20, 32, 188
Lewis, Ivey, 189
Lexington, Virginia, 188
Liberal arts colleges, 275
Lilienthal, David, 113
Lincoln, Abraham, 52, 206
Lippmann, Walter, 244, 255
"Little People," 203
Livestock Industry, 62, 162, 168
Llewellyn Park, 85
Lodge, Henry Cabot, 54
Long, Huey, 47, 203
Louisville Courier-Journal, 8, 156
Louisville & Nashville Railway, 122
Lynching, 63, 154
MacArthur, General Douglas, 89
McCormick, Anne O'Hare, 226
MacCracken, Henry Noble, 194, 199
McCrory, Wm. Malcolm, 27
MacDill Field, 80
McGuire, Chaplain, 84
MacRae, Hugh, 165

Manners, 197
Marshall, General, 125
Marshall, Mrs. Thomas W., 253
Martin, Telfair, 34
Martin, Thomas W., 74
Masterly inactivity, 233
Maybank, Burnett R., 9, 243
Mencken, Henry L., 5
Mexico, Gulf of, 83
Miami Beach, 100
Miller, Francis P., 66
Miller, Commander Louis N., 94
Milton, George Fort, 9
"Mind of the South, The," 204
"Miscarriage Room," 215
Mississippi State College, 74, 97
Mitchell, Margaret, 10
Monkey-doings at Dayton, 257
Montgomery Advertiser, 156
Moore, Major General George F., 91
Moses, 68
Mountain Brook Country Club, 73
Mountain Lake, 189
Murder capital, 15
Music, 46
Nashville Banner, 9
Nashville "Fugitives," 176
National Association for the Advancement of Colored People, 123, 127, 128, 132, 153, 270
National Cotton Council, 73
National Negro Congress, 153
National Resources Committee, 164
Natural gas, 117
Navy recruiting, 82
Negro education, 152
Negro health, 153
"Negro March on Washington," 128
Negro vote, 242, 245
Newcomen Society, 73
Newfound Gap, 191
New Deal, 57, 117
New England Society, 52
New Orleans, 40, 184
New Republic, 177, 208, 209
New York Times, 226
Ninety-first Psalm, 95, 258
99th Pursuit Squadron, 133
Nixon, H. C., 66
North Carolina Mutual Life Insurance Company, 154

North Carolina, University of, 150
Noyes, Alfred, 36, 182
No. 1 Economic Problem, 66
Odum, Howard, 16, 66, 190, 212, 221
Office of Price Administration, 265
Oglethorpe, General, 205
O'Hara, John, 106
O'Hara, Scarlett, 21
Old Faithful, 101, 102
"Old Sawney," 118
Oleomargarine, 62, 171
Orange Bowl, 101
Oxford Group, 253
Oxygen tent, 105
Pass Christian, 183
Paternalism, 46
Paternalistic system, 112
Patrick, Luther, 5
Patterson, F. D., 66, 133, 134
Pavlichenko, Jr. Lieut. Liudmila, 215
Pearl Harbor, 84
Percy, William Alexander, 39, 206, 258
Pepper, Claude, 4
Perkins, Secretary of Labor, 65
Perry, John Lester, 61
Petroleum, 117
"Pickaninnies," 120
Pickens, William, 133
"Pittsburgh Plus," 60
Plymouth Rock, 252
Poe, Clarence, 66, 162
Poe, Edgar Allen, 71
Point Clear, 93, 183
Poll tax, 63, 159, 238, 240, 241
Praise the Lord and pass the ammunition!, 99
Pritchard, William S., 64
Problem of Problems, 264
Progressive Farmer, 162
Promised Land, 69
Purchasing power, 67, 158
Race riots, 29, 139
Raleigh News and Observer, 156
Ramsay, Erskine, 198
Ramsey, D. Hiden, 8, 190
Randolph, A. Philip, 124, 127, 128, 130, 135
Raper, Arthur, 66

Redding, J. Saunders, 150
Regionalism, 236
Republican Party, 105
Revelation, Book of, 78
Revivals, 254
Reynolds, Senator, 4
Richardson, Major-General, 12
Richmond News-Leader, 8
Richmond Times-Dispatch, 8, 156
Roberts, Captain Arthur Meredyth, 94
Roberts, David III, 94
Roberts, Mrs. David, 95
Roberts, John Sharpe, 94
Rome, Georgia, 187
Rommel, Marshal Erwin, 92
Roosevelt, Franklin Delano, 77, 128
Roosevelt, Mrs. Franklin, 139
Roosevelt Revolution, 110, 115
Roosevelt, Teddy, 21
Rose Bowl, 71, 90, 101
Rosenwald, Julius, Fund, 153
Rushton, Marion, 243
Salty voice, 75, 77, 86
San Antonio, 89
San Antonio Express, 89
Santa Claus, 210
Saturday Review of Literature, The, 221
Scottsboro Case, 160, 187, 208
Sectionalism, 236
Segregation, 120, 125, 159, 160
Shaw, George Bernard, 254
Shepard, James E., 133
Sherman, William Tecumseh, 52
"Silver Taps," 91
Sinkwich, Frank, 97
"Slovenly Peter," 23
Smith, Major Charles E., 27
Smith, Cotton Ed, 129
Smith, Craig, 245
Smith, Kate Duncan, School, 87
Smith, Ross, 193
Smith, T. V., 250
Southern accent, 41
Southern Association of Colleges and Secondary Schools, 156
Southern birth rate, 220
Southern Conference for Human Welfare, 160

Southern Conference of Universities, 156
Southern gentleman, 200
Southern Methodist, 90
Southern Party, 247
Southern Railway, 101
Spanish-American War, 21
Spies Clinic, 167
Spies, Dr. Tom Douglas, 167
Sportsmanship, 198
Stahlman, James G., 9
States' rights, 276
Stein, Gertrude, 256
Steve, Uncle, 28
Stone Mountain, 187
Strode, Hudson and Theresa, 186
Stockton, Gilchrist B., 41, 243
Sugar Bowl, 101
Supreme Court, 133
Talladega Kiwanis Club, 245
Talmadge, Eugene, 43, 120, 140, 151, 175, 259
Tampa, 80
Tatem Hotel, 100
Teche Country, 184
Technological advance, 268
Tennessee Coal, Iron & Railroad Company, 61, 169
Tennessee, University of, 90
Tennessee Valley Authority, 113, 187
Tepelini, 79
Texas Agricultural and Mechanical College, 91, 97
Texas State Legislature, 167
Texas, University of, 167
Thick Blood of Youth Movement for the Preservation of the Purity and Honor of the White Bloodstream, 145
Thompson, Dorothy, 5, 63
"Tobacco Road," 40, 165, 169, 170
Tobruk, 92
Tontitown, 184, 185
Town Meeting of the Air, 5, 58, 224, 250, 274
Traffic lights, 268
Tunney, Gene, 216
Turner, Reverend John, 88
Tuscaloosa, 185
Tuskegee, 123

Tuskegee Institute, 133, 154
Two-Thirds Rule, 249
"Umpired Competition," 110, 267, 269
Underwood, Oscar, 44
United Auto Workers, 224
United Daughters of the Confederacy, 234, 236
United States Employment Service, 135
United States Steel Corporation, 60
V-for-Victory, 99, 101
Vance, Rupert, 66
Vanderbilt University, 10, 97
"Veterans of Future Wars," 230
Vicksburg, 73, 185
Victoria, Queen, 20, 106
Vienna, 71, 92
Vigilantes, Inc., 151
Virginia Tech, 97
Virginia, University of, 97, 181, 189
Von Bock, General, 100
Wade, John D., 30
Wage differentials, 63
Wainwright, General, 90
Wallace, Vice President Henry, 269
Waller, Odell, 124
"Warrior Bold," 31
Warsaw, Mayor of, 70
Washington and Lee University, 188
Watson, Thomas E., 21, 44, 51, 53
Webb, William R., 118
White, Walter, 128, 133, 135
White, Brother Woods, 35
Wickard, Claude R., 173
Wilkins, Roy, 127, 132
Wilkinson, Horace C., 121
Williams, John Sharp, 44
Willkie, Wendell, 19, 113, 115, 123, 253
Wilson, Woodrow, 7, 8, 14, 36, 44, 110, 115
Women Welders, 213, 214
Wood, Guy, 186
Woodward, C. Vann, 66
Worship, 252
"You Have Seen Their Faces," 179
Young, Stark, 10
Youth, 116
Zorina, Vera, 212